THE GROWTH AND DEVELOPMENT
of NURSE LEADERS

Angela Barron McBride, PhD, RN, FAAN, FNAP, is well prepared to write a book on the growth and development of nurse leaders. A mental health nurse and a developmental psychologist, she has long demonstrated an ability to write about complicated matters in a personal and accessible way, starting with her first book *The Growth and Development of Mothers*, which was recognized as one of the best books of 1973 by both *The New York Times* and the *American Journal of Nursing*. In the intervening years, she has provided leadership as dean of Indiana University School of Nursing, president of both Sigma Theta Tau International and the American Academy of Nursing, and a member of the board of Clarian Health, the largest hospital network in Indiana and one of the largest in the United States. For her contributions, she has been honored with various professional awards and honorary doctorates, elected to the Institute of Medicine, and designated as a "Living Legend" by the American Academy of Nursing. Passing on her leadership savvy, she designs the annual leadership conference of the John A. Hartford Foundation's Building Academic Geriatric Nursing Capacity Program and chairs the national advisory committee for the Robert Wood Johnson Foundation's Nurse Faculty Scholars Program.

As important as her professional credentials are, her personal story contributes even more to her understandings about work–life balance, overcoming difficulties, and lifelong learning. From the age of 13 years until well into her college years, she worked weekends and summers as a nurse's aide on various services—medical, surgical, and newborn. Shaped by a Polish grandmother who dared as a young girl to arrange her own passage to the United States, a seamstress mother who never achieved her dream of becoming a schoolteacher, and a policeman father who wound up getting his GED at the age of 60, she grew up seeing education as the key to changing her circumstances. In 1965, she married philosophy professor Bill McBride, whom she credits with always asking her that stretch question "What do you want to do next?" They have two daughters, both now university professors, and two grandchildren. Over her career, she has worked every configuration of part-time, full-time, and double-time, and there was even a stretch of more than a dozen years when her round-trip commute was 124 miles, so she is no stranger to the challenge of juggling time for self and time with others.

THE GROWTH AND DEVELOPMENT *of* NURSE LEADERS

ANGELA BARRON McBRIDE, PhD, RN, FAAN, FNAP

SPRINGER PUBLISHING COMPANY

NEW YORK

Springer Publishing Company, LLC
11 West 42nd Street
New York, NY 10036
www.springerpub.com

Acquisitions Editor: Allan Graubard
Cover design: Joe Pisano
Composition: S4Carlisle Publishing Service

ISBN: 928-0-8261-0241-6
E-book ISBN: 928-0-8261-0708-4

10 11 12 13/5 4 3 2

The author and the publisher of this Work have made every effort to use sources believed to be reliable to provide information that is accurate and compatible with the standards generally accepted at the time of publication. Because medical science is continually advancing, our knowledge base continues to expand. Therefore, as new information becomes available, changes in procedures become necessary. We recommend that the reader always consult current research and specific institutional policies before performing any clinical procedure. The author and publisher shall not be liable for any special, consequential, or exemplary damages resulting, in whole or in part, from the readers' use of, or reliance on, the information contained in this book. The publisher has no responsibility for the persistence or accuracy of URLs for external or third-party Internet Web sites referred to in this publication and does not guarantee that any content on such Web sites is, or will remain, accurate or appropriate.

Library of Congress Cataloging-in-Publication Data

McBride, Angela Barron.
 The growth and development of nurse leaders / Angela Barron McBride.
   p.; cm.
 Includes bibliographical references.
 ISBN 978-0-8261-0241-6
 1. Nurse administrators. 2. Leadership. I. Title.
 [DNLM: 1. Nursing, Supervisory—organization & administration.
 2. Education, Nursing. 3. Leadership. 4. Nurse's Role. WY 105]
 RT89.M425 2010
 362.17'3068—dc22

                                                                                2010029981

Special discounts on bulk quantities of our books are available to corporations, professional associations, pharmaceutical companies, health care organizations, and other qualifying groups. If you are interested in a custom book, including chapters from more than one of our titles, we can provide that service as well.

For details, please contact:
Special Sales Department, Springer Publishing Company, LLC
11 West 42nd Street, 15th Floor, New York, NY 10036-8002
Phone: 877-687-7476 or 212-431-4370; Fax: 212-941-7842
Email: sales@springerpub.com

Printed in the United States of America by Gasch Printing.

This book is dedicated to
my sisters in blood and friendship—

Cecilia Rose Barron, Sarah Evans Barker,
Rhetaugh Graves Dumas, Mary Cleary Fleener,
Doris H. Merritt, and Fran Miller.

Contents

Foreword

F. Scott Fitzgerald once noted that "the test of a first-rate intelligence is the ability to hold two seemingly contradictory ideas in mind at the same time . . . and function effectively." For decades, Angela Barron McBride has not only lived the paradox of "the concrete and the theoretical," as she describes it but, in the process, has also shaped the thinking of thousands of nurses, professional colleagues, and thought leaders to help them embrace paradox, challenge conventional wisdom, and lead effectively. "I was never very fond of either/or approaches to anything. Life is more complicated than that and all grown-ups need both head and heart to succeed."

The seeds of *The Growth and Development of Nurse Leaders* were planted almost 40 years ago when Dr. McBride wrote the landmark book *The Growth and Development of Mothers,* selected by both *The New York Times* and the *American Journal of Nursing* as one of the best books of 1973. As she noted in *Conversations with Leaders* (Hansen-Turton, Sherman, & Ferguson, 2007, p. 188), that early success gave her the confidence of "taking [her] own experience seriously as a lens through which to analyze what may be the generic issues of the day. Instead of taking as gospel what you read or what authorities tell you, you are willing to reflect on your experience, looking for insights into understanding the phenomenon under study."

Fortunately, she has turned to the phenomenon of nursing leadership and, drawing on her vast experience as an internationally known nurse scholar and pragmatist, she has shared her reflections and recommendations that have relevance for nurses at all levels. One of Dr. McBride's strengths is her ability to connect with both the student nurse and the experienced academician, to have something meaningful to say to the chief nurse officer and the novice nurse. In this current book, she offers numerous insights that are comfortingly familiar while others are refreshingly new. One of the former insights for me was that "Most of us have some trouble even envisioning that there are people who actually like to do what we don't like to do, because we tend to think of our own behavior as normative." *How true!* On the other hand, a refreshingly new insight was that "If you ask for more help than someone can reasonably give, the person is annoyed and may distance him/herself from you." *Interesting*. Each reader will find his/her own *How true!s* and *Interestings* woven throughout the book.

As a textbook, *The Growth and Development of Nurse Leaders* offers a wonderful array of learning products, such as frameworks (e.g., career stages and mentoring needs, developmental tasks by career trajectory); a table comparing the changes in paradigms affecting health care delivery and academia over the past century; and key take-away points at the end of each chapter. Students at all levels will learn much about becoming nurses and leaders from Dr. McBride's writings. More importantly, as a treasured book that one turns to again and again, *The Growth and Development of Nurse Leaders* will provoke new thinking and insight with each reading, inviting the reader to underline meaningful passages and write in the margins. Nurses at all levels will learn much about becoming leaders. Life is complex, and Dr. McBride's wisdom enriches and simplifies the leadership journey for everyone.

Joanne Disch, PhD, RN, FAAN
Director of Katharine J. Densford International Center
   for Nursing Leadership
Katherine R. & C. Walton Lillehei Chair in Nursing Leadership
University of Minnesota
and
President-Elect of the American Academy of Nursing

Acknowledgments

This book took a long time to birth, so I have many people to thank for their support along the way. Ursula Springer had read a paper* I had published, which looked back then forward a quarter century, on breakthroughs in nursing education, originally commissioned to celebrate the 25th anniversary of the founding of the American Academy of Nursing. She thought that what I had to say lent itself to a book-length treatment of the subject. I was interested in writing such a book that would be both retrospective and futuristic, but the timing wasn't right. Meanwhile, my conceptualization of the book began to change thanks to Vernice Ferguson's urging that I not focus just on academic leadership but treat the subject more generally. When I got down to serious writing in 2007, Allan Graubard was my editor and he encouraged me to go in the new direction. His own abilities as a playwright supported my inclination to use both the anecdote and the scientific citation to make my points.

I dedicate the book to my nurse–psychologist sister, Cecilia Rose, and to other long-standing friends who over time have been like sisters to me, three of whom are no longer alive (Dumas, Fleener, and Miller). I don't think you can juggle all that you need to careerwise without friends with whom you laugh, cry, and complain, and then laugh, cry, and complain some more on the way to figuring out what you are going to do next. I would not have finished the book if it were not for my friends who listened to me grouse, always with that right balance of sympathy and get-on-with-it. My aquacise group—Michelle Denney, Peg Dunkle, Linda Froberg, Tina Joseph, LuAnn Lamie, Kitty Mills, Mary Jo Risk, Beth Spencer, and Ruth Wukasch—cheered me on as I sought to keep the arthritis at bay. During that long period of intense writing, Debbie Collins, Joan Lietz, Mary Ann Nester, and Beverly Skinner helped me keep up with my other responsibilities.

---

*McBride, A. B. (1999). Breakthroughs in nursing education: Looking back, looking forward. *Nursing Outlook, 47*(3), 114–119.

A number of colleagues have been encouraging along the way—Joan Austin, Marion Ball, Marion Broome (who suggested the title of the book), Joanne Disch, Marsha Ellett, Linda Everett, Catherine Gilliss, and Sherry Sims in particular—but the two people who helped me the most in getting clear about my ideas were my older daughter Cammie and my husband Bill. My daughter, who is associate editor of a couple of journals, gave me the most insightful feedback as to where to expand and where to shift the emphasis. My husband read every word using his superb editorial abilities to question my wording and insert commas when pauses were in order.

I also want to acknowledge all the colleagues in nursing and other fields who have taught me so much about leadership—classmates, teachers, peers, bosses, and students—through both conversation and observation. I am particularly grateful to the John A. Hartford Foundation and the Robert Wood Johnson Foundation for inviting me to be involved with their leadership-development programs because the experiences gave me many ideas about what to include in this book. In these efforts, I have been particularly touched by my dealings with Claire Fagin, Pat Archbold, Patty Franklin, Rachael Watman, Marcus Escobedo, John Beilenson, Jackie Campbell, Mary Joan Ladden, Sue Hassmiller, Amy Rial, Shirley Chater, and Marie Michnich.

Career

Career—
résumé lines,
but more than a long list.
What's core is the sum total of
meaning.

Mentored,
then mentoring.
The challenge is to give
away self as you build substance
in place.

Introduction

I have been interested in writing a book about the growth and development of nurse leaders for a long time because I've long thought that the subject wasn't covered adequately in a practical way. We talk a great deal about expecting nurses to be leaders, but declaring that isn't the same thing as making it happen. I have never forgotten the panic that I felt as a new RN when asked to do a procedure I didn't know how to do. At the time, I thought going ahead and muddling through would demonstrate my worth rather than speaking up to admit shortcomings, which I now know would have been the real demonstration of my professional abilities. I remember, as if it were yesterday, my first year of teaching when I was told at the start of the second semester that I had been a disappointment because I hadn't yet obtained grant funding. I now know that the expectation was unrealistic and that such impractical expectations can kill leadership potential before it can bud. Out of these experiences and many more, I have formed the opinion that leadership only develops over time when individuals have a road map for thinking about their professional progress, one that pays particular attention to the basics that don't get discussed out loud enough.

Over the years, I have written on various aspects of leadership development (McBride, 1972, 1988), but I wasn't sure until now that I had enough experience to have the credibility to pen a book-length manuscript. My expectations were high. I wanted to write something that would be generally useful to all nurses, no matter where they worked, but didn't want to spout meaningless generalizations. I wanted to pepper the book with both personal reflections and scholarly references because my mind typically seesaws between the concrete and the theoretical. Although I am very aware of the huge general literature on leadership that is certainly relevant to nurses, more needs to be said that's geared to the special situation of nursing as a gendered profession still largely peopled by women. This is an issue even for the men in our field.

The first time that someone called me a "leader," I started to deny that was the case because I thought that the profession was in trouble if I was one of its leaders. I don't do that now because being described that way doesn't seem foreign anymore. But even though I have served in many capacities—as a committee chair, an administrator (charge nurse, department chair, associate dean, dean), and an elected officer (president of both Sigma Theta Tau International and the American Academy of Nursing)—I do understand why being called a leader can leave even the most experienced person feeling a trifle ambivalent. So much is expected of leaders these days that you have to be a brave soul to admit to being one. What is more, many of us still erroneously equate being a leader with not making mistakes. Even though we know better, we still may not be comfortable either referring to ourselves as a leader or being referred to that way, if we are still not yet the incarnation of perfection. Of course, if you think that way, then you're destined never to be a leader because you'll never be perfect! And ruminating on one's inadequacies is likely to fuel anxiety more than adequacy.

As a woman of a certain age who entered the field before Friedan's *The Feminine Mystique* (1963) started the latest round of the Women's Movement, I was socialized from childhood to believe in universal masculine–feminine distinctions. For example, men were supposed to be the head of the family and women were the heart; men were instrumental and aimed for mastery and women were supposed to be supportive, more emotionally sensitive. It is not surprising then that I largely equated nursing in my early professional years with facilitating relationships and being creatively supportive—not qualities then associated with serious leadership.

I was valedictorian at my college graduation, and my commencement remarks emphasized nursing as service to others. When I received an honorary doctorate from my alma mater decades later, I did not repudiate that emphasis but talked about how my career had encompassed so much more. Nursing proved to be full of opportunities to express every aspect of my person from my creative bent to my taste for adventure. To just emphasize that nurses "have heart," as some advertisements do, simply doesn't do justice to either the intellectual challenges or the vibrancy of our field.

Simone De Beauvoir's *The Second Sex* (1952) was a revelation to me when I finally read it in the late 1960s because she questioned repeated descriptions of men's work in transcendent terms and women's work in terms of maintenance activities, on the grounds that all should be responsible in the here-and-now and be concerned with future developments. This made sense to me because I was never very fond of either/or approaches to anything. Life is more complicated than that, and all grown-ups need both head and heart to succeed. You need to maintain the best of what is in place at the same time that you greet new challenges.

I do not think that it's just nurses of my generation whose identity has been shaped to value caring over mastery, thus inadvertently making them skittish about becoming leaders. Nursing as a gendered profession has frequently been described in terms of professional domesticity (Roberts & Group, 1995). The Nightingale Pledge, neither written nor condoned by Nightingale, emphasizes sacrifice, service, and loyalty to the physician (Reverby, 1987). By contrast, the historic Nightingale was the founder of public health statistics, wrote the definitive statement on organization of military hospitals, shaped the field of sanitation, and was, if anything, much more politically astute than touchy-feely (Nauright, 1984). I find it interesting that Prince Albert met her and commented on her modesty, but Queen Victoria remarked on her mind, wishing she was part of the War Office (Strachey, 1963).

Although there have been many social changes since I first became a nurse, the ensuing feminist revolution has done a much better job of encouraging women to enter fields previously considered to be the province of men than it has of making visible the leadership that must be exerted to achieve the complicated missions of still gendered professions such as nursing, social work, and K-12 teaching. One way this plays out even now is for nurses to be given considerable responsibility without corresponding authority. For example, it has been found that physicians and administrators assign primary responsibility for patient safety to nurses (Cook, Hoas, Guttmannova, & Joyner, 2004) but may simultaneously not make them members of the decision-making team concerned with quality improvements (Mason, 2004). To the extent that nursing is largely viewed as providing "coverage" for an institution, then the field is seen in static, not leadership, terms.

When I was growing up, you wanted to do your best but you didn't think in terms of leadership because if you were a woman you were more concerned with the question: Should you work outside the home once you married and have children? When I announced that I wanted to be a nurse, both my parents were pleased with that decision. My mother said, "Good, you can always use that learning in raising your family," and my father said, "Nursing is a good thing to fall back on in case you marry a drunkard." Having grown up in East Baltimore where there were saloons every few blocks, I knew what they both meant. To my parents, getting married and having children should be my real aims in life, but a nursing background would serve me well, particularly if I was unfortunate enough to marry someone who couldn't provide for his family. Nursing as a fallback position, however, isn't a leadership stance!

There have always been women who have had continuous work lives outside the home, but mine was a watershed generation when large numbers of married middle-class women began to have continuous work lives, even if we didn't work full time each and every year. When many nurses worked until they became mothers, then returned to work only when the children were launched, their interrupted work patterns meant that they might never leave entry-level positions, thus never be offered the leadership opportunities that are available over the course of a full career. Now that the overwhelming majority of nurses have continuous work lives, individuals are still concerned with taking care of patients and their families but are also increasingly involved in making changes where they work so as to improve the care received, and this organizational focus requires a sense of strategy and tactical skills not traditionally emphasized in descriptions of the nursing profession.

Nursing schools have historically provided more course work on sound management rather than leadership for a variety of reasons: in nursing, the emphasis has been on collective 24-hour responsibility rather than on individual leadership; nursing roles have typically been described as *in service* to the patient and the physician; and leadership has been equated with graduate education and administrative roles rather than with the rank and file, who may not have those degrees or hold such titles (Scoble & Russell, 2003). Nurses have historically seen themselves as helpers more than leaders because representing oneself as the latter might even sound above your station and the antithesis of being a caring person.

Whatever else they believe, I think just about everyone who enters nursing wants to be perceived as a caring person. As a group, we are idealistic and dedicated to improving patient well-being. Raised, as I was, in a very religious family, the focus on humility—not getting a big head—meant that I was more oriented to service than to leadership and wary of appearing ambitious even though I always was determined to succeed. What I didn't understand at the time is the extent to which you need to be masterful to provide effective caregiving. In addition, many nurses are the first in their families to be educated beyond high school; this fact, however, may mean that our orientation is more likely to be directed at getting the degree(s), an achievement in itself, rather than on using that degree and obtaining others to play a transformative role in changing the future of health care.

I was the first person in my family to go to college. I knew that I wanted to become a nurse, but I also wanted to be college educated, someone at home in the world. I did well in school, but like many others without professional role models growing up, I kept thinking I was just lucky to get good grades, so I worried in grammar school about being adequate in high school, then worried in high school about my performance in college, with the same wonderings surfacing when I sought a master's then a doctoral degree. When I eventually read about the "imposter phenomenon" (Clance & Imes, 1978), I recognized myself. Every time I was successful, I kept thinking they just don't know how much I don't know. I kept wondering long after I should have whether I would be discovered to be a fraud, that is, not as good as I may appear to be. The biggest problem with that kind of thinking is that you remain focused primarily on your adequacy when you should be using your abilities to achieve important goals.

It's not that I lacked some measure of self-esteem, or otherwise I couldn't have accomplished what I did. It's just that each success was accomplished without the self-doubts disappearing. I didn't lack ambition but I always thought that I should hide those impulses—so as not to scare away prospective dates or blow my cover as a sweet person— and, in the process, I didn't always see the assets in my own person as something stable, something I could count on having and purposefully use. Consequently, it took me some time to learn how to use my advantages deliberatively to achieve the important goals that I had as a member of the nursing profession.

Mind you, I don't assume that everyone in the nursing profession suffers from the same psychology, but being comfortable enough with your strengths and limitations to use them deliberately for constructive change is not as common as one would wish. You can exert leadership while feeling insecure (e.g., setting up a service that is needed by a particular patient population), but you have to get over being surprised that you got this far if you are going to be able to exert transformational leadership, and work to change "what is" into "what could be" (Bennis & Nanus, 1985). Pushing for real change requires some moxie which you won't be capable of in any measure if you are still largely self-absorbed and concerned with making ripples.

Over the course of my career, these matters have been further complicated by the fact that nursing has spent a great deal of energy striving to become fully professional. We have moved from apprentice training to degree-based education, specialty knowledge has been developed with certification processes in place to validate those skills learned in master's programs, and the knowledge base of nursing has grown with the development of doctoral education and nursing research. These developments reflect our determination to build the profession so our perspective can exert more influence in shaping health care, but this focus on infrastructure development had the inadvertent effect of making us more aware of our limitations than our strengths. We are finally, however, at a point in history when there can be no doubt that nursing is fully professional, and our task now is to harness our field's competence in service to quality health care that is both accessible and affordable.

When the emphasis is on getting up to speed, then it is less likely that each individual will be thinking of how she or he can exert leadership. You're more likely to think that you will make a difference, but at some future time, which may never arrive. I remember being part of a panel on research mentoring at a conference about 20 years ago. The discussion was animated, but everyone who spoke seemed to want a mentor, and no one seemed ready to be a mentor. It was as if each person didn't feel grown up enough to play that developmental role. Alas, a field that is peopled with the needy will be limited in the extent that it can address the needs of others boldly.

What tipped me into finally getting comfortable with being a leader? It was becoming a Kellogg National Fellow in 1981. The W. K. Kellogg Foundation celebrated its 50th anniversary the year before by designing a new kind of leadership-development program. Scholars in a range of fields were selected to attend two week-long seminars on interdisciplinary topics each year for three years; they were also expected to complete an individual project for which they received released time (25%). The experience was intended to encourage under-40 individuals with promise to become prepared for leadership, with the program designed to highlight the bigger-picture issues that do not belong to any one field, for example, use of technology, economic development, and the aging of society.

When Group II was selected, I was the only nurse in it, though the legendary Rozella Schlotfeldt was on the advisory committee to that class, and she took me under her wing. One sign of the times was that in our cohort of 40, there were only nine women, and I was the only "traditional" one, by which I mean married to the original husband and with children. (The original age restriction was later lifted because the women in the program successfully argued that it was limiting; women's careers do not necessarily proceed lockstep from college through graduate school, so women might only demonstrate their full leadership potential after 40 years.)

This leadership experience changed me in profound ways, and I found my voice as that fellowship program intended me to do (Matusak, 1996). I came fully to terms with residual concerns that I was only "bright for a nurse" and realized that I had talents that weren't limited by any qualifier. In this group of prospective leaders, I wound up taking charge of designing the final seminar. Having come of age in the 1960s when you were more likely to be suspicious of the establishment than comfortable with becoming part of it, I saw how apprehensive my whole generation was about assuming leadership, so it wasn't just my personal problem. I also began to appreciate how unattractive and off-putting it is for able individuals to deny their leadership potential and to resist taking on new challenges.

Three years of being repeatedly told in different ways that we were leaders had the desired effect on us. It also convinced me that a powerful way to develop leaders is to tell people with potential that they are leaders, then help them act accordingly. The next time a major leadership opportunity came my way—being asked to run for the board of Sigma Theta Tau International, the honor society of nursing—I was willing to stand for election and conscientiously visited every chapter's booth in a concerted effort to introduce myself to the delegates.

This going after votes was an about-face for me. As a freshman in high school, I had run for class office but didn't vote for myself because I thought it was egotistical to do so. I lost that election by one vote and learned that you cannot be passive about going after what is important to you. Leadership isn't about being lifted up by others; it requires you to assume some responsibility for the heavy lifting.

Eventually becoming president of Sigma Theta Tau International during the time when the first chapters outside the United States were chartered and a headquarters was built taught me a great deal: use your strengths to shape what you'll emphasize during your tenure in office, fundraising is an important leadership activity, it is important for the leader to stay on a message for those in the organization to hear the message, and being involved internationally helps you understand your home situation better (McBride, 2005). Success in this experience made me more willing to accept other leadership positions and to expand my abilities further, learning to forge community connections and function effectively on boards where I sometimes was the only nurse.

In my striving to become adequate to the requirements of leadership, I have become something of a student of leadership, intrigued by what makes some people very successful in leadership positions and others quite the opposite. I've come to believe that leaders come in all forms and that no one leader can be all things to all people, despite the fact that we all have our juvenile moments when we wish for a leader who will save us from the problems and dislocations our institutions face, only to be disappointed because real flesh-and-blood people regularly fall short of expectations.

My musings have convinced me that the ancient advice, "know thyself," is a good starting point for leadership because understanding your strengths and limitations will help you get clear about what you can do best and where you need to shore up your abilities as you go about the central task of leadership, which is "inspiring and catalyzing others to realize shared values in a complex world that is constantly changing and requiring us to design new ways of achieving our goals." This definition of leadership is useful, I believe, no matter what the level of leadership at which you are operating, from staff nurse to executive director of a professional association to president of a university.

If you unpack this definition, it is clear that the exercise of leadership involves communication, collaboration, morale building, understanding the demands of the larger environment, thinking in a fresh way about the issues, strategizing how to address goals then designing processes to achieve them, developing needed resources (human and financial), evaluating outcomes, and using any success in furtherance of the next round of aspirational goals. Some aspect of all these skills is taught in schools of nursing.

What to Expect

With this introduction, let me now proceed to describe what you can expect in the chapters ahead. I have stressed in the title "the growth and development" of nurse leaders because my perspective is that of my background as a master's-prepared mental health nurse with a doctorate in developmental psychology. This preparation has enabled me to understand the importance of mind sets that either assist one in realizing one's full potential or get in the way of doing so. For example, there are many normal-crazy thoughts that can limit your leadership potential if you don't come to terms with them.

Something is normal-crazy if it is believed by most of us but more or less irrational. A good example of normal-crazy thinking is "I must be perfect" because it is an impossible objective and acting as if perfection is possible is only likely to get in the way of actually achieving what is doable. Albert Ellis (2001), one of the first to highlight the importance of thinking differently to act differently, emphasized the need to tackle core irrational beliefs in order to achieve mental health, and I think you need to do likewise in order to reach your leadership potential.

This book, however, isn't just about the leader's mental health or personal qualities. There are three sections to the book and they collectively address the three major views of leadership that have occupied center stage in recent decades. Early attempts at defining leadership focused on the qualities all leaders share, so the first four chapters concentrate on the *personal*. Chapter 1 looks critically at "the right stuff" leaders are supposed to have. Self-knowledge is the most important quality that leaders need to possess, so chapter 2 focuses on coming to terms with one's strengths and limitations. Sustaining career optimism in the face of disappointments and challenges is vital, so chapter 3 discusses strategies for staying optimistic and not being waylaid by anger. As leadership implies full career development, chapter 4 considers what it means for an individual to have a career, and not just a job, and the stages of a career.

The second section of this book concentrates on leadership as *achieving organizational goals*. You can be a charismatic figure, but if you are not successful in helping your institution achieve its mission, values, and goals, you aren't much of a leader. Because stereotyped views of nursing continue to downplay the contributions of our field, chapter 5 discusses how important it is for nurses to be able to name what they do to meet the mission of their work setting. The next four chapters tackle specific skill sets essential in promoting organizational effectiveness— being clear about expectations, processes, and direction (chapter 6); interpersonal and communication effectiveness (chapter 7); resource development (chapter 8); and an ability to appreciate and develop others (chapter 9).

Achieving an institution's long-standing goals has itself been criticized as insufficiently dynamic in a quickly changing world. That is why the focus of the third section is on leadership as *transformational*. In this view, the very meanings of what constitute health and quality of life keep changing, so leaders must have an understanding of these matters and a strategic vision that enables them to create new ways of addressing emerging challenges and opportunities. The third section begins with an overview of what nursing has accomplished in recent decades with a view to energizing nurses to exert additional leadership in the future (chapter 10). The next two chapters tackle the importance of strategic vision (chapter 11) and of choosing excellence as a change strategy (chapter 12). Chapter 13 focuses on how the leadership that nurses exert cannot be limited to what they do within nursing (discipline specific) positions. To be transformative requires interdisciplinary savvy, and there are many leadership positions that do not belong to any one field and nurses are moving into them. The epilogue is future oriented, focusing on why this is the very best time to be a nurse leader.

A further word about my slant and the methodology of this book. Because my orientation is developmental, I subscribe to the view that personal narrative and reflection on one's lived experience is an appropriate research method (Ellis & Bochner, 2000). Introspection, for the purpose of understanding underlying themes and issues, has often been used by women to develop insights in those areas where their experience may vary from that of their male counterparts (Reinharz, 1992). Accordingly, I will share some personal experiences when I believe they bring into sharp relief issues that are important, but my discussion of these matters will also draw on the literature written on the subject. My hope is that the approach of the book, combining as it does personal reflections with academic backup, will serve some of the same functions that a mentor does in sharing both book learning and insights forged from practical experience.

In recent years, I have taught a doctoral course on leadership and have been involved with a number of leadership programs, most notably the Robert Wood Johnson Foundation's Nurse Faculty Scholars Program and the Building Academic Geriatric Nursing Capacity Program managed by the American Academy of Nursing and funded by the John A. Hartford Foundation (McBride, Fagin, Franklin, Huba, & Quach, 2006). As a result of these experiences, I have learned how much participants value tips for leadership. Ending a review of the issues with a final summing up can be a helpful way to remember key matters. Accordingly, I end all chapters, except for the epilogue, with a listing of take-away points.

Let me close this introduction by admitting that I have not handled each and every leadership challenge presented to me as well as I would have wished. When I make recommendations in this book, the authority behind the words comes from some successes but also from having, many a times, struggled unsuccessfully with these matters. It is a truism to say that sometimes the biggest learning comes from making mistakes, but it is, indeed, true.

Early in my deanship, I had an irate faculty member come to see me about something that I hadn't handled well. She walked into my office prepared to tell me the error of my ways. As soon as she said what she was angry about, I responded with an acknowledgment that I had not handled the situation well. The acknowledgment turned a critic into a supporter and taught me a valuable leadership lesson: If you make a mistake, admit it right away then move the discussion on to how the situation might be improved the next time around. Leadership is a constant struggle for improvement—a nursing value in itself and one of the major reasons why nurses make good leaders.

I hope this book encourages each reader to give some thought to her or his situation. Do you see what you are doing on a daily basis as an opportunity to exert leadership? Have you come to terms with how you can make a difference, or are you still thinking that leadership is someone else's responsibility? Do you still, mistakenly, equate leadership with being an administrator? What do you need to do to move yourself to the next level of professional development? Are you bold enough in thinking about "what could be"? Do you know how what you do contributes to the mission of the organization in which you serve? Are you waiting to be "empowered," or are you clear about how you can act in the here-and-now on the authority you already possess? Do you read broadly enough to have a sense of key trends likely to shape our world and our profession in coming years? What is the area in which you can be personally excellent? What are the areas in which your organization can be first-rate? Do you know how to operate effectively in interdisciplinary forums?

REFERENCES

Bennis, W., & Nanus, B. (1985). *Leaders: The strategies for taking charge.* New York: Perennial Library.

Clance, P. R., & Imes, S. (1978). The imposter phenomenon in high achieving women: Dynamics and therapeutic intervention. *Psychotherapy Theory, Research and Practice, 15,* 241–247.

Cook, A. F., Hoas, H., Guttmannova, K., & Joyner, J. C. (2004). An error by any other name. *American Journal of Nursing, 104,* 32–43.

De Beauvoir, S. (1952). *The second sex* (H. M. Parshley, Trans.). New York: Bantam Books.

Ellis, A. (2001). *Feeling better, getting better, staying better. Profound self-help therapy for your emotions.* Atascadero, CA: Impact Publishers.

Ellis, C., & Bochner, A. P. (2000). Autoethnography, personal narrative, reflexivity. In N. K. Denzin & Y. S. Lincoln (Eds.), *Handbook of qualitative research* (2nd ed., pp. 733–768). Thousand Oaks, CA: Sage Publications.

Friedan, B. (1963). *The feminine mystique.* New York: Dell Publishing.

Mason, D. J. (2004). Who says it's an error? *American Journal of Nursing, 104,* 104–107.

Matusak, L. R. (1996). *Finding your voice: Learning to lead anywhere you want to make a difference.* San Francisco: Jossey-Bass.

McBride, A. (1972). Leadership: Problems and possibilities in nursing. *American Journal of Nursing, 72,* 1445–1447.

McBride, A. B. (1988). Angela Barron McBride. In T. M. Schorr & A. Zimmerman (Eds.), *Making choices, taking chances. Nurse leaders tell their stories* (pp. 261–266). St. Louis, MO: C. V. Mosby.

McBride, A. B. (2005). Angela Barron McBride. In Sr. R. Donley (Ed.), *Reflecting on 30 years of nursing leadership: 1975-2005* (p. 37). Indianapolis, IN: Sigma Theta Tau International.

McBride, A. B., Fagin, C. M., Franklin, P. D., Huba, G. J., & Quach, L. (2006). Developing leaders via an annual leadership conference. *Nursing Outlook, 54,* 226–230.

Nauright, L. (1984). Politics and power: A new look at Florence Nightingale. *Nursing Forum, 21*(1), 5–8.

Reinharz, S. (1992). *Feminist methods in social research.* New York: Oxford University Press.

Reverby, S. (1987). A caring dilemma: Womanhood and nursing in historical perspective. *Nursing Research, 36,* 5–11.

Roberts, J. I., & Group, T. M. (1995). *Feminism and nursing. An historical perspective on power, status, and political activism in the nursing profession.* Westport, CT: Praeger.

Scoble, K. B., & Russell, G. (2003). Vision 2020, part 1: Profile of the future nurse leader. *Journal of Nursing Administration, 33,* 324–330.

Strachey, L. (1963). *Eminent Victorians* (pp. 129–196). New York: Capricorn Books.

THE GROWTH AND DEVELOPMENT
of NURSE LEADERS

Part I

Leadership as Personal

Chapter 1

"The Right Stuff"

I was once asked in an interview, "When did you first know that you were a leader?" The interviewer wanted to find out whether I had been a leader in my early years, but I found that question difficult to answer, as it seemed improper for me to admit that I grew up thinking of myself as in any way exceptional. Before college, I had been selected to give a speech welcoming the bishop at our confirmation and had been the first girl to be president of a parish youth group, but these experiences didn't make me think of myself as a leader. My view of leadership, even at the time of that interview, was still shaped by some residual notion of a leader as "the great one," because while I was growing up I had been encouraged to read the lives of statesmen, scientists, and saints for inspiration. Since I didn't see myself becoming president of the country, destined for a Nobel Prize, or ready for martyrdom, I didn't see myself as prime leader material. I wanted to be a good nurse, but back then I didn't see nurses as leaders who could inspire movements or headlines.

Characteristics of Leaders

Historically, leaders have been described in *heroic* terms. Read the literature on the characteristics shared by leaders, and you might conclude that they are some combination of the following traits: intelligent, responsible, persistent, perceptive, self-confident, sociable, articulate, dominant, determined, cooperative, trustworthy, dependable, friendly, tolerant, influential, motivated, outgoing, upright, tall, and masculine (Northouse, 2004, pp. 1–34). Although some of these traits seem to apply equally to women—being responsible, trustworthy, and friendly—others clearly do not. You can imagine women being perceptive more than dominant, and this difference gives women leaders a documented advantage in settings that place a premium on collaboration and a disadvantage in those that value power plays (Eagly, 2007).

In more recent times, the leadership literature has seriously questioned the longstanding exclusive emphasis on whether the person in charge has the right stuff on the grounds that leaders are substantially influenced by the situations they encounter, including their ability to harness their followers. In this view, a person might be an effective leader in one situation but not in another one. However, even those who think that a cataloging of attributes isn't enough to explain leadership tend to put forward their own lists of desired traits (Hackman & Wageman, 2007). And those lists can be off-putting because they usually include more positive attributes than most ordinary people see themselves as possessing or are likely to acquire in a lifetime devoted to self-improvement.

Admitting that you are a leader takes considerable self-assurance, but owning up to having leader-like virtues may be even more difficult, particularly if you have been raised to be self-effacing, as many women have. Quite recently, I heard of a woman physician who was a semifinalist for a prestigious grant and who answered the question "We are going to have a hard time selecting next year's awardees from this talented pool, so tell us what makes you special?" with "Oh, the pool is talented and I don't think I'm any more special than anyone else." Needless to say, the final decision didn't go in her favor.

Nursing has not been untouched by the fascination to break leadership down into certain attributes of personality and character. Like other fields, our profession has studied acknowledged leaders to try to figure out what the accomplished have in common. Intrigued by the subject as a result of their experience in the Robert Wood Johnson Foundation's Executive Nurse Fellows Program, Houser and Player (2004, p. xv) interviewed 12 nurse leaders who were widely recognized for their achievements and concluded that each was visionary, scholarly, resilient, committed, courageous, responsive, creative, innovative, thoughtful, and humble. Although their positive regard for humility runs counter to the preferential weight usually given in the leadership literature to dominance, their selection of that trait does demonstrate a dilemma for many nurse (and women) leaders: they are expected to be the best but simultaneously also expected not to be self-important. All of the other traits Houser and Player saw as characterizing the group they interviewed had much in common with the literature on leadership and were qualities that are useful across a range of situations.

The longing to figure out who has "the right stuff" and how it can be taught to others is powerful. Even those who resist inventories of qualities concede that some sets of attributes are important. Sternberg (2007) argues that leaders synthesize *wisdom* (seeking common good, balancing personal aspirations with helping others, attending to short-term and long-term needs), *intelligence* (academic, practical, and emotional), and *creativity* (problem redefinition, problem analysis, risk taking). Yukl (2006) and Zaccaro (2007) emphasize other sets of leader attributes: *cognitive capacities* (creativity, general intelligence, grasp of complexity), *personality qualities* (openness, sociability, risk tolerance), *motives* (drive for power, need for achievement), *social capacities* (emotional and social intelligence), and *problem solving* (problem statement and solution generation).

What is comforting about the search for what constitutes "the right stuff" is that there is considerable overlap in the list making of various experts. They all emphasize some combination of astuteness, ingenuity, and cordiality. What is also obvious is that one is not born with most of these traits. Although heredity may make you more or less intelligent and extroverted, family life, experience, and education hone the raw material. You can learn how to meet and greet, even if you are naturally shy. Eleanor Roosevelt proved that. You can learn to look at situations in more than one way even though you first learned that there was one correct way of doing things. That is why critical thinking is a staple of professional education. You can learn negotiation skills even if you don't know much about the give and take of such exchanges while starting out.

I find it useful not to think of leaders as destined to succeed, because thinking of them as born that way keeps them beyond reach. The more that leaders are defined as innately special, the more we can excuse ourselves if we're not like them and rationalize our passive behavior by saying, "I'm not cut out to be a leader." If we think we can grow the dispositions and skills they have over time, then the focus is on what we're going to do to move in that direction, and moving forward occupies our attention. This produces better momentum.

The reality is that nurses as a group have in a large measure what leaders are supposed to possess. First and foremost, we are taught to value problem solving (i.e., the nursing process), systems thinking, and the common good. Even if some of us aren't extroverts, we are all socialized to develop empathy, value interpersonal relationships, and respect cultural differences, all of which are central to emotional and social intelligence. Integrity is a core leadership trait, and Americans consistently give nurses the highest marks when asked to rate the honesty and ethical standards of various professions ("Nurses top list," 2006). Given the competitive nature of admissions to nursing schools, today's nurses do not lack academic intelligence, but their IQs may be less critical to their leadership potential than their strong practical intelligence.

Practical intelligence, which has been described in military structures as applying knowledge gained from experience to the solution of everyday predicaments, is almost a definition of nursing (Hedlund et al., 2003).

Learning to Be Taken Seriously

Nurses as a group may not be as prepared for leadership in some respects. More nurses than physicians and lawyers start out as the first in their families to have completed postsecondary education, so they may lack the social ease and graces that individuals growing up in more educated and affluent families possess, for example, being comfortable with nonfamily members in a broad array of circumstances or expecting that the influential will pay attention to you if you ask for something. The less educated and poorer you are, the more you tend to be fatalistic, the exact opposite of thinking that you can make a difference.

I have thought a great deal about the difference it makes if you grow up with role models and in family circumstances where you are used to holding your own. I happened to go to high school with Nancy Pelosi (2008), the first woman to be Speaker of the House. Her family of origin was not wealthy, but her father was Mayor of Baltimore for 12 years after serving five terms in Congress. She was also the only daughter after six sons (one died young), which made her more comfortable from the start, I think, in dealing with men than I was growing up in a decidedly matriarchal family. Before she had finished high school, she had met many famous people, including Jack Kennedy.

I remember talking with her over the phone one time when I was visiting San Francisco well before she was elected to Congress. She was then head of the Democratic Party in California and recommended that I get in touch with a very famous physician to get some help from him in an area that we had discussed. I thanked her for the recommendation, but got off the phone knowing that I was not going to follow up and call him as she had suggested. I didn't think he would care to be bothered by someone like me even if I told him Nancy Pelosi told me to call. I tell this story because I have thought about the situation many times since her rise to power. The 21st century me would now make the phone call. Since then I have learned that people pay attention to you if you act as if they should, but it was to take me more years and more experience before I really began to think that someone like him would pay attention to me.

I contrast my own experience with that of Afaf Meleis, dean at the University of Pennsylvania School of Nursing, who grew up in Egypt watching her mother become the first Egyptian nurse to obtain a doctoral degree. She learned early on to be fearless, persuading the Chancellor of the University of Alexandria to let her matriculate there at age 15; 16 years was the minimum age, but she argued successfully that 15 years was 16 years in the Arabic calendar. After coming to the United States for a master's degree, she wanted to stay on to get her doctorate. However, she didn't want to be away from her nuclear-engineer fiancé any longer, and Egypt wasn't letting young scientists like him leave the country. Anguished about the matter, she decided to write to the Egyptian President Gamal Abdel Nasser. She didn't tell her fiancé what she had done, so imagine his surprise when he was called into his boss's office and handed a note written by Nasser that read, "Could you please take care of this and let him out of the country?" (Tiger, 2008). That much success early on in getting institutions to bend to your will would reinforce that you are the kind of person to whom people pay attention.

I don't want to leave the impression that one or two successes in getting what you have lobbied for will transform anyone into a confident person who will never again settle for either the status quo or an initial negative response. You have to learn to keep trying, noticing along the way that the proverb "ask and you shall receive" requires you to ask in the first place. The more you push what is important to you, some measure of what you ask for will come to pass, and each success builds confidence that you can effect change. Over time, residual hesitancy dissipates, in part because you soon realize that no one is successful all the time.

Nurses are taught to make good judgments, but we are not expected to be decisive in the "ordering" way that physicians learn, so our resolution may even look different. Our tendency to insinuate information— implying a course of action without giving a definite opinion—may seem indecisive just because our speech is more indirect (Stein, 1967; Stein, Watts, & Howell, 1990). Because our practice is structured by professional standards and institutional policies/protocols, what we do is likely to look more programmed than it is, with the consequence that our ingenuity in applying standards is sometimes underappreciated and unrecognized even by us.

The overall tendency in nurses to be indirect in their speech has itself been shaped by the larger issue of how women's and men's conversational styles affect their language choices, who gets heard in our society, and who gets credit (Tannen, 1994). The conversational differences between women and men have consequences even within nursing.

I have seen men in nursing use simple-declarative sentences, and their female counterparts mistakenly (and angrily) hear them as ordering them around. I have seen women in nursing use complex compound sentences, and their male counterparts not hear them as providing the intended direction. The string of "would you" and "could you" phrases in the request obscured the underlying message that the woman thought she was sending.

Although there are big differences between what is true of nursing as a profession and what is true of nurses as individuals, it can be helpful to consider where our professional values dovetail with expectations of leaders and where they do not as you calculate your personal strengths and challenges. In circumstances where you do not feel like a leader, it may be helpful to remember that you are part of a profession with many desirable attributes. It may also help to remember that feelings may not be the most accurate indicator of your abilities. You can be very effective and still feel subpar because of lack of sleep and exercise. What matters more is that you understand the overlap between what you have been taught to do professionally and what leaders are expected to do.

In my opinion, the whole issue of energy is often left unaddressed in the leadership literature, yet we all vary in how healthy we are—stamina changes with age and/or chronic illness—and how much time we can put into work. I have worked every configuration of part time, full time, and double time, and my schedule in any year was determined by a host of factors, for example, family responsibilities, length of commute, life stage, and drive. Simply put, motivating others to accomplish a mission and then figuring out how to get there requires an assortment of behaviors, and that goes well beyond what it takes to maintain what is already in place. When I was a new graduate, it took all of my concentration to do what I had learned to do in school. When I was a new mother, I was creative but limited my work investment, so I could juggle family and job. When I was an empty nester, I was able to take on all sorts of new challenges, because by this time I was experienced and not weighed down by home responsibilities. Although energy and time are not the same, you may be less likely to take on new challenges during those periods when juggling work and family seems all consuming.

Leadership is associated with drive, and one's investment in guiding others will depend on the time available. The former means that one must take care of oneself—attending to nutrition, exercise, sleep, relaxation, and frame of mind—so as to have the energy to concentrate on other matters. The latter means that one is likely to embrace the demands of leadership differentially at different stages. Mothers in academia, for example, spend 23% more time on household tasks and 75% more time on caregiving than fathers in academia, so it is not surprising that they wind up devoting 8% less time per week to their professional responsibilities than do their male counterparts (Mason & Goulden, 2002).

In some circumstances, professional women may devote somewhat less time to professional responsibilities than their male counterparts, but that doesn't mean that they aren't enriched by the seesawing back and forth between the pulls of work and family. Juggling roles can be enriching or depleting depending on whether the combination is energizing or overwhelming, with both men and women experiencing more enrichment in the shift from their traditional sphere of influence to the nontraditional domain—work to family for men and family to work for women (Rothbard, 2001).

If anything, I found renewed pleasure in employment when I became a mother because that pursuit got me away from being swallowed up by the home front, but my investment in family also gave me some sense of perspective when I was bothered by job-related anxieties. When my teenage children sometimes treated me as if I didn't know the ways of the world, having a regular paycheck was a comfort; when I had to deal with a convoluted personnel matter at work, I took an added measure of pleasure in how straightforward the delight of a daughter's hand-drawn card saying "I love you" can be. This notion that you are enhanced when you "don't put all your eggs in one basket" is in keeping with the longitudinal findings of Maas and Kuypers (1974) who studied adult development from 30 to 70 and found that those who aged best were not one sided.

When you are in the early years of a career, it may also take some time for you to recognize the extent of your own ambition. It was only after I had accomplished what society (and my parents/in-laws) expected of me—that is, getting married and having the requisite two children—that I began to come to terms fully with my own ambitions. I was fortunate enough to have a husband who regularly asked "What do you want to do next?" even when I wasn't raising the question myself. What surprised me was the fact that I always had an answer when he posed that question, often one that took me aback because I didn't see it coming. My answers surprised me and forced me to give more thought to what I wanted to make of the rest of my life.

I didn't set out to be a leader, but I also began to see over time that I had some abilities in that direction. The first time you think "Even I could do better than that," you mean that more as an insult to the person you're criticizing than you mean it as a compliment to your own abilities. However, if you find yourself regularly thinking some version of "I could do better than what is now in place," then you should, in my opinion, redirect your energies away from the disapproving part of that stance and seriously contemplate your own leadership potential. You may just be right—you could do better! Said or implied often enough, "Even I could do better" is likely to get you invited to assume more leadership, and refusing to accept this challenge will look more unseemly over time. You (and others) reach a point of "put up or shut up."

I recently heard France Córdova, president of Purdue University, talk about her career trajectory. The oldest of 12 children, she found her studies to be a respite from all the babysitting that occupied her early years. An English major in college, she eventually followed her Apollo 11–inspired passion with the stars and became an astrophysicist. She did not set out to become an administrator but pursued opportunities when offered. She described herself as fearless, a quality she came to value in herself as she saw how many people were riddled with fears. Whether owing to her firstborn status in a large family or other experiences, she came to appreciate the "take charge" aspects of her own personality. As I listened to her speak, I was impressed with how so many of the "take charge" experiences that she had had were comparable to those most nurses have in dealing with people riddled with fears. Even if you are able to function well in situations that distress others, you may still shy away from accepting leadership challenges.

It is so much easier to criticize others than to assume the responsibilities of leadership. I can do a really good analysis of a situation, and take pride in that ability, but that's not the same thing as figuring out how to improve matters and then moving forward in that new direction. Going on to next steps is scary because criticizing allows you to cling to your moral superiority indefinitely (I know what "better" looks like); doing something about the situation leaves you open to criticism from others if things don't go as expected. In addition, assuming the challenges of leadership can expose any residual ambivalence you may have about exerting power.

Power Isn't a Dirty Word

It took me a long time to get comfortable with the word "power." I wanted to exercise influence, but going after power struck me as incompatible with being caring. Exerting power did not seem as unladylike after I read French and Raven's (1959) classic description of different kinds of power. The first three—reward power, coercive power, and legitimate power—are typically conferred by the organization in which you work. You may have a title that legitimates your sphere of influence in that institution, and that position may carry with it the ability to reward some (recommending for special opportunities) and penalize others (disapproving merit pay increases). There is also the power that comes from the person. Expert power is wielded by virtue of education and experience; if you are knowledgeable, then the information you possess is a form of power. Finally, there's referent power, meaning the influence you have when others want to be like you or admire you. A good example of the latter is society's aforementioned high regard for the integrity of nurses, a trust that can be converted into authority in certain situations.

Many nurses are not comfortable admitting they have power because the word seems more associated with dominance than tending to others (Rafael, 1996), and I was no exception. Only gradually did I understand that without power what I wanted to do would not be accomplished. And if nurses didn't move forward nursing's long-treasured values, who would? The mistake I made originally was thinking that power equaled telling others what to do, and that tactic didn't strike me as likely to be successful in most circumstances. And it isn't! Once I realized that the exercise of power could take many forms other than swagger and bluster, then I became more comfortable in exerting my authority. I even came to enjoy exercising authority that didn't look on the face of it like old-fashioned autocratic power. Many times I have said something strong or difficult prefaced by the words, "It would be remiss of me as _____ [use any title you have] if I didn't point out that _____." In these instances, I have deliberately used my position to legitimate my opinion, moving the issue out of the personal domain and framing my strongly expressed opinion as part of just doing my job.

Nurses exercise an enormous amount of power by doing their jobs. If you think about power not as coercion but as influence, then it is clear that nurses of every stripe shape countless matters every day. They determine whether mistakes are caught, problems are noticed before they do damage, families know what to do when a member goes home, and hospitals get accredited. They do triage in the emergency room, explain what the doctor meant when patients are puzzled by jargon, and help provide meaning at the end of life. The issue isn't whether nurses have influence but whether they act as if they make a difference and don't hesitate to point out where they do (nicely of course).

The other word typically associated with discussions of power in nursing is "empowerment," meaning the development, within the situation in which you operate, of a climate that encourages you to do what you believe needs to be done professionally (Manojlovich, 2007). Does the environment in which you work value nurses who give voice to their viewpoints? You are considered to be empowered if you can achieve some measure of control over the content, context, and competence expected of nursing.

I have mixed feelings about this construct. On the one hand, I truly believe that you need to have that kind of control to get the job done and settings do vary in how supportive they are. However, on the other hand, there remains about that word "empowerment" the suggestion that some external force will shape whether you feel emboldened to act on your existing authority, and that's too passive for my taste. I have seen nurses argue that the environment did not empower them as a justification for what they weren't able to accomplish, and I've never been sure whether they could have accomplished more if they hadn't believed that they first had to be empowered. Like leadership itself, should the focus be on having "the right stuff," in this case being empowered by the organization, or on moving to act in terms of the authority you already professionally have?

Complex person–environment interactions shape one's perceptions of empowerment. Take the example of self-esteem, which waxes and wanes over the lifespan—growing in childhood when views of self may be unrealistically positive, dropping (particularly for girls) during adolescence with social comparisons and external feedback, then growing during the adult years as power and status build, and declining with age as retirement and loss take hold (Robins & Trzesniewski, 2005). Self-esteem does not necessarily predict achievements, but self-views do matter because they play a major role in organizing our perceptions of reality, which then influence our subsequent behaviors (Swann, Chang-Schneider, & McClarty, 2007).

Simply put, if you think that you have authority in a situation and make a difference, then you are more prepared to act accordingly, even in the face of difficulties. If you feel unsure of yourself, you are all the more likely to handle perceived rebuffs ineffectually (Sommer & Baumeister, 2002). What is particularly fascinating is that there is some evidence that people keep putting themselves in circumstances that reinforce how they already see themselves, so those with positive self-views prefer to interact with those who see them positively and those with negative self-views too often continue to associate with those who see them negatively (Robinson & Smith-Lovin, 1992).

This tendency of the depressed to associate with the depressed and the optimistic to associate with the optimistic has profound consequences in how empowered each of us might feel by our environments. I had a running dispute with someone who used to report to me. She would regularly argue that our university was not properly supportive to some people, and I would respond by reminding her that it was like all institutions just a bureaucracy, and what varied the most was not the university but how faculty and staff responded to opportunities. Some of my colleagues seemed to apply for every opportunity that was posted, whereas some others always said that they hadn't received the e-mail message that went out to one and all describing the opportunity. Obviously, I am being glib in de-emphasizing the role that supportive environments can play in encouraging risk taking and acting authoritatively, but it is to make the larger point that it is "seeing the opportunity" that may vary more than what is in place.

I have been greatly influenced by the range of all those models that emphasize the importance of explanatory style in shaping hopelessness or optimism and subsequent expectations and behaviors (Abramson, Seligman, & Teasdale, 1978; Peterson, Seligman, & Maier, 1993). Do you, for example, blame a failure on something stable and global ("I'm not cut out to be a leader") or on something unstable and specific ("Last Tuesday, I did not handle that situation well")? The former explanation means that you are not likely to try again, whereas the latter is likely to lead to another effort. We all have the inalienable right not to be at our best each and every day! Do you explain success in terms of something unstable and external ("I lucked out") or in terms of your own competence ("I'm good in that area because nurses are well prepared to handle such situations")? The latter is likely to make you think that this success is repeatable, and with repetition you develop even more confidence in your abilities.

Optimism is important to leadership, not in a mindless "happy face" pin kind of way, but constructing a worldview that is not defeatist is an important component of effectiveness. In workshops, I have asked attendees to imagine for two to three minutes everything in their lives that is positive and then to take another two to three minutes to do the same for everything in their lives that is negative. The only stipulation I have is that they have to be scrupulously honest with themselves. They usually write feverishly in both segments. After the time has elapsed, I remind them that they live out their lives suspended somewhere between those two versions of reality, and they can choose every day which pieces to focus on as they meet their professional responsibilities. The point of the exercise is to help them see that so much is dependent on whether they focus on their strengths or their limitations.

Pretending Can Be a Leadership Strategy

Maybe you think I have come dangerously close to maintaining that there isn't such a thing as objective truth and it's all in your head. I assure you that I don't believe that. I do believe, however, that what story you tell about your reality—"they never listen to nursing" versus "nursing is appreciated by most"—will shape what you can make of your reality. In my own life, I've gone so far as to say to myself, "They may all be organized against me, but I choose *not* to think that's true, because if I do then I don't know where to go from there." In my view, it is better to overestimate support than to feel paralyzed by indifference, and "pretending" there is support may sometimes even get nonsupporters to act that way in the long run.

I have many times had the experience of asking to join a group where I wound up being either the only nurse or the only woman, and hardly anyone spoke to me at the beginning. Instead of assuming that they did not value my input, I kept coming back and sitting with different people at different times. Over the months, more people talked to me; over the years, I even became an important member of the group and no one remembered that they had initially invited me to join the group with reluctance. The self-consciousness at the onset was difficult to handle, but my behavior changed the behavior of others. If I had assumed at the start that they simply didn't care, then the transformation simply wouldn't have happened.

I take "pretending" very seriously because I once knew a new PhD who was hired at Harvard to work on a major research project supported by the National Institute of Mental Health. She was thrilled by the position because it would give her an opportunity to work with a very famous psychologist; let's call her Marcia. A few months after she arrived, however, Marcia died suddenly and my friend became with much trepidation the principal investigator. Years later when the book resulting from the project was being universally praised, I asked her how she managed to accomplish what she did straight out of graduate school. She said that she often didn't know what to do, being so new to such responsibility, so she would regularly ask herself what Marcia would do. She always had a sense of what Marcia would do in a difficult situation, even when she didn't know how to provide leadership herself in that situation.

Her strategy made sense to me. When you are new in a leadership role, you may not feel comfortable at the start, acting from your own authority, yet you know enough to have a sense of what that mythical creature "the good leader" would do in that situation. I have used that ruse in my own life. When I was a brand-new dean and didn't know how to handle something, I would regularly ask myself, "What would a good dean do in this situation?" and that ploy helped me brainstorm ideas. Over time, you need to do this less as the distance between who you are in relation to some idealized leader narrows.

In many ways, this chapter may seem a bit perverse. Instead of elaborating on "the right stuff" leaders should have, I have spent more time admitting that the assumption of leadership can be scary and that you might start off just pretending to be a leader. Admittedly my approach has been shaped by the disenchantment many nurses have expressed about assuming leadership positions: "Don't know if I can do it," "Not sure the effort is worth it." I have heard doctorally prepared nurses say that they would rather write a grant proposal than attend a leadership conference, because they don't intend to become leaders. In most instances, they're equating leadership with some administrative position that they would prefer not to occupy. My own view though is that you can either be an ineffective leader or an effective leader, but nurses do not have a choice about becoming a leader because *inspiring and catalyzing others to achieve shared values and goals in a complex world that is constantly changing* is a requirement of being professional. My intention in this chapter has been to make it seem less daunting—attributes can be cultivated; ambition can develop; and power need not be exercised in an uncaring way.

There is, however, one attribute I do value more than any other, and that is *perseverance*, meaning that you are prepared to persist in trying to realize your core values no matter what the obstacles. Perseverance isn't a stylish, elegant quality, but it is the one that matters in the long run. The "Teach for America" Program has found that a history of perseverance is the best predictor that someone will make a great teacher (Ripley, 2010). If you are not the smartest or bravest or most eloquent person you know, you can still become a great leader if you persevere. I think the August 2009 period of mourning for Senator Ted Kennedy brought that lesson home. He was by his own admission deeply flawed, but he persisted after public humiliations that would have stopped others in their tracks, and his legislative determination in service to core values made a huge difference to the country. I like him as a role model because he personifies a view of greatness to which we can all aspire, one that is shaped by thousands of steps all directed toward public benefit.

Let me end this chapter with what might be either the ultimate perversity or the ultimate comfort—a reminder about the wisdom of crowds. Large groups that meet certain conditions—diverse, independent, decentralized, and capable of being canvassed—have a collective wisdom that is smarter than their leaders, meaning that no matter how brilliant the leader is, the group as a whole is better at problem solving, innovation, and predicting the future (Surowiecki, 2004).

Because nurses are used to working with others (patients, their families and communities, and other professionals) in order to obtain what is best for the patient, they have many opportunities to draw the best out of the collective wisdom. In this view, one doesn't have to worry about being the smartest or loudest to achieve the objective. Leadership ceases to be having the right stuff and becomes getting the right stuff out of others, a task for which nurses are generally well prepared. If you ask key stakeholders what they think should be done, chances are that you will get some very good ideas about how to proceed, and what is more, those you canvassed are likely to think highly of you because you had the sense to ask them for their opinions. Meanwhile, you have also bought yourself some time to weigh the issues thoughtfully, and that in itself is likely to make the resulting plan better.

Key Take-Away Points

- Leaders develop over time rather than being born with "the right stuff."
- Nurses as a group possess many of the abilities that leaders are expected to have, for example, integrity, practical intelligence, and systems thinking.
- Thinking "Even I could do better than what's in place" may be an indicator of readiness for new leadership challenges.
- Nurses see themselves as caring so they may be uncomfortable with exercising power, but if they do not take control of their practice they will not be able to achieve what is important to them and their patients.
- Beware of the dangers of waiting to feel empowered before acting on the authority you already have professionally.
- Self-views matter because they organize how we see reality, which, in turn, influences the next round of what we do.

- Never hesitate to "pretend" to be a leader.
- Leadership is less a matter of brilliance and more a matter of persistence and being able to access and use the collective wisdom of others.

REFERENCES

Abramson, L. Y., Seligman, M. E. P., & Teasdale, J. D. (1978). Learned helplessness in humans: Critique and reformulation. *Journal of Abnormal Psychology, 87*, 49–74.

Eagly, A. H. (2007). Female leadership advantage and disadvantage: Resolving the contradictions. *Psychology of Women Quarterly, 31*, 1–12.

French, R. P., Jr., & Raven, B. (1959). The bases of social power. In D. Cartwright (Ed.), *Studies in social power* (pp. 150–167). Ann Arbor, MI: University of Michigan Press.

Hackman, J. R., & Wageman, R. (2007). Asking the right questions about leadership: Discussion and conclusions. *American Psychologist, 62*, 43–47.

Hedlund, J., Forsythe, G. B., Horvath, J. A., Williams, W. M., Snook, S., & Sternberg, R. J. (2003). Identifying and assessing tacit knowledge: Understanding the practical intelligence of military leaders. *The Leadership Quarterly, 14*, 117–140.

Houser, B. P., & Player, K. N. (2004). *Pivotal moments in nursing: Leaders who changed the path of a profession.* Indianapolis, IN: Sigma Theta Tau International.

Maas, H. S., & Kuypers, J. A. (1974). *From thirty to seventy.* San Francisco: Jossey-Bass.

Manojlovich, M. (2007, January 31). Power and empowerment in nursing: Looking backward to inform the future. *OJIN: The Online Journal of Issues in Nursing, 12*(1), Manuscript 1. Retrieved August 30, 2010, from http://nursingworld.org/MainMenuCategories/ANAMarketplace/ANAPeriodicals/OJIN/TableofContents/Volume122007/No1/Jan07/Looking Backward to Inform the Future.aspx

Mason, M. A., & Goulden, M. (2002). Do babies matter? The effect of family formation on the lifelong careers of academic men and women. *Academe, 88*(6), 21–27.

Northouse, P. G. (2004). *Leadership: Theory and practice* (3rd ed.). Thousand Oaks, CA: Sage Publications.

Nurses top list in honesty and ethics again in Gallup poll. (2006, February–April). *ISNA Bulletin, 32*, 1.

Pelosi, N. (2008). *Know your power: A message to America's daughters.* New York: Doubleday.

Peterson, C., Seligman, M. E. P., & Maier, S. F. (1993). *Learned helplessness: A theory for the age of personal control.* New York: Oxford University Press.

Rafael, A. R. (1996). Power and caring: A dialectic in nursing. *Advances in Nursing Science, 19*(1), 3–17.

Ripley, A. (2010, January/February). What makes a great teacher? *The Atlantic, 305*(1), 58–60, 62–65.

Robins, R. W., & Trzesniewski, K. H. (2005). Self-esteem development across the lifespan. *Current Directions in Psychological Science, 14,* 158–162.

Robinson, D. T., & Smith-Lovin, L. (1992). Selective interaction as a strategy for identity maintenance: An affect control model. *Social Psychology Quarterly, 55,* 12–28.

Rothbard, N. P. (2001). Enriching or depleting? The dynamics of engagement in work and family roles. *Administrative Science Quarterly, 46,* 655–684.

Sommer, K. L., & Baumeister, R. F. (2002). Self-evaluation, persistence, and performance following implicit rejection: The role of trait self-esteem. *Personality and Social Psychology Bulletin, 28,* 926–938.

Stein, L. I. (1967). The doctor-nurse game. *Archives of General Psychiatry, 16,* 699–703.

Stein, L. I., Watts, D. T., & Howell, T. (1990). The doctor-nurse game revisited. *New England Journal of Medicine, 322,* 546–549.

Sternberg, R. J. (2007). A systems model of leadership: WICS. *American Psychologist, 62,* 34–42.

Surowiecki, J. (2004). *The wisdom of crowds.* New York: Doubleday.

Swann, W. B., Jr., Chang-Schneider, C., & McClarty, K. L. (2007). Do people's self-views matter? Self-concept and self-esteem in everyday life. *American Psychologist, 62,* 84–94.

Tannen, D. (1994). *Talking from 9 to 5: How women's and men's conversational styles affect who gets heard, who gets credit, and what gets done at work.* New York: William Morrow.

Tiger, C. (2008, December 29). The Energizer Dean. *The Pennsylvania Gazette.* Retrieved September 4, 2009, from http://www.upenn.edu/gazette/0109/PennGaz0109_feature2.pdf

Yukl, G. A. (2006). *Leadership in organizations* (6th ed.). Upper Saddle River, NJ: Pearson Prentice Hall.

Zaccaro, S. J. (2007). Trait-based perspectives of leadership. *American Psychologist, 62,* 6–16.

Chapter 2

Knowing What You Know and What You Don't Know

In the previous chapter, the focus was on the qualities that leaders are expected to possess, and being self-aware is an ability that makes most lists of leadership qualities. Can you analyze your strengths and limitations so as to maximize assets and not get caught off balance by flaws? From the ancient Greeks and Romans—Heraclitus, Marcus Aurelius, Pythagoras, Socrates, and so forth—to *The Matrix* film series to the Robert Wood Johnson Foundation's Executive Nurse Fellows Program (The Center for the Health Professions, 2008), "know thyself" has been regarded as the key to effective leadership. This is easier said than done, because self-scrutiny can be painful and lopsidedly geared toward the negative.

To be simplistic, you typically spend the toddler-to-teenage years trying to figure out who you are. What kind of personality, temperament, and interests do you have? Aided by parents, teachers, counselors, and significant others, you begin to develop some notion of your talents, inclinations, and ambitions. If these elders have focused on your strengths you are fortunate, because you have some sense of how you are special. If they have focused on your weaknesses or on what they would like you to be regardless of your inclinations, your self-confidence may be in short supply, so you may end this period of self-scrutiny surer of what you aren't than confident of your strong points.

I was part of that generation of women socialized not to have a "big head"—unseemly in a woman who should instead have a big heart—which I think was detrimental to my getting a head (and ahead), because I was more preoccupied early on with what I wasn't than sure of what I was. If you ruminate on flaws, then you are not thinking much about what you will do with assets. You approach each new situation as if any success was a matter of quixotic luck rather than innate ability, so you are not sure that it will reoccur, and every new challenge can be a source of anxiety. This is counterproductive because you eventually need to get to the point where you recognize that problems and challenges are the inevitable stuff of everyday life and not proof positive that you're not handling matters well. Every person, every family, every institution, and every country has problems and challenges. That you and yours have them is less important than how you (and if you) address them.

I look back on my Catholic girlhood, with its emphasis on regular confession, as useful in preparing me for a lifetime of self-examination, but limited because more stress was placed on the discovery of errors than virtues. I would fret that I wasn't consistently generous or athletic or smart, and then I would just get sick and tired of being overwhelmed by my imperfections. (That's when a cookie seemed to be the answer to a sweeter life.) If you asked me what I was good at, I would have regarded the question as a difficult one to answer, because you weren't supposed to tout your merits. It's a shame that I didn't know then one of the fundamental concepts of mental health counseling, *the good-enough person,* that is, someone who is not perfect but is good enough for day-to-day living and loving. If I had just realized that I was "good enough" to make contributions, I would have been primed to proceed sooner. (This is another way of saying what Voltaire did so elegantly, "The perfect is the enemy of the good.")

What Are You Going to Do With Your Gifts?

That struggle with whether I was worthy began to change for me when I sought a master's degree at Yale University in the1960s. Unlike my previous schooling, the teachers there cared more about the state of my career than the state of my soul. In dozens of ways, the faculty assumed that you must be talented or you wouldn't have been admitted to that august institution as a graduate student, so the question always asked directly or indirectly was, "What are you going to do with your gifts?" That focus redirected my energies in a way that I found liberating. I stopped being so reactive and became more proactive.

It's not that I gave up working on my limitations, but I was able to concentrate more on what my special contributions might be. At least I began to ask myself that question. Ultimately, that shift enabled me to give up feeling responsible for everything in exchange for assuming responsibility for some things. When you feel responsible for everything, you generally feel overwhelmed because there is no way that you can do everything well. Having a self-chosen focus can be energizing, because working on what interests you is inherently engaging.

It is for these reasons that I have subsequently counseled all new nursing students to use their basic preparation as an opportunity to figure out what piece of the profession appeals to them. No nurse is good at all aspects of nursing, yet we don't make much of that fundamental truth. We still act regularly as if all nurses should be interchangeable, and that attitude limits work satisfaction, because it makes you feel more like a functionary providing coverage than a professional with specific skills. I have also counseled graduates to be mindful of the person–environment fit when they apply for positions and not treat all workplaces as alike. You want to be "planted" in an institution that values your strengths and lives your values.

When I look back on my career, I wish that someone had told me right from the start that I didn't have to be good at everything. It would have saved considerable wear and tear as I struggled to confront my failings. I am a klutz, not particularly good with my hands, so I was miserable in the operating-room rotation when it was important to hand the correct instrument with an economy of motion. I don't like to work under pressure, so I worried all the time when I was in critical care or the emergency room about responding quickly enough in a crisis. On the other hand, I'm good at putting people at ease and talking my way through situations. I know how to take bits and pieces of information and weave them into larger ideas. I like to write. Nursing, of course, needs all of those skills, and many more, and the profession will have maximum impact when each one of us in the field does what she or he does best and can count on others to do the same.

You usually make the career decision to go into nursing because you or others see some fit between your interests and abilities and the nursing profession. At this point, the connections are usually stated in general terms—"You will be good because you are so caring" . . . "You know how to calm people who are anxious" . . . "You remind me a lot of the nurse who helped my father when he was hospitalized." The emphasis at this point is on whether you are a good match, not on the strengths you will bring to the field, so the orientation at the start of a career is on "fitting in," not on whether you are likely to be someone who will eventually shape the future of the field. Unlike a physician-in-training, regarded historically as preparing to become the captain of the health-profession team, the nurse-in-training was prepared for teamwork, not leadership. This group orientation has advantages because nurses have more of a systems orientation, and that can be enormously helpful in effecting institutional change. There can, however, be a downside, when everyone is thought to be responsible and no one is driving the needed change or when you think everyone has to agree for change to take place.

Understanding what you are good at is enormously important to leadership, because you will never excel in anything if you are still trying to be good at everything. One of my biggest leadership challenges came when I was president-elect of Sigma Theta Tau International (1985–1987). Vernice Ferguson, then chief nurse of the Veterans Administration, was president; she oversaw more than 65,000 nurses in her job and spoke with impressive authority. She had succeeded Lucie Kelly, Carol Lindeman, and Sr. Rosemary Donley, all of whom had transformed the organization, making it more strategic during a period of intense growth. I fretted about being in their league and only managed to quell my fears when I stopped worrying about being like them and tried to figure out what I could uniquely contribute.

As it happens, the organization was going through an intense growth spurt, and the modal member was like me, a married woman with children. I understood the difficulties of juggling work, family, and commuting, so I made those and other related issues of career development the theme of my presidency and was therefore able to make a special contribution to the organization. For example, "Sustaining Career Optimism" was the theme of every regional assembly during the biennium I was president, and that topic generated record-breaking attendance.

Failing to build on strengths is a common problem. The positive psychology movement has criticized some of the assumptions made in the leadership literature, pointing out that most organizations make the mistake of taking their employees' strengths for granted and focusing instead on their weaknesses. An emphasis on weaknesses presupposes that a uniform workforce, all the members of which have the same relevant general competencies, is most desirable; for example, an RN workforce is best defined in terms of general RN competencies. That approach may be useful in setting minimum expectations but is not useful in maximizing potential. The best human resources policy a leader can have is to try to place all personnel in positions that will use their skill sets to maximum advantage.

Expressing the ideas of the positive psychology movement, Buckingham and Clifton (2001) have encouraged the identification of strengths for the purpose of using each person strategically where she or he will do best and then managing these strengths. For them, a strength is a talent that is expanded by acquiring knowledge and developing the skills necessary to practice. Childhood experiences and genetic inheritance leave you with certain predispositions, and focusing on dominant talents is the best way to achieve the greatest potential.

There are 34 themes to Clifton's StrengthsFinder, developed during his tenure at the Gallup International Research and Education Center and based on data collected from 2 million individuals. There is a proprietary Web site (http://www.strengthsfinder.com) where you can figure out your strengths so you can leverage them in your development. I have used that instrument to identify my dominant strengths. I've also taken the Myers-Briggs Type Indicator, which is designed to measure how you perceive the world and make decisions, as part of leadership-development programs. The advantage of this instrument and several related free online methods for assessing strengths in terms of Jungian types is that they provide a means of understanding your preferences better (see http://www.human-metrics.com/cgi-win/JTypes2.asp and http://www.kisa.ca/personality/).

One can also use such personality assessments to tailor messages to others in terms of their preferences and hand out assignments in terms of people's strengths (Slowikowski, 2005). When I was a dean, I organized annual leadership retreats so that all of us administrators would spend at least one day each year together trying to get better as managers and leaders. I still remember the time when we all completed the Myers-Briggs, shared our profiles with each other, and then considered our group profile. The biggest learning from that exercise was realizing that the colleagues who annoyed us most were our opposite in how they approached matters. We liked best those who were most like us. Not surprising, since all of us are comforted by the familiar. We also found out that a number of types were missing in our group profile. Those of us who had gravitated toward academic careers certainly didn't represent the full spectrum of perspectives. Those were valuable insights because we each became a bit more tolerant of standpoints unlike our own and realized in a new way that our overall point of view wasn't as diverse as the total viewpoint of our many constituents.

Addressing Limitations

Building on strengths doesn't mean that you can ignore your limitations. If you have to take certain courses to achieve a coveted degree, then that's what you have to do, even if you are not good in that subject matter. You can learn a great deal about yourself even when you watch yourself struggle with difficulties. It is particularly important, I think, that you learn to be honest about limitations. Instead of trying to deny them—denial has long been my favorite defense mechanism—I have learned that it is often better to admit them early on and try to deal with them instead of spending years afterward trying to hide them.

When I went back to school for my doctorate, I was ill prepared for doctoral-level statistics. I hadn't had any math since high school (no trigonometry or calculus there), and my master's statistics course 14 years before was at the level they were now teaching to undergraduates. Instead of starting with some needed remedial work, I decided that I would bluster my way through, because I was a "mature" student with time constraints (two young children) who didn't want to have to do anything extra. The irony, of course, is that I didn't save time. I learned to mimic the teacher in solving problems, but I never mastered the underlying theory, and I spent much more energy in the long run covering my failings instead of tackling them. I did learn a good deal from that experience, but it didn't have anything directly to do with statistics. I learned that you are wiser to admit your flaws right from the start and try to do something about them.

As a leader, however, the biggest reason you need to understand your limitations isn't so much to eliminate them but to address them by surrounding yourself with individuals who do well what you find to be difficult. Most of us have some trouble even envisioning that there are people who actually like to do what we don't like to do, because we tend to think of our own behavior as normative. Our behavior is what we are familiar with; we think of it as normal, so what we think must be the norm! The person who prefers creative expression to managing lots of details tends to think that anyone who likes the latter is deadly dull, whereas the detail-oriented person often complains that imagination doesn't necessarily get things done. I know it took me more years than it should have to realize that the world was full of good people who liked to do what I didn't, and I just had to hire them.

When you are not good at something or don't like to do something, you also tend to put off dealing with the matter, and that can be a serious vulnerability. When I was a dean, there were certain meetings that I didn't like to chair because they were full of bureaucratic matters (at least that's how I saw them), and I found organizing them to be tedious. These same meetings, however, only went well when attention was paid beforehand to all the details. Committee work needs to be carefully organized so there is a structure for effective decision making. Groups, in my experience, cannot go from jawing to voting on matters without preparation, and I was ultimately responsible for that preparation. Only when I recognized my resistance as a liability was I able to work out a system for effectively using others to get the needed preparation completed in timely fashion.

I think supervisors don't always ask the right question of those who report to them. They tend to note that an associate has certain abilities and certain limitations, and then spend evaluation time on how this person can improve, but they never ask the real question, "Since you are not particularly good in this area, what are you doing to see that someone else gets the needed work done?" Too often the focus is on the person's drawbacks, not on pressing the person either to extend his or her abilities or figure out how to work around inadequacies, which is a more realistic approach. What we forget is that leadership doesn't have to mean being good at everything yourself but means working with others to envision and then act on all that needs to be done.

Because nursing is largely peopled by women and nurses have long been described as caregivers, we tend to take particular pride in being practical and getting things done, but that predisposition has its shadow side. Our first thought when tackling a new challenge tends to be "I don't want to do that; I already have enough on my plate," rather than to start brainstorming about how we are going to address the matter at hand without the solution necessarily being to do the work ourselves. Our group appreciation for the complexities of implementing a new strategy can leave us with a reverse snobbery of sorts about the work of strategizing, dismissing it as easier than implementation. However, if you regularly define your real work as "doing" rather than "strategizing," you will be severely limited by what you personally like to do and can do in solving problems and encouraging innovation. Moreover, you don't really want to be constrained by those limitations.

The reality is that you will be limited by who you are no matter how substantial your gifts and how few your weaknesses. If you were some exotic combination of Florence Nightingale, Sojourner Truth, Margaret Sanger, Clara Barton, Walt Whitman, and Golda Meir (all nurses), you would still have limitations and would still need help from others to address the challenges before you. In chapter 1, I mentioned Surowiecki's book, *The Wisdom of Crowds* (2004) in which he explores the notion that the many can be smarter than the few, particularly when a diversity of opinions is encouraged. Diversity isn't important because it is politically correct. It is important because diversity of all sorts—racial/ethnic, disciplinary, generational, gender, religious, educational, and so forth—ensures that the problems under consideration and resulting solutions will be viewed from a range of perspectives. In complex organizations with very complicated problems, comprehensive

solutions will never take shape without a spectrum of opinions informing the decision making.

The nursing world needs thinkers and doers, artists and analysts,
those who do not shy away from conflict, and those who value ritual. We
need different personality types to look at issues and organizational matters through different lenses. Bolman and Deal (2003) have proposed four
frameworks through which leaders can address the range of organizational challenges. Their *structural* framework values leaders comfortable
with analysis and concerned with whether the organization is effectively
and efficiently designed. Their *human resource* framework emphasizes
service-oriented leadership that empowers others. Looking through their
political frame, one recognizes that some organizational problems require
a focus on conflict resolution, negotiation, and coalition building. Using
their *symbolic* lens, a leader would be mindful of the need to inspire and
use symbols/ceremonies to communicate larger meaning.

Not every challenge requires all four approaches, but leaders need
to be sure to approach problems mindful of the appropriate tactics.
Since none of us is good at everything, this means that input from a
broad array of sources is crucial. That makes infinite sense, but most
of us are so busy that we don't think we have time to get this feedback.
Even closer to the truth, most of us don't really like feedback, even if we
recognize that it is important.

Feedback—The Key to Professional Development

Ask bright people for feedback, and what do they do? They give you
feedback, but do you really want it? I would argue that most of the time
we ask for feedback hoping in our heart of hearts that the person will
respond by saying that our idea, paper, or proposal is already the incarnation of perfection. When we get more feedback than we bargained for,
our first impulse may be to argue about why some of the suggestions
don't make sense or really don't matter. That is our first impulse because
criticism feels like repudiation, instead of what it is, the lifeblood of
professional development.

The knee-jerk equation we all make of criticism with something
negative is so pervasive that we often forget what criticism should
involve. To be critical is to recognize, first and foremost, what is positive about a product or activity—"you have demonstrated an innovative
approach to handling a pileup of patients at busy hours" . . . "your paper

has zeroed in on a clinically important topic" . . . "Your analysis of how we can recruit more minority students to our graduate program is more far reaching than anything else we have ever attempted."

Criticism also involves articulating the limitations of a product or activity, but that doesn't necessarily mean being negative. You can note that a project has limited patient sampling or that more stage 3 skin ulcers are happening above the neck and not only on the backside without implying that the project or the patient care is without merit. Alas, most of us respond to such comments as if they were disapproval rather than assessment, because we hear it as "Gotcha" or "I'm smarter than you are" more than as helpful advice.

Feedback isn't always helpful because we're all better at making judgments than following them up with either reasons why something works or concrete suggestions for improvement. Journal editors and funding agencies have gotten steadily better at instructing reviewers to note the positive and point out limitations, supporting both with examples and specifics, but the rest of us haven't followed suit. I think we haven't gotten better at this in day-to-day life because we still cling to the notion that the skillful clinician or the first-rate manager or the accomplished educator will be beyond criticism. Hence, we resist feedback because we hear it as "You're not first rate," when the reality is that none of us is so good that we cannot get better.

There's always a *next level* of development for all of us, and obtaining feedback serves many purposes. Seeking advice early on saves time in the long run. Ideas always get more comprehensive with commentary. Evaluation is a feature of the nursing process, the research process, and every other problem-solving process. Peer review is an accepted practice in the development of clinical, teaching, and scholarly excellence, and providing peer review is a means of staying current and learning from others. What is more, building regular feedback into ordinary processes provides face-saving opportunities for rethinking matters without having to declare that what is in place is awful or insufficient.

Everything I wrote in the preceding paragraph is something I deeply believe in, but I still don't like criticism, so I have had to deal with the gap between what I accept as true and how I actually respond to criticism. I have come to treat seeking feedback as necessary medicine, sometimes bitter but good for me. I build feedback into timelines, understanding that some days must elapse before I am able to respond constructively to comments and move forward. I try not to act immediately on my first thoughts and feelings because it takes me some time to admit that the points made have any validity. It takes time for new ideas to sink in and for me to figure out what I'm going to do with them. Not surprising when you think of it, because I probably would have incorporated the suggestions in my initial statement, if I had thought of them in the first place.

Coming to terms with my own way of processing criticism hasn't been easy. I remember once asking an associate dean for her opinion of a document I wanted to circulate the next day. She gave me feedback and told me that it needed more work, and I started arguing with her. What I had really wanted her to say is that the proposal was complete, because I was tired of working on it. When she didn't say that, I started disagreeing with her. As I thought about the matter afterward, I realized that I needed to take what she said seriously, because she was right. And I needed to apologize to her, which I did the next day, or otherwise she would stop giving me feedback, and that is a death knell for a leader. As you are about to step off a metaphorical cliff, you need to be surrounded by colleagues who won't hesitate to tell you to move in another direction.

I have learned a number of tricks in dealing with criticism. Generally, I try not to argue with critics, realizing that that kind of defensive behavior just makes me look touchy. You continue to look like the one in control of the situation, however, if you respond by asking for clarification or for examples of how to improve, so you have the time to take in more information before you react. Ask more experienced colleagues for help in understanding and responding to criticism. When you read what reviewers have said about your first grant proposal or the first manuscript you submit for publication, you can feel overwhelmed by negative comments and are likely to need help even seeing the positive and figuring out how to respond to any suggestions made.

Always remember that it is the recipient's job to figure out if the criticism is worthwhile. Just because someone says something disapproving doesn't mean that it's actually true. It may just mean that you haven't been clear enough for the person to understand your central point. Some feedback is idiosyncratic and doesn't make sense even after giving the criticisms their due. Some comments are too general and unfocused to be that helpful. But when more than one person points out the same thing—"There is no real ending to your paper; it reads as if you got tired and just stopped writing"—then you need to take that observation seriously.

I have come to believe that the smarter you are, the more you may have difficulty with feedback in life after graduation, because you didn't learn how to handle constructive criticism earlier in your life. A+ students have a history of acing courses and wowing teachers, so they get used to ready applause. Their elders may have been so pleased with their perform-ance in comparison with others that they never pushed them to consider how something mastered can always be moved to the next level of devel-opment. Eventually even the brightest people hit some ceiling because projects increase in complexity over time, but the steady diet of kudos in the past may have skewed their judgment, causing them to equate any criticism with "not being any good," when all that has happened is that they have now reached the point where speed and brains aren't enough.

If all of us got better at giving criticism, maybe we could profit from it more. The psychologist who was my major professor when I was working on my dissertation, Kathryn Norcross Black, was particularly good at saying tough things in an ego-enhancing way. She had a style that implied, "You are destined for greatness, but there are just these 57 things that you have to attend to before getting there." She would regularly say, "As you and I both know . . . " before pointing out how I needed to improve, always communicating that I was smart enough to know that I had this problem and smart enough to do something about it. I didn't always know what she was driving at, but I appreciated her acting as if we were partners in addressing a shared concern.

There was something about her overall style that I wish I could have bottled. She never looked nervous giving feedback; it was always delivered in a businesslike, forthright manner without a lot of angst. I, on the other hand, can get very nervous and anxious when I have to talk to someone about a needed improvement. I once delivered my observations and had an employee express relief at how the session had gone, because she had noticed my twitchy behavior beforehand and the reality of what I had to say wasn't nearly as difficult as what she had imagined I might say. This experience shouldn't be surprising, because uncertainty can be more stressful than clear negative feedback (Hirsh & Inzlicht, 2008).

I have improved since then, trying to emulate the style of my men-tor and coming to terms with my own crazy thinking about criticism. Part of me was still stuck in a world that equated criticism with not being nurturing or supportive when the opposite is true—if you really care about someone, then you help them grow and develop. The more I looked into my discomfort, the more I also realized that the whole proc-ess of having to give criticism made me angry—angry that the object of my criticism didn't know better in the first place. Why should I have to tell an assistant to let me know when she has completed arrange-ments? She should know I need to be assured that arrangements have been made. Why should I have to tell someone that I felt "set up" in a particular meeting? He should have known that his words put me in a quandary because they implied that I had been a party to the decision making when I hadn't.

I recognized this behavior in myself because I observed it in others. I've seen faculty get angry at secretaries for not doing something and say, "I don't know why she cannot do that; even I know how to do that." And I've had to remind them that they are better paid and more educated, so it's not surprising that they can do some of the things that they are expecting staff to do. If you see having to tell someone how to improve as an imposition, you feel one way about these matters. If you see telling someone how he or she can improve as a sacred professional obligation, part of mentoring, you handle matters differently. I think my mentor was as good as she was about giving feedback in an encouraging way because she assumed that learners are open to suggestions, and being a teacher meant that she had an obligation to be helpful.

There is real value in creating an environment where not being good at something is not regarded as proof positive that you are either dumb or difficult. In the early 1990s when my school decided to move aggressively in the direction of becoming savvy about information technology (IT), my colleague Diane Billings designed a very successful train-the-trainer program that presupposed that all faculty and staff in the School of Nursing needed development in this area. About a dozen early adopters received special training, and then they provided 16 hours of IT mini-courses over the course of two months to all the rest of us faculty and staff alike. The courses were offered at all hours, so no one could say they didn't fit into his or her schedule. We went that summer from most of us not knowing how to use a computer to becoming IT savvy. And I think the success was due to the fact that all could admit ignorance without being regarded as ignorant—an approach in keeping with the key to giving and getting criticism in a respectful way.

One of the things that I like best about the last decade's emphasis on clinical quality and safety is that physicians and nurses are slowly but steadily moving to the point where you can raise a question about what someone is doing or not doing without automatically being accused of picking on the person and being a pain in the butt. There have been so many examples when someone had misgivings and group-think prevailed—the surgeon started operating on the wrong leg but the circulating nurse didn't say anything; NASA (National Aeronautics and Space Administration) shrugged off indications of O-ring failure leading to the shuttle disaster—that feedback/criticism is increasingly being elevated to the status of essential to effective leadership. Where once good nursing was described as following doctor's orders, now professional behavior is generally equated with questioning because that could be the crucial difference between life and death. We are fast learning that questions aren't a judgment about where matters now stand but an investment in future success.

A Lifelong Journey of Discovery

The ancient admonition to "know thyself" seems at first glance to be rather straightforward, but on reflection you begin to realize what a lifetime project that discovery process will be. It takes experience, reading, talking, contemplation, education, and mentoring to identify your strengths and develop them further while attending to the shadow part of who you are. We all have a shadow part, meaning that our strengths always come with some built-in limitations. If you are good with people, then you may not value strategic analysis as much and therefore not provide for it when it is warranted. If you take pride in being able to analyze matters strategically, then you may not see the point in getting the opinions of others before unveiling a new initiative and you may live to regret that omission. If you try to be cordial with everyone because you grew up in an angry household, you may have some difficulty listening to others who are justifiably angry with you.

I once participated in a strategic-planning retreat that included some analysis of everyone's leadership abilities. The resulting feedback told you how you tended to respond under conditions of success and conditions of failure because most people respond differently depending on the situation. The facilitator told me that I had the special ability of responding to failure by redoubling my energies. Most people hunker down when things don't go well, but I go in the opposite direction. I never forgot her final comment, though, because it gave me insights into my shadow self. She said that my persistence and creativity were wonderful assets, but the positive features of this approach had to be balanced by the fact that I tended to confuse others when I went from one approach to another. What she said resonated with me, because it reminded me of occasions when I had confused others by trying one thing and then another, because the first approach didn't work. My colleagues didn't see the logic of moving from one tactic to another so quickly; they thought I was just frenetic.

Thankfully, the more you build on your strengths, the more others want to use them, making them grow even more, and the more your limitations don't matter as much as they did at the start. They don't matter because over time you know more and more colleagues who are good at what you are not. One of the best rewards of a full career is that you can eventually answer every question in nursing. What you know personally is still limited by the finite nature of your strengths, but over time you get to the point where you either know who will know what you do not, or you know whom to contact to get the name of the person who will know.

The cultivation of self-knowledge has, therefore, to go hand in hand with the cultivation of a network of colleagues. Some will be people with whom you went to school; some you will meet occasionally at conferences or on task forces; some will be the people your mentor introduced you to; some will be co-workers. Collectively, they will serve as the resource base that will shore you up when you've reached your limitations. Best of all, that network will include a few longtime friends with whom you can be completely honest about your misgivings and wonderings. You will repeatedly use these colleagues as sounding boards for sharing anxieties and rehashing what happened in committee meetings. These are the colleagues who will agree with you that the time isn't right, family-wise, to accept an out-of-town opportunity; at other times, they will goad you into accepting an organizational challenge, reminding you that you are ready for a new position.

Self-knowledge isn't just a matter of introspection. It involves looking at yourself through the eyes of others—their comments, kidding, compliments, and criticisms—and learning from watching yourself in different situations (conditions of failure vs. success; small groups vs. big groups). For example, you can recognize that you have been wrong every time you acquiesced to a decision that did not feel right, learning eventually to say, "I am uncomfortable with going forward with this right now. I honestly cannot give you all the reasons why I'm reluctant, but I do know that it never works if I ignore such misgivings. I need to think about this more before taking action."

Self-knowledge isn't easy, and it is never complete. It requires you to contemplate with candor your faults and eccentricities and your strivings and ambitions (Bennis, 2003). The aim is not so much to hold self-perceptions that match perfectly with reality but to get in touch with your personality, motivation, and talents so this awareness can be used to advantage (Wilson & Dunn, 2004). For example, if you notice that your first impressions usually tend to be spot on, then you trust them more over time; if you notice that decisions made when you are worn out never work out, then you learn to buy time when you are tired and put off decision making for another day.

Most formal leadership programs require participants to do some self-assessments or get 360-degree feedback from supervisors, peers, and subordinates (Alimo-Metcalfe, 2002) as they seek to use themselves in new ways. The assumption is that you cannot take on more responsibility and authority if you don't have a handle on your strengths and limitations. From experience, I would say that it is particularly important to have a handle on how needy—for support, compliments, and recognition—you are before you start working to develop others and the organization itself, because excessive neediness may mean that you are not likely to be available to others. If you are still needy in a particular area, it is better to address that lack forthrightly than to have your inadequacy seep out in ways that aren't constructive.

In a real sense, self-knowledge is the continuous improvement process of leaders (London, 2002), the means by which they ensure their own growth and development as they strive to do the same for others. The best leaders understand this and remain open enough to listen to what others have to say to and about them. They may never come to feel good about criticism, but they know that its absence doesn't mean that all is well, because feedback keeps you abreast of what others think and feel, and that is invaluable.

Key Take-Away Points

- Since ancient times, self-knowledge has been regarded as the key to effective leadership.
- No nurse is good at all aspects of nursing; therefore, each one needs to figure out what will be his or her area of special contributions.
- Instead of focusing largely on weaknesses, organizations should identify their employees' strengths for the purpose of using them strategically and then managing to those strengths.
- It is better to admit one's limitations early on, and deal with them, rather than spend years trying to hide them.
- As a leader, you don't have to be good at everything; you just have to be good at using others to complement your limitations.
- No one really likes criticism, but criticism is the lifeblood of professional development and improvement; therefore,

leaders need to know how to give and accept criticism in an ego-enhancing way.

• Self-knowledge is never complete; it is achieved through ongoing introspection, candor, figuring yourself out in different situations, and looking at yourself through the eyes of others.

REFERENCES

Alimo-Metcalfe, B. (2002). 360-degree feedback and leadership development. *International Journal of Selection and Assessment, 6*(1), 35–44.

Bennis, W. (2003). *On becoming a leader: The leadership classic.* New York: Basic Books.

Bolman, L. G., & Deal, T. E. (2003). *Reframing organizations: Artistry, choice, and leadership.* San Francisco: Jossey-Bass.

Buckingham, M., & Clifton, D. O. (2001). *Now, discover your strengths.* New York: The Free Press.

Hirsh, J. B., & Inzlicht, M. (2008). The devil you know: Neuroticism predicts neural response to uncertainty. *Psychological Science, 19,* 962–967.

London, M. (2002). *Leadership development: Paths to self-insight and professional growth.* Mahwah, NJ: Lawrence Erlbaum.

Robert Wood Johnson Foundation. (2010). *Robert Wood Johnson Executive Nurse Fellows.* Retrieved August 31, 2010, from http://www.rwjf.org/reports/npreports/enfp.htm

Slowikowski, M. K. (2005). Using the DISC behavioral instrument to guide leadership and communication. *Association of periOperative Registered Nurses Journal, 82,* 835–838.

Surowiecki, J. (2004). *The wisdom of crowds.* New York: Doubleday.

Wilson, T. D., & Dunn, E. W. (2004). Self-knowledge: Its limits, value, and potential for improvement. *Annual Review of Psychology, 55,* 493–518.

Chapter 3

Sustaining Optimism
and Managing Anger

When you think of the lofty qualities that leaders are supposed to have, you think of high-powered ones such as integrity, creativity, courage, and intelligence. You don't think of sustaining optimism and managing anger, because they seem more like givens than a stretch toward greatness. However, one of the most difficult but important aspects of leadership from the personal side is to take responsibility for managing your emotions so that you can stay optimistic enough to energize others.

What I call "sustaining optimism" may not seem all that substantive at first glance, but a considerable portion of the discussion about leadership in the 2008 presidential race touched on this subject. Which candidate had the right temperament? Who had the best strategy for addressing the complexities ahead? Who can work with all the factions in this country? The editors of *The New Yorker* (13 October, 2008) supported Obama's election for many reasons including temperament, describing him as self-aware, able to concentrate on essentials, balanced, and exuding calm and hopefulness. These qualities, I argue, are important to nursing leadership, too.

I grew up thinking that some people were naturally optimistic and hoped I would be one of them, but I feared that I belonged in the inclined-to-be-despondent camp. My family was more likely to complain about what wasn't in place than to express gratitude for what was, partly because we were superstitious enough to think that any expression of satisfaction would quickly be followed by some disaster hurled by an angry god determined to put you in your place. If you muttered enough about your lot in life, then maybe the celestial accounting system would have enough tribulations already listed to balance the pleasures without need for more problems.

It is easy to get into the habit of muttering about how awful things are, particularly if you grew up in modest circumstances where autocratic bosses and the grinding monotony of never-ending work were the main subjects of dinnertime conversation. Complaining can for some people turn into a way of life. In my experience, nurses are particularly good at grumbling. A nurse might complain at 6:00 P.M. about being tired, saying, "I'm exhausted because I've been here since 8:00 A.M.," only to have a colleague respond, "Well I've been on my feet since 6:30 A.M.," with someone else chiming in, "You think you've got it bad; I just worked a double shift and my drive home is 50 miles." I have sometimes thought that our profession's competition was for who was most miserable rather than who was most successful. This behavior is not surprising in a field where the historic emphasis has been on service and working hard; you proved your mettle through sacrificial effort more than achievement. All of this is understandable, but these tendencies are counterproductive in exerting leadership. No one wants a leader who spreads gloom; you want the leader to be optimistic that tomorrow can be better than today.

Unlearning Helplessness/Learning Hopefulness

Where I once believed that you were stuck with your predispositions and mindsets, I eventually came to believe that you are obligated to assume responsibility for managing your emotions in the same way that you are duty bound to take responsibility for brushing your teeth. Sustaining career optimism is an important component of being fully professional. You have to understand and manage how you think about matters, because how you construct reality affects your emotional state, which in turn affects your expectations for the future and follow-up behaviors. If you are not optimistic about what can be done to improve matters, then you will have difficulty motivating others to achieve a preferred future. This doesn't mean that you should be unrealistic about barriers ahead. To put it simply, it means that you should tend to see the proverbial glass as half full rather than half empty, so you recognize that you have some resources in place on which to build the future.

As I mentioned in the previous chapter, I was moved to appreciate the importance of positive psychology by all that I read that collectively emphasized the importance of identifying and changing dysfunctional thinking (Beck, 1999; Ellis & Dryden, 2007). There are ways of constructing experience that can be counterproductive—for example, discounting the positive and ruminating on the negative. The more you dwell on what you cannot do, the less likely you are to do anything substantive, because it may not seem worth the effort.

Day-to-day depression is associated with learned helplessness, believing generally that you are powerless to change your situation—"Nothing will work" . . . "We tried that before and nothing happened" . . . "You're naïve if you think we have any control over our hours/jobs." The reality is you hardly ever are in a situation where you truly have no control; that is certainly not the case when you have some professional authority of your own, as nurses do. If Gandhi could confront the British Empire, nurses can do something about patient care. Instead of grousing, I came to believe that professional life was more productive (and fun) if you did what Martin Seligman (1991) urged, and I realized that an understanding of learned helplessness could become the basis for learning how to sustain optimism: If ruminating on your limitations makes you more depressed, then why not focus on your opportunities, possibilities, and resources to become more optimistic? There are a host of concrete strategies for feeling good about yourself and your work that you can adopt to keep your perspective on an even keel; more about that at the end of this chapter (Burns, 1980; McKay, Wood, & Brantley, 2007).

Such strategies assume particular importance in a field largely peopled by women because gender-connected issues of confidence remain an issue in the 21st century. For example, women medical students, who are the intellectual peers of their male counterparts, report increased anxiety and decreased self-confidence over the course of their studies (Blanch, Hall, Roter, & Frankel, 2008). Their less confident style, it is hypothesized, may have downstream consequences for their advancement, including whether their judgments are perceived by others to be authoritative. It is a fact that both women and men still have a preference for male bosses over female bosses, and this penchant holds across all of the 22 nations surveyed by Gallup (Eagly & Karau, 2002, Table 1). Although it is not clear whether this partiality is a response to women's actual lack of confidence or due to stereotyped thinking, or the result of some complicated combination of the two, the fact remains that people expect leaders not to exude worry and despondency.

The Battle for Emotional Control

Women in general worry about losing control and aspire to self-regulation, because the stereotype so often portrays them as very emotional and undisciplined, and they don't want to be regarded negatively (Chrisler, 2008). The superwoman of media fame successfully juggles multiple roles, but real women are regularly overwhelmed by task overload, leaving them feeling unsure and inadequate even when they are more than adequate. It is no wonder that women fall particular prey to rumination, hoping to get more insights into their situation by replaying past grievances and how distressed they felt, but that tactic is more likely to lead to depression and reduced self-confidence, not problem solving (Nolen-Hoeksema, Wisco, & Lyubomirsky, 2008). The more you think about some slight or grievance in terms of "I cannot believe what happened," the more you keep trying to plumb the unfathomable and drown in a sea of feelings.

On the whole, women worry more than men about losing control, in part because angry men are more likely to be rewarded whereas angry women are penalized. In a series of studies, the videotaped performance of male CEOs was ranked the highest in competence and salary regardless of their emotional levels; unemotional women were regarded next best; with angry women ranked lowest in competence and salary (Brescoll & Uhlmann, 2008). What was most striking about that research, given the extent to which women objectively continue to have so many reasons to feel straightjacketed by their environments, is that women's anger was more often attributed internally—"she is an angry person"—while men's emotional reactions were more likely to be attributed externally to contextual circumstances. When the angry woman in a follow-up study provided objective external reasons for her feelings, she evoked less negative reactions, suggesting that women fare better when they know how to explain themselves.

Women are perceived to be more emotional than men (Plant, Hyde, Keltner, & Devine, 2000), and displays of emotion are thought to convey weakness and incompetence (Tiedens, Ellsworth, & Mesquita, 2000). Even Madeleine Albright (2003) spoke about this issue in her memoir and how she successfully worked to keep her voice unemotional so as not to tap into this stereotype. Though it is a shame that she had to worry about this matter while attending to affairs of state, high-powered individuals do tend to react more selectively (Van Kleef et al., 2008). It is not that they are insensitive to the concerns of others, but they are shaped more by their goals and values than by emotions (Keltner, Van Kleef, Chen, & Kraus, 2008). Women in general, and women nurses in particular, may consequently have a more difficult time balancing the caring attitude expected of them with the discriminating attention required of leaders.

A major problem for women seeking to exert leadership, particularly women in nursing, is that they operate in a health care system where they still are regularly underappreciated for their contributions, giving them ample reason to be angry about their situation. Yet anger is an expression permitted without penalty only to those with status and power. Get angry, and a woman is quickly labeled a banshee, harpy, fury, bitch, or worse, and those labels can take on a life of their own. However, how many women can notice slights repeatedly with emotional equilibrium?

One nursery rhyme captures this psychological conundrum: "There once was a girl who had a curl right in the middle of her forehead. And when she was good, she was very, very good. And when she was bad she was horrid." I understand that girl because I am she. I, too, have had the experience of trying to handle reoccurring snubs or slights with equanimity; then the same thing happens for the 16th time that month and I get really angry. Anyone looking at me would wonder where that explosion came from, since the response didn't seem proportional to the immediate stimulus.

From my point of view, I was a saint in how I handled the first 15 times I had to deal with the situation, but I couldn't keep up the good behavior. Anyone observing me would explain my behavior as overwrought, not unlike the respondents in the previously mentioned studies. Of course, every time you blow up out of proportion to the immediate circumstances, you are scared by your own behavior; you wonder if you really aren't a crazy lady, so you tamp down your emotions further, resolving to do better, and the stage is set for the next explosion. In addition, getting angry causes you to lose whatever moral authority you originally had, for you become the problem people can see instead of the identified problem being the original issue.

It was in analyzing my attempts to not get angry, always followed by an anger that eventually surfaced at inappropriate times, that I came to understand how important it was to deal more constructively with my anger if I wanted to be effective. I would get angry at how unfairly nurses are sometimes treated (ignored and overlooked), try to put a lid on those boiling emotions, and get so focused on this inner drama that I lost my strategic edge. When this happened, I kept rethinking the past and emoting in the present, which made me ill prepared to seize the future.

My own experience is in keeping with the findings of Sandra Thomas (1993, 2001, 2005, 2008), who has extensively studied women/nurses and anger. She found that powerlessness (not being listened to) and injustice (being treated unfairly) were the themes behind anger-producing situations. Rather than responding constructively, many women rehash their grievances. This ruminating only fuels their resentments and, presumably, engenders some distancing behaviors on the part of friends, family, and co-workers who are tired of listening to rehashed complaints (Nolen-Hoeksema & Larson, 1999).

Thomas also noted a male bias in measuring anger. Hitting is regarded as an expression of anger but crying is not. I mention this because, in my own attempt to decipher the patterning in my behavior, I came to realize that being teary-eyed was a reliable indicator that I was seething inside, not that I was sad. Alas, if you have tears in your eyes, you are mortified that you look like the female stereotype (someone who cannot handle things), which can make you more upset. In addition, you cannot be strategic if you are fixed on the notion of tears not spilling over in front of a person who has gotten to you.

Before I move away from discussing Thomas's work, I need to recount one story that confirms the importance of her insights. In the early 1990s when I was president of the American Academy of Nursing, we decided to host a session at the biennial convention of the American Nurses Association. Imagine our consternation when the only time made available to us was 7:00 A.M. on a Sunday morning, not an auspicious time to attract a large crowd. Dr. Thomas' first book on women and anger had recently been reviewed very favorably by the *Washington Post*, so I decided that she was the perfect person to invite to be our breakfast speaker. The topic produced a sell-out crowd, proving that anger is a serious problem for us all, so much so that we will get up early on our day of rest to try to get a handle on the problem. Interest remains high; there are now continuing education programs for nurses on this subject (ISNA, 2007–2008).

Anger isn't in and of itself negative. As you strive to be in tune with your thoughts and feelings, as opposed to being overwhelmed by them, you can use anger as an indicator of intensity, one that forces you to figure out why you are upset. Anger can have instrumental benefits when it provides motivation for action or confrontation (Tamir, Mitchell, & Gross, 2008). The trick is to use the energy of the emotion in service to important goals, in much the same way as you are supposed to use your anxiety before making a speech to energize your presentation.

To harness emotion on behalf of some greater good requires some very practical skills. Do you know how to call a *HALT* and not act poorly when you are *hungry, angry, lonely, and/or tired*? Do you have friends who will help you vent in the immediate moment but who will also push you to figure out the next constructive action? What do you do to "let off steam" so it doesn't build up to an uncontrollable point? To what extent have you engaged others in tackling a shared issue so neither the problem nor the solution has to rest just on your shoulders? Do you know how to be properly assertive—describing what happened factually without accusing the other person of bad faith, noting how it made you feel, specifying what you hope will happen next, and the consequences of addressing or not addressing the matter? It should be noted that much of what I have said thus far about the relationship between women and anger tends to hold for minorities of any kind and anger, because powerlessness and injustice tend to fuel their responses, too.

Managing anger is a part of sustaining optimism, but so are many other things. I'm not arguing that everyone can be optimistic all of the time, nor that a positive attitude is the only shaper of events, but there is evidence that how one sees matters can be a factor in what happens about 40% of the time (Lyubomirsky, 2008), and that motivational margin can have significant consequences. You can maximize that 40% by artfully promoting your personal health and hardiness and thinking about matters in a way that promotes hopefulness. Let me now elaborate on these learnable skills.

Taking Care of Yourself

Keyes (2007) has described mental health as the interplay between and among emotional well-being (mostly satisfied), psychological functioning (self-acceptance, purpose in life, mastery, positive relations), and social integration (contributing to society). Flourishing physically is a matter of taking seriously all that you already know about good health habits—diet, exercise, sleep, relaxation, moderation—and applying that knowledge to your own situation. This means regarding yourself as an executive who deserves to be encouraged, developed, and well maintained.

All of this makes sense, but nurses are notoriously bad at following the advice that they freely give others, in part because many of us have absorbed those super-person images that focus on all we should do—juggling career, family/friends, and community engagement—with nary a mention of how we sustain and renew ourselves (Pesut, 2008). We describe ourselves as caring for others, but the prevailing conceptualization is simplistic, because it all too often ignores how much the caregiver needs to be sustained in order to maintain the ability to provide care. We would do well to remember that airline instructions caution you, in case of a drop in pressure, to place the oxygen mask over your face before attending to the needs of others, because if you're in distress you'll be less effective in helping anyone else.

To be honest, I tell a better story about these matters than I have lived. It took a certain amount of living for me to believe that I "deserve" to be taken care of because I grew up in an environment where only rich people took care of themselves; the rest of us took care of them. I had some class prejudices against any pampering of self because I equated it with being useless. Even though I know better, I have tended to treat healthy habits as if they were an option instead of a necessity. Like many others, I would get overwhelmed at the gap between my everyday diet/ exercise behavior and what I should ideally do, and my lack of perfection paralyzed me, keeping me from doing better. The biggest thing that I learned in my own personal journey is the importance of figuring out what is right for you, that is, what physical-fitness routine keeps you even keeled. If you have no small-motor skills, then taking up jewelry making isn't likely to reduce stress; if your joints hurt like mine, then exercising in the water (aquacise) is likely to be a better choice. The one choice you do not have is to do nothing, because if you lead a full life you will be regularly stressed, and you have to deal with pressures and tensions so they don't interfere with realizing what you want to accomplish.

Just as I believe that leaders need to manage their anger so they are not caught off guard by their emotions, I also believe it is important to cultivate body listening in general. Can you recognize when you are depleted or exhausted before that vulnerability gets you into trouble? This monitoring may even assume greater importance if you are a person who usually has an enormous amount of energy, functioning well most of the time, but who can crash when you collapse rather quickly, surprising yourself and those around you. When I was younger, I was like that, and it took me some time to learn how to decode subtle clues indicating that breakdown was imminent and with it a dramatic slide from high performance to the exact opposite.

After a colleague once told me that the stress was showing, I resolved to get better about monitoring myself. I decided that I shouldn't have to be told by others when I'm not handling things well; I should be able to do that for myself. As I tried to figure myself out better, I came to realize that I have some tendency to get paranoid when sleep deprived. From then on, I made myself get extra sleep each time I thought someone was "against me" and realized that my suspicions always disappeared with rest.

Without understanding the consequences, I went through my peak adult years thinking that sleep was overrated, priding myself on being able to manage with five hours of sleep each night. In hindsight, I realize that sleep deprivation wasn't a badge of courage; it is more likely to make one insulin resistant, hungry, and vulnerable to developing

Type 2 diabetes (Spiegel, Knutson, Leproult, Tasali, & Van Cauter, 2005; Yaggi, Araujo, & McKinlay, 2006). I wonder now how much more I might have accomplished, with less physical cost, if I had taken self-care more seriously at the start. Taking good care of yourself is not being selfish; it is the key to high performance.

Part of thriving also involves attending to your financial future. Nurses do not make exorbitant salaries, but they do make salaries substantially above the American median. In 2008, the average nurse salary was $66,973, up more than about 16% from 2004 (Bureau of Health Professions [BHPR], 2010). Although it is changing, a sizable number of married women persist in seeing their incomes as an "extra" available to the family instead of as a significant resource for them to manage. The trouble with thinking of your salary as optional is that you don't think strategically about your money, often failing to take full advantage of employer-supported retirement plans and the like, because you see the dollars as a help to others as opposed to resources that you need to deploy strategically. I hate to admit it, because it is not seemly behavior for a self-professed feminist, but I saw the salary I made as "helping out the family" longer than I should have. It was only when I realized that I managed my organization's resources better than I did my own that my behavior changed, and I began to take better control of my financial future.

The mindset that you are working "to help out" also gets in the way of obtaining needed supports at crucial times. I have known women who resist having to pay for child care, cleaning help, prepared foods, gym memberships, and even additional education, because they think "it doesn't pay for me to work if I have to shell out so much money to do so." Such supports, particularly in the early career years of raising a family, can make all the difference in whether you stay in a field to progress to higher pay, better hours, more interesting assignments, and exciting opportunities. If nurses are to exert leadership, then they need to see themselves as worthy of investment.

There is a substantial literature examining the interconnection between health and hardiness (Judkins, Massey, & Huff, 2006; Kobasa, Maddi, & Kahn, 1982). There have even been attempts to create hardy occupational environments where workers have more control over their situations (Hockey & Earle, 2006; Judkins, & Furlow, 2003). Although there is considerable variation in the effectiveness of attempts to strengthen hardiness, there are four "Cs" that are mentioned regularly as important: You are more likely to be resilient if you are *committed* to what you do, believe you can significantly *control* what happens, regard *change* as likely to yield some good, and stay connected to *community*.

People who are engaged in life, not apathetic, and committed to values tend to be involved in their neighborhoods and professional communities. They are likely to associate with other optimistic people, network effectively, celebrate achievements large and small, and appreciate the supports provided by professional organizations—meetings, Web sites, journals, newsletters, and grants. Committed and connected individuals are not likely to regard all change as necessarily bad; they are more likely to see the possibilities of shifting situations. If someone retires or is recruited elsewhere, you can mourn her leaving, but also see this as an opportunity to hire someone else with more up-to-date skills. If there is a move to an electronic health record, there will be some difficulty learning to use the new system, but there is an opportunity to have the system do things for you that you couldn't do in a paper-and-pencil world. Implicit in such conceptualizations is the notion that you can control what happens to you. You are not a pawn in the health care system but someone who can exert strategic influence.

It has become almost a truism to argue that while you cannot control others, you can control your own response to events and people. You can control whether you wallow in pity or force yourself to do something. You may not be able to control whether someone irritates you, but you can try to figure out why that person always sets you off. You can go to a meeting and be ignored and still decide that you are going to respond to the call for feedback even if you have not been personally asked for your opinion.

The chief nurse officer (CNO) of our hospital system (Sonna Ehrlich Merk) and I once did something like this. About three years after a large community hospital and our academic health center were consolidated into a new hospital system, there was an effort undertaken to obtain feedback from the physicians regarding what they liked and did not like about the new structure. No one asked nurses for their opinion, but the two of us, as CNO and dean, decided to respond, "pretending" that we had been asked. We began our joint letter to the CEO and COO saying that we knew that the system valued nursing, so we thought we would provide an update on progress to date since the consolidation, ending with a summary of what we thought needed to happen in the future. One of the things we wanted to push was moving to achieve Magnet hospital status. Our letter was never publicly discussed, but over time everything we recommended came to pass. We had planted ideas that eventually became part of larger conversations.

Whether change is always a thorn and control always seems elusive may be a function of how sure you are as a result of your upbringing. If you experienced a series of losses, you may be suspicious about having any control since most of the changes in your life seemed negative. The important thing to realize, however, is that it is counterproductive for you to rail against change or assume lack of control. Regardless of how true it is objectively or not, it always helps to believe that you can control matters and change can bring advantages, because a positive default position ensures that you will at least try to make a difference or find the good in something new. Even unrealistic optimism has some value, especially in a health care system where power is not something nurses possess until they gain and claim it (Armor, Massey, & Sackett, 2008).

Do nothing and nothing will happen. Try something and it might not work, but if you don't try, for sure nothing will happen. Although I once worried that if I tried something, I ran the risk of not succeeding, I now am more likely not to worry all that much about not succeeding, because I see trying as an important professional activity in its own right. As with so many things, you have to keep trying, because only some percentage of efforts will pay off, and you don't know which ones will do so. This shift was an important one for me because it marked a move away from fear of failure to an appreciation of what really goes into success—lots of effort mixed with false starts. When we look at successful people, we tend to assume that success came easily to them—"they don't know the troubles I've known"—but if you ask them about their journeys, you are likely to hear a narrative full of persistence rather than one that is trouble free.

Monitoring How You Think

Much of learned optimism involves being careful about how you think. Here are some additional strategies that work:

- *Don't overgeneralize.* If you didn't handle something well in a particular situation, it is better not to say "I was never cut out to be a nurse" or "I'm a lousy mother." It is better to say to yourself and others, "I didn't handle that well" and go on from there, because all of us have the inalienable right not to be at peak performance every day. Overgeneralize and you've made yourself the problem, not what you did or didn't do at a moment in time, and that is more difficult to address.
- *Don't ruminate.* Every time you focus just on the negative, you are ignoring most of everyday life, which is without incident, and taking the positive for granted. There was a time when I commuted long

distances and would arrive home usually late to have my husband ask "How was your day?," and I rarely responded with some description of my triumphs. Instead I regaled him with the disappointments of the day. There came a time when I realized that all my daughters ever heard about my work life was negative, and they must wonder why I ever bothered to leave home. Because I liked my husband's sympathy at the end of a long ride, I was shortchanging the day by not sharing my triumphs, and in the process turning into a lousy role model for what it means to be a woman. Physical activity is one of the major strategies for cutting off rumination, because it is physically impossible to exercise for an hour and still feel as bad as you did when you started.

- *Regularly count your blessings.* It has been found that people who force themselves to recall their blessings on a regular basis have a more positive approach to life. Individuals who hold negative self-perceptions can be taught to reflect on their personal value with long-term positive consequences (Cohen, Garcia, Purdie-Vaughns, Apfel, & Brzustoski, 2009).

- *Learn to reframe.* As a developmentalist, I have long appreciated the value of reframing a problem as a developmental challenge; having a problem sounds grim, but experiencing a developmental challenge suggests that what you are going through is normal. As part of reframing when I need to recall that a failure can be an opportunity in disguise, I say "I'm so grown up that I cannot tell the difference between failure and life experience." I have reminded stalled students that "The bright know what the ideal might look like, so it is not surprising that they regularly feel inadequate in the current situation," in order to help them see their blues in a positive light (you have to be smart to see the gap between what is and what could be). In dealing with my boss, I often reminded myself that "A *no* can be helpful in the next round of negotiations." This is a reframing I learned from my children who would ask metaphorically for the sun and moon, get refused, then chide us for being unduly negative when we didn't come up with at least one star, which we usually did to avoid the uncaring label.

- *Confront irrational beliefs.* All of us want to be liked; all of us want to be perfect; all of us want a life free of problems/demands. Recognizing that you are prone to such irrational beliefs can be a quick way of realizing that your expectations for a situation are unreasonable. Just admitting that you still hope everyone will like you and realizing that there is no way you can please everyone can lead you to take a more realistic look at how you handle some situations.

- *Be careful how you explain matters.* On the whole, women are less likely to make self-serving explanations for their success and failure than men, attributing their achievement to "lucking out" and their lack thereof to something intrinsic. In this respect, they may be reflecting the attributional bias of the observers who regarded men's anger as due to circumstances and women's anger as personality driven. However, one consequence of this pattern is that women may not own their success the way you do when you see a clear connection between effort, ability, and something going well; conversely they may believe that their failure is immutable if they are quick to explain something not going well as their fault. Women nurses may be more prone in this direction because the collectivistic culture of the profession discourages prideful explanations of success and encourages taking personal responsibility for failure (Roese & Olson, 2007). This attributional style can be good for society because you want professionals who assume responsibility for their actions, but hard on the individual who would do better emotionally by being slower to take personal blame, particularly when constructive changes in the environment are warranted.
- *Triage daily.* Because nurses have been socialized to think in terms of meeting all of their patients' needs, they regularly feel inadequate when they cannot meet every demand. Covey's (1989) notion of putting first things first, one of his habits of highly effective people, suggests that triage is in order on a daily basis. You can feel less overwhelmed when you organize your time in terms of his urgent/important management matrix. If something is both urgent and important, then it needs immediate attention. The goal is to work more on matters that are important but not urgent, activity most likely to be strategic. Don't saddle yourself with doing anything that is neither urgent nor important; it's busy work. If you decide something is urgent but not important, it usually means someone else is trying to make this your problem so resist fixing things that you don't perceive as in need of repair.

The point of this chapter has been to call attention to the importance of self-regulation in being ready for the challenges of leadership. If you are run down, quick to anger, and predisposed to explain problems as due to fixed causes, then you are likely to be self-conscious, overwhelmed, and disinclined to think creatively about alternative ways of changing your environment. Feeling powerless, whether real or imagined, means you are shaped by your constraints rather than your values and goals (Smith, Jostmann, Galinsky, & Van Dijk, 2008), and you are probably not managing your time well. What is more, your sense of humor is not likely to surface much under these conditions. And being able to make light of the human condition and the distortions we are all prone to when we are beleaguered can be another way of managing anger and sustaining optimism.

Key Take-Away Points

- An important aspect of leadership is taking responsibility for your emotions, so you can stay optimistic enough to energize others.
- Women as a group may have added difficulty managing their emotions because they are prone to rumination and regarded more negatively when they are emotional.
- For women/nurses, the themes behind most anger-producing situations are powerlessness and injustice.
- Crying, in women, is often an indicator of anger; realizing that can help all concerned deal more effectively with tears.
- Anger can have benefits when it provides motivation for realistic confrontation of a problem.
- Body listening is an important part of self-regulation; the better you get at figuring out your own energy fluctuations, the more likely you are to use them to advantage.
- Hardiness is associated with being committed to what you do, believing you can control what happens in some respects, regarding change as likely to yield some good, and staying connected to community.
- You need to be careful about how you think about matters, because you are listening to yourself, and you may take your overgeneralizations more seriously than you should.

REFERENCES

Albright, M. (2003). *Madam secretary: A memoir.* New York: Miramax.

Armor, D. A., Massey, C., & Sackett, A. M. (2008). Prescribed optimism. Is it right to be wrong about the future? *Psychological Science, 19,* 329–331.

Beck, A. T. (1999). *Prisoners of hate: The cognitive basis of anger, hostility, and violence.* New York: HarperCollins.

Blanch, D. C., Hall, J. A., Roter, D. L., & Frankel, R. M. (2008). Medical student gender and issues of confidence. *Patient Education and Counseling, 72,* 374–381.

Brescoll, V. L., & Uhlmann, E. L. (2008). Can an angry woman get ahead? Status conferral, gender, and expression of emotion in the workplace. *Psychological Science, 19,* 268–275.

Bureau of Health Professions. (2010, March). *The registered nurse population. Initial findings from the 2008 National Sample Survey of Registered Nurses.* Retrieved March 20, 2010, from http://bhpr.hrsa.gov/healthworkforce/rnsurvey/initialfindings2008.pdf

Burns, D. D. (1999). *Feeling good: The new mood therapy.* New York: William Morrow.

Chrisler, J. C. (2008). 2007 presidential address: Fear of losing control: Power, perfectionism, and the psychology of women. *Psychology of Women Quarterly, 32,* 1–12.

Cohen, G. L., Garcia, J., Purdie-Vaughns, V., Apfel, N., & Brzustoski, P. (2009). Recursive processes in self-affirmation: Intervening to close the minority achievement gap. *Science, 324,* 400–403.

Covey, S. R. (1989). *The 7 habits of highly effective people.* New York: Simon & Schuster.

Eagly, A. H., & Karau, S. J. (2002). Role congruity theory of prejudice toward female leaders. *Psychological Review, 109,* 573–598.

The Editors. (2008, October 13). The choice. *The New Yorker,* pp. 51–52, 54, 56, 58.

Ellis, A., & Dryden, W. (2007). *The practice of rational emotive behavior therapy.* New York: Springer Publishing.

Hockey, G. R. J., & Earle, F. (2006). Control over the scheduling of simulated office work reduces the impact of workload on mental fatigue and task performance. *Journal of Experimental Psychology: Applied, 12,* 50–65.

Judkins, S., & Furlow, L. (2003). Creating a hardy work environment: Can organizational policies help? *Texas Journal of Rural Health, 21*(4), 11–17.

Judkins, S., Massey, C., & Huff, B. (2006). Hardiness, stress, and use of ill-time among nurse managers: Is there a connection? *Nursing Economics, 24,* 187–192.

Keltner, D., Van Kleef, G. A., Chen, S., & Kraus, M. (2008). A reciprocal influence model of social power: Emerging principles and lines of inquiry. *Advances in Experimental Social Psychology, 40,* 151–192.

Keyes, C. L. M. (2007). Promoting and protecting mental health as flourishing. A complementary strategy for improving national mental health. *American Psychologist, 62,* 95–108.

Kobasa, S. C., Maddi, S. R., & Kahn, S. (1982). Hardiness and health: A prospective study. *Journal of Personality and Social Psychology, 42,* 168–177.

Lyubomirsky, S. (2008). *The how of happiness: A scientific approach to getting the life you want.* New York: Penguin Press.

McKay, M., Wood, J. C., & Brantley, J. (2007). *The dialectical behavior therapy skills workbook. Practical DBT exercises for learning mindfulness, interpersonal effectiveness, emotion regulation & distress tolerance.* Oakland, CA: New Harbinger Publications.

Nolen-Hoeksema, S., & Larson, J. (1999). *Coping with loss*. Mahwah, NJ: Erlbaum.

Nolen-Hoeksema, S., Wisco, B. E., & Lyubomirsky, S. (2008). Rethinking rumination. *Perspectives on Psychological Science, 3,* 400–424.

Pesut, D. J. (2008). The wisdom of renewal. Put balance back in your life, using reflection, wisdom, and renewal. *American Nurse Today, 3(7),* 34–36.

Plant, E. A., Hyde, J. S., Keltner, D., & Devine, P. G. (2000). The gender stereotyping of emotions. *Psychology of Women Quarterly, 24,* 81–92.

Roese, N. J., & Olson, J. M. (2007). Better, stronger, faster self-serving judgment, affect regulation, and the optimal vigilance hypothesis. *Perspectives on Psychological Science, 2,* 124–141.

Seligman, M. E. P. (1991). *Learned optimism*. New York: A. A. Knopf.

Smith, P. K., Jostmann, N. B., Galinsky, A. D., & Van Dijk, W. W. (2008). Lacking power impairs executive functions. *Psychological Science, 19,* 441–447.

Spiegel, K., Knutson, K., Leproult, R., Tasali, E., & Van Cauter, E. (2005). Sleep loss: A novel risk factor for insulin resistance and type 2 diabetes. *Journal of Applied Physiology, 99,* 2008–2019.

Tamir, M., Mitchell, C., & Gross, J. J. (2008). Hedonic and instrumental motives in anger regulation. *Psychological Science, 19,* 324–328.

Thomas, S. P. (Ed.). (1993). *Women and anger*. New York: Springer Publishing.

Thomas, S. P. (2001). Teaching healthy anger management. *Perspectives in Psychiatric Care, 37,* 41–48.

Thomas, S. P. (2005). Women's anger, aggression, and violence. *Health Care for Women International, 26,* 504–522.

Thomas, S. P. (2008). *Transforming nurses' anger and pain: Steps toward healing* (3rd ed.). New York: Springer Publishing.

Tiedens, L. Z., Ellsworth, P. C., & Mesquita, B. (2000). Sentimental stereotypes: Emotional expectations for high- and low-status group members. *Personality and Social Psychology Bulletin, 26,* 560–575.

ISNA. (November 2007, December 2007, January 2008). Tips for managing anger constructively. *ISNA Bulletin*.

Van Kleef, G. A., Oveis, C., Van der Lowe, I., LuoKogan, A., Goetz, J., & Keltner, D. (2008). Power, distress, and compassion. Turning a blind eye to the suffering of others. *Psychological Science, 19,* 1315–1322.

Yaggi, H. K., Araujo, A. B., & McKinlay, J. B. (2006). Sleep duration as a risk factor for the development of type 2 diabetes. *Diabetes Care, 29,* 657–661.

Chapter 4

Orchestrating a Career

In my opinion, the most important development bearing on leadership during my years as a nurse has been the latest round of the Women's Movement. The unprecedented number of women entering the workforce in the last third of the 20th century changed all fields, including nursing. Where before many women entered nursing thinking of it largely as good preparation for marriage and motherhood rather than as embarking on a career, now 84.8% of licensed registered nurses (RNs) practice, most working full time (63.2%). In the last four decades, the number of nurses has tripled, going from about 1 million to 3.1 million, and the number of men in nursing has dramatically increased, though their number is still relatively small compared to their female counterparts, but it is growing. Women outnumber men 15 to 1, but of those entering nursing after 1990, the ratio is 10 to 1 (Bureau of Health Professions [BHPR], 2010; McBride, 2007).

Kalisch and Kalisch (1987) have written extensively about the changing image of the nurse in the 20th century, describing various portrayals—ministering angel, girl Friday, battleaxe, and sex object—that preceded the latest one, nurse as careerist. They describe the careerist as a knowledgeable, respected professional who is goal oriented. However, that isn't how nurses are always perceived. For example, middle-school students' perceptions of a career in nursing are different from their view of an "ideal career" with regard to autonomy, respect, compensation, and "busyness" (Cohen, Palumbo, Rambur, & Mongeon, 2004). An ideal career, like an ideal leader, is still seen as having a forceful valence, somewhat at odds with even today's representations of nursing, but perceptions are far from static (Jinks & Bradley, 2004).

Ethicist Norman S. Care (1984) shaped my thinking enormously when he described a career as a long-term commitment through which self-realization and service to others may be achieved. Nursing has long been depicted as providing service to others, but our profession has not consistently been described as a pathway to self-realization. Traditionally, nurses were seen as having a vocation to serve others—patients, their families, physicians, and their communities—but were expected not to be much concerned about career matters such as salary, promotions, and work conditions if they "really cared."

All of the staff and office nurses whom I admired as I grew up were good at their jobs, but they did essentially the same thing year in and year out. Their effectiveness was usually described in terms of giving an injection without it hurting and getting all of the tasks completed by the end of their shifts. In any career, there is supposed to be an overlap between personal development and professional goals, but I do not remember much attention being paid to the nurse's own strivings. Like the good mother, she was supposed to "do" for others without asking much in return, occasionally receiving a box of chocolates for her efforts.

If you lined up the values that a careerist should have along with the prevailing views about our field in the second half of the 20th century, you would find considerable disparity between the way nurses were seen back then, and even saw themselves, and what has been emphasized in other established professions. Begin with the notion of whether nursing is a long-term commitment. To the extent that nursing has been seen by a substantial number of its practitioners as something to fall back on in case they needed to work outside the home, some of the workforce could be characterized as "washing machine" or "refrigerator" nurses (i.e., individuals who work only to be able to afford to buy things they want) because they did not have an overtime orientation.

The more the growth and development of the nurse is taken seriously, the less likely it is that the minimum entry-into-practice educational qualifications will dominate all academic debates, as they have for so many years in nursing, because minimum standards are a small part of discussions regarding career trajectories. A career by its very nature presupposes development over time, including the likelihood of additional education. Lifelong learning ceases to be a slogan and becomes a professional expectation, even when continuing-education credits are not mandated for continuing licensure. Even the way one discusses mentoring changes. Instead of the focus being on the personal generosity evidenced by a select few, the emphasis switches to the obligation everyone in the field—even those with curmudgeon tendencies—incurs in guiding future generations. In addition, the more the growth and development of nurses is taken seriously, the growth and development of nurse leaders is of concern.

Some of us may not have had a careerist orientation from the start because we were not totally convinced that nursing qualified as a true profession, even though some of the criteria for evaluating a profession used by Flexner (1910) in his watershed study of medical education has been trotted out in every issues-oriented nursing class for almost a century. In classroom analyses, we typically conclude that nursing at its core requires mastery of well-defined and complex knowledge and skills, so nursing is a learned profession. However, not everyone has bought into that conclusion. Many continued to see nursing as "a profession that doesn't have its act together" (Schorr, 1981a), though that is changing, because in recent years we have undergone an extensive process of professionalization—developing ethical guidelines and practice standards, establishing graduate programs, and engaging in research (Bureau of Health Professions [BHPR], 2004, Figure 2.1).

The reasons that nursing is sometimes seen as a profession betwixt and between are complex. The RN is not an academic degree like the MD (Doctor of Medicine) and this licensure is arrived at in different ways, so we do not all proceed from a shared socialization to the role the way physicians or dentists do. Even though nurses occupy a special niche in their dedication to those they serve, they may still be invisible in listings of the learned professions because the language used to describe some of their work (e.g., following doctors' orders) downplays their independent functioning and ignores their legal liability (Pellegrino, 2002).

The impact that a nurse can have as a leader remains constrained even today by the lack of attention paid to how a nurse changes over the course of a full career. How do you move over time from developing yourself to developing others, the setting in which you work, and the field? Every nurse whose principal role is not direct caregiving has had the experience of being asked, "When did you used to be a real nurse?" That equation of "real" nursing only with one view of nursing has had a chilling effect on nurses being able to envision themselves in leadership positions and on prospective nurses imagining that the profession can be a satisfying route to realizing an array of career ambitions. I remember being repeatedly whether I was still a nurse when I completed my doctorate, so I developed a pat answer, "I am a mental health nurse and I want you to know that I practice my specialty each and every day!" That glib answer, however, masked how upset I was to be in a learned profession yet one where you were assumed to have left the field if you became an educator, scientist, policy maker, or administrator.

I wish I had had someone at the start of my career who could have explained to me what a full career might look like. I can still remember a cartoon that I saw in a nursing journal in the 1960s. It featured a student nurse, lamp in hand—à la Florence Nightingale—sauntering into her future saying that she was prepared to play a host of roles: mother surrogate, patient advocate, therapist, educator, researcher, change agent, policy maker, and the like. This was the period when all the roles a nurse could or should play were much discussed, and the implication always seemed to be that a new graduate should be capable of doing it all from the start. I looked at that cartoon figure and wondered how long her enthusiasm would last, particularly if she went into a beginning position expecting to be an instrument of institutional transformation from the start. She would probably get her comeuppance in short order.

Benner's watershed book (1984) on how a nurse passes through five levels of ability—novice, advanced beginner, competent, proficient, and expert—on the way to complete professional development was one of the first writings to make clear that there is a journey all practitioners undertake in life after obtaining the RN license. Her work forced the field to give up unrealistic expectations that proficiency and excellence can be achieved at the start with a sound education. And those insights prepared the way for a careerist perspective to take hold. (It should be noted that no one expects new MDs to be capable of practicing on their own the day after graduation.)

The advantage of a career framework, complete with multiple stages, is that one doesn't start out expecting to be fully developed at the beginning. It is a relief when an individual doesn't have to feel burdened by that expectation. There isn't any role that you cannot master, but there are developmental themes to each stage. Just like other developmental models, whether it's Erikson's stages of ego development or Piaget's stages of cognitive development or Kohlberg's stages of moral development, a career framework is a heuristic device for outlining central developmental tasks. Understanding the main objective of a period helps you develop realistic expectations for what you can accomplish at any one time, but it also pushes you to consider what your next challenge might be.

The remainder of this chapter is an overview of the career model that I have fleshed out over time, greatly influenced by Dalton, Thompson, and Price's classic article (1977) on stages of a professional career. Table 4.1 outlines five career stages and the role mentoring plays in each; I have come to believe that wise counsel and coaching are needed throughout a career, not just in the early period when you are getting a handle on the field and your place in it.

TABLE 4.1 Career Stages and Mentoring Needs

Stage	Central Developmental Task	Means	Role of Mentor
I. Preparation	Learning—Assimilating values, knowledge base, and clinical/inquiry skills of chosen profession and specialty	• Analysis of personal strengths and limitations • Formal education • Socialization experiences • Licensure • Certification	• Model values and practices • Encourage problem-solving skills • Help set career goals • Guide to experiences that build skills and expand vision
II. Independent Contributions	Moving from novice to competence—Demonstrating ability to work independently and interdependently in chosen area of practice	• Build collegial network, intra- and interdisciplinary • Deal with inevitable gap between ideals learned and realities of work setting • Demonstrate ability to think, synthesize, and act critically • Mentor less experienced and less educated	• Help navigate inner workings of institution/profession • Open doors of opportunity • Direct to resources • Facilitate networking • Keep focus on meeting institutional/professional benchmarks of success
III. Development of Home Setting	Moving from competence to expertise—Assuming responsibility for development of others and of setting	• Engage in strategic planning • Develop tolerance for ambiguity and political savvy • Build home setting's image, infrastructure, and resources • Mentor in more complex aspects of role	• Share successes, failures, and tips • Provide feedback regarding strategy • Teach how to delegate • Develop mentoring abilities • Nominate for awards
IV. Development of Field/Health Care	Shaping profession and health care—Exercising power of authority and creating a vision for the future	• Consult in area of expertise • Serve as advisor to local, regional, national, and/or international efforts and organizations	• Discuss strategy and likely future scenarios • Recommend for opportunities • Sponsor for honors
V. The Gadfly Period	Continuing to shape profession and health care when no longer constrained by institutional obligations	• Coach current generation of leaders • Take on special projects that require high-level integrative abilities • Articulate strong positions that might not have been possible when constrained by institutional affiliation	• Assist in envisioning postretirement prospects • Recommend for opportunities

Preparation

The first career stage is appropriately named "preparation," because the central task is absorbing the values/standards, learning the basics, and developing the clinical/inquiry skills of one's profession or specialty. Formal education is the best way to master a body of knowledge, but you also need socialization experiences—clinical rotations, internships, assistantships, apprenticeships, counseling, mentoring, group relations training, workshops, and the like—in order to test yourself in real-life situations and hone your problem-solving skills. I've always thought you go to school to "read the lines," and you count on a variety of social-ization experiences to begin to "read between the lines." Both kinds of learning are enhanced by an honest appraisal of your strengths and limi-tations (the point behind chapter 2).

Different levels of education prepare you for different kinds of prac-tice. Undergraduate education is the typical preparation for licensure as an RN, and that level of instruction enables you to know a little bit about all aspects of the field, so you can decide what kinds of settings and patient populations appeal to you the most. Licensure is a statement of minimum competency; you have the basics on which to build a nurs-ing career. For many nurses this practice as a generalist isn't sufficient, so they return to school for a graduate degree that prepares them to specialize, for example, as a clinical nurse specialist, nurse practitioner, nurse midwife, nurse anesthetist, or nurse informaticist. Whereas the undergraduate degree stresses learning something about all aspects of nursing, the focus of graduate education [MSN (Master of Science in Nursing)] [DNP (Doctor of Nursing Practice)] is on learning a great deal about some specific area. The resulting specialty knowledge is typically confirmed by certification, a credential validating defined expertise.

Being a learned profession means that some nurses also need to seek the PhD (Doctor of Philosophy) or DNS (Doctor of Nursing Science) degree, the level of education concerned with moving beyond what is known to the next step, tackling important practice-relevant questions for which we do not yet have good answers. This level of preparation is concerned with developing the profession's knowledge base—figuring out efficacy (what works under controlled conditions) or effectiveness (what works when research findings are applied in real-life environments). Increasingly, nurses wishing an academic career seek postdoctoral research training, so they can launch their programs of scholarship under the tute-lage of an accomplished researcher focused on the same area.

Course work is only a part of undergraduate preparation. Schooling is a time when you should be figuring out workable strategies for personal stress management, developing habits of precision (e.g., learning to manage time and organize files for later retrieval), discovering how to network, polishing your writing/communication skills, and extending your command of information technology. Honors options, international experiences, volunteer work, and independent studies may help you "try out" interests that can be pursued further in graduate studies. Some may wish to get involved in governance—serving as a student representative on a faculty committee—to learn more about organizational mores.

Graduate education needs to be undertaken with an eye to such socialization experiences as much as or even more than undergraduate education. If you intend to become an educator or an administrator, then there is no substitute for working closely with someone who already has mastery in your area of interest. The biggest thing that you learn as a teaching assistant (TA) or research assistant (RA) is that if things can go wrong, then they are likely to go wrong. When you are early in a career, you tend to assume that eloquent speakers, gifted writers, astute negotiators, and funded researchers all found easy what you find difficult. Work closely with accomplished persons, and you will find that their eloquence is predicated on over-preparing for a speech, their writing takes multiple drafts to reach finished shape, not all of their negotiations are successful, and their research is currently supported by an important agency but it took repeated submissions to get it funded.

When you are becoming prepared, mentoring is crucial in all sorts of ways: modeling values and practices, assessing holes in the protégé's background, providing graded challenges that test abilities without overwhelming, welcoming the individual to the profession/specialty, and teaching what is typically not taught in class, for example, how to construct a curriculum vitae, prepare a budget, and follow up. Mentoring over the course of a career can take many forms—guiding, advising, protecting, focusing, sponsoring, challenging, coaching, facilitating, introducing, recommending, sharing, and so forth—with different needs emerging as a career unfolds. You can also learn a great deal by simply observing effective people in a range of situations and trying to figure how they manage to accomplish what they do when we all get the same 24 hours each day. Some of my greatest insights came from studying what makes some nurses successful and others ineffective and then trying to emulate the best role models (and avoid the shortcomings of the unsuccessful).

Historically, mentoring was seen as a single, sustained hierarchical relationship occurring during the school years, but that is being challenged now. Over the course of a career, a person will have multiple relationships of various lengths that are important to advancement, and, at best, collectively constitute an evolving network of support (Chandler & Kram, 2007). The mentors you meet through educational experiences may introduce you to leaders in the field, and those individuals can provide important assistance as you seek consultation for a project or think about whom to telephone for advice when joining a board.

Joining appropriate professional organizations is important at this stage, since you can take advantage of student discounts in trying out some, in order to figure out which ones will be of greatest support to you in life after graduation. Which ones will help you network with likeminded colleagues, and offer interesting annual meetings and informative journals, newsletters, or Web sites? With doctoral preparation, you will want to consider joining at least one interdisciplinary organization because most research areas can be well understood only in terms of how the interests of individual professions overlap and diverge. For example, the pediatric nurse researcher may wish to join the Society for Research in Child Development; the geriatric nurse researcher would be interested in the Gerontological Society of America; the cardiac nurse researcher would want to be involved in the American Heart Association, and so forth.

Before tackling the next career stage, a word is in order about how the developmental tasks of each stage might vary by career trajectory. Table 4.2 outlines how each stage generally differs depending on whether one is orchestrating a clinical or an academic career. Although there is more that each trajectory has in common, and that commonality increases as one advances, there are differences. For example, mentored presentations, publications, and small grants are important in learning to be a faculty member, but they do not have the same primacy in the formative preparation of a clinician. Certification has a prominent place in the preparation of a master clinician, though it is obviously also important to the faculty member teaching a clinical subject at the graduate level.

Independent Contributions

Preparation is never over, because all nurses must stay prepared to meet current-practice expectations, but you cannot stay a student forever. You must eventually move on to the next stage of using what you have

TABLE 4.2 Developmental Tasks by Career Trajectory

Stage	Master Clinician	Faculty Member
Preparation	• Formal education—undergraduate, MSN, DNP, PhD • Internships, apprenticeships • Licensure/Certification • Join appropriate professional organizations	• Formal education—undergraduate, MSN, PhD, post-doctoral research training • TA (teaching assistant) experience/teaching portfolio • RA (research assistant) experience • Mentored presentations, publications, small grants • Join appropriate professional organizations
Independent Contributions	• Ensure that personal practice reflects best practices and outcomes set by organization • Build teamwork • Participate in governance structure • Preceptor students • Demonstrate emotional intelligence	• Build research team and program of scholarship—interdisciplinary connections, refereed presentations and publications, external funding • Integrate teaching, research, and service commitments • Advise/mentor students • Demonstrate emotional intelligence
Development of Home Setting	• Engage in strategic planning • Lead quality-improvement efforts • Develop junior colleagues • Build home setting's image (presentations/publications), infrastructure, and resources • Obtain additional preparation for leadership	• Engage in strategic planning • Lead curricular and program initiatives • Juggle multiple grants/projects • Develop junior colleagues • Build home setting's image, infrastructure, and resources • Obtain additional preparation for leadership • Extend own program of research

(continued)

TABLE 4.2 (*continued*)

Stage	Master Clinician	Faculty Member
Development of Field/Health Care	• Consult in area of expertise • Serve as advisor to local, regional, national, and/or international efforts and organizations • Assume leadership roles in professional organizations • Develop next generation of leaders • Speak out about issues of the day locally, regionally, and nationally • Testify regarding needed policy changes	• Consult in area of expertise • Serve as advisor to local, regional, national, and/or international efforts and organizations • Assume leadership roles in professional organizations • Develop next generation of leaders • Write editorials and papers geared toward stimulating debate and discussion • Testify regarding needed policy changes
The Gadfly Period	• Take on special assignments • Serve as a consultant • Coach current leaders • Push dialogue and challenge to new ways of thinking	• Take on special assignments • Serve as a consultant • Coach current leaders • Push dialogue and challenge to new ways of thinking

learned. In the second career stage, the focus is on demonstrating the ability to work independently and interdependently with nurse colleagues, other health professionals, and a broad array of staff/technicians. Probably the first career crisis all of us face is dealing with the inevitable gap between the principles learned in school and the realities of work settings (Pellico, Brewer, & Kovner, 2009). You go to school to learn ideals, never thereafter to be in a situation that is ideal, so the rest of your career is applying what you know to the current situation as best you can.

The response to this gulf between the ideal and institutional realities isn't always productive. New nurses often either bemoan their choice of workplace, believing that they would be able to function better in another setting, or conclude that they were never cut out to be a nurse and should instead pursue another career. Although those impulses are natural, they can get in the way of addressing the central developmental task of this career stage. If you are disillusioned with the institution, you are not likely to try to figure out how to be successful within the constraints that you are experiencing. If you are angry with your own performance, you are not likely to be thinking critically about how you might improve and what support you need. Mind you, you may have planted yourself in the wrong setting for your personality and abilities, but if you jump immediately to that conclusion, the biggest problem may be that you are still holding on to fairy-tale notions that there is such a thing as the perfect job.

It is perfectly normal to think "I would be a better mother if only my children were better" or "I would be a better nurse if this hospital would only get its act together" or "I would be a better faculty member if only the students tried harder" or "I would be a better dean if I only had better faculty." That kind of thinking, however, only delays the confrontation all of us must have with the fact that we are all planted in settings that fall short of the ideal and we are all not as good as we are going to be someday after learning from experience.

What you learned in school is like the colors and shapes in a kaleidoscope. Every patient, every student, every co-worker, and every challenge provides you with an opportunity to shake the kaleidoscope of your knowledge and skills and see if you can use that background to decipher the patterns in a particular situation. You went to school and heard a great deal about critical thinking, but the need to think, synthesize, and act critically is now. The mark of a smart person isn't never making mistakes; the mark of a smart person is doing something you think will work, but doesn't, no more than three times, and then rethinking the whole situation.

At the beginning of a career, there is so much to learn about the institution's culture that you didn't expect to have to worry about when you
started out, and I don't mean what is taught as part of formal orientation:
Should you go out of your way to eat with colleagues in order to get to
know them better? Where are the personality rubs so you don't get caught
in the cross fire? Who should you cultivate as allies? Particularly in the
health care professions, there is a great deal of tacit knowledge about how
you respond differently in different settings that isn't spelled out in policy
statements, but is important to functioning (Coffield, 2000; Sternberg &
Horvath, 1999). The new graduate is more likely to be thinking in terms
of applying skills that were learned in school but not as much about the
context of care, which can be overwhelming. Work in critical care, and
you have to be super-fast and know a great deal about machines/devices;
when you move to wound care, patients want to talk and you spend a
great deal of time negotiating with insurance companies to secure necessary equipment. Understanding and prioritizing important versus less-
valued aspects of the job is going to make a big difference in your success,
but you can learn these things only in the context of a specific position.

With rare exceptions, nurses in this career stage operate within the
confines of an organization. Your practice is shaped by the values, history, policies, resources, and mores of the home setting. That is why the
mentoring you need at this stage largely has to do with helping you nav-
igate the functioning of the institution and your profession by opening
doors of opportunity and keeping you focused on meeting institutional
and professional benchmarks of success. For the clinician, this means
ensuring that your personal practice reflects the best practices and outcomes set by the organization. For the academic, this means building
a program of scholarship in keeping with the tenure and promotion
expectations of the university.

All nurses must be concerned at this stage with building teams—
working with less-educated and less-experienced personnel; learning
how to take advantage of peer colleagues who are good in areas that you
are not; using those who know more than you know as consultants. At
the start of a career, many are reluctant to take advantage of the expertise
of others because admitting what you don't know may make you feel
vulnerable. You tend to hide your ignorance at the start more than you
will later on, because you don't yet appreciate that the skill involved in
learning from others is far more important than having a photographic
memory of all the facts you have ever read.

I remember reading long ago about the political value of asking for
help. If you ask for more help than someone can reasonably give, the

person is annoyed and may distance himself/herself from you. However, if you ask for a reasonable amount of help in the area of the person's expertise, the person may even feel more connected to and supportive of you and your career. After all, you were smart enough to recognize his or her proficiency! In my own experience, this approach works. Although sometimes a person is truly too busy to be helpful, I have found that the best and busiest people usually are of the greatest assistance. Many of them have a strong investment in nurturing the next generation of leaders because they either have experienced mentoring along the way and now want to "pay it forward" or have had bad experiences themselves and don't want them repeated.

Knowing how to read others is an essential leadership skill, so this career stage requires you to demonstrate appropriate emotional intelligence. Do you know how to interpret your own emotions and those of others correctly and how to manage these feelings so that you can bring out the best in people? There is a growing literature on the importance of emotional intelligence in sizing up situations and helping others find meaning (Goleman, Boyatzis, & McKee, 2004; Mayer & Salovey, 1995; Salovey & Mayer, 1990), and demonstrating this ability is important at this stage as you seek to build your competence in a particular setting through interactions with others.

Because you are a novice, you are likely to be more self-absorbed than you will be with experience. Consequently, you may have little tolerance for the foibles of others, particularly those who should already in your opinion know better. Alas, that stance can get in the way of your success, because being self-centered can lead you to write off people prematurely, not understanding their contributions to the organization because you think they don't handle some things as well as they should. Being caught up with your own novice status may also leave you reluctant to get involved in anything that you don't have to, for example, institutional governance. You think, "I don't have to bother with that and would do well to just focus on getting better myself." That approach has some merit, because you do not want to take on more than you can reasonably handle, but you also do not want to appear removed from larger concerns because both clinical and academic nursing leadership require some active engagement in the affairs of the institution.

In this stage when you are most concerned with moving from novice to competence, you are not likely to believe that the organizational culture is your responsibility to change. You are likely to see what is in place as a reflection of how good others are. That's only natural, but it is important to recognize from the start how much the organizational culture supports or hinders what you personally are able to do. You need to become familiar with institutional governance to figure out how the mandates that affect you and your work are shaped. If you wanted to improve matters, how would you go about garnering support for needed changes and then incorporating them into the culture? Thinking about how the structure can support better practice and how matters can be improved propels you to the next career stage.

Development of Home Setting

In this stage, you continue to be concerned about how to be more effective as a clinician or educator, learning how to be more of a boundary spanner, and how to juggle more responsibilities/projects. The big difference is that now you also assume more responsibility for development of others and the setting, and in the process you move from competence to expertise. In seeking to improve the status quo and build supports/resources, you learn new lessons about striving for excellence. In the previous stage, your focus was on the here and now; in this stage, you have one foot in the present but another in the future. What needs to be done to better serve various stakeholders (e.g., patients, the public, students, and alumnae) or to enhance the institution's reputation?

When you become more involved in planning the future, your orientation switches in several respects. You have to develop a tolerance for ambiguity. No one, perhaps with the exception of Moses, ever looked to the future with a well-developed 10-point plan in hand. When you contemplate the future, you see trends, but it takes time, effort, and lots of conversation with others for clarity about how to proceed to emerge. The fuzziness of strategic planning can be uncomfortable for nurses who, as a group, are action-oriented people more comfortable with getting things done than talking seemingly endlessly about them. It is necessary, therefore, at this career stage that you learn more about the dangers of rushing to conclusions before you have engaged an assortment of stakeholders in reaching broad agreement about needed new directions.

Strategic planning is important no matter what kind of a nursing career you have. In clinical settings, an enormous amount of effort is going into quality-improvement efforts, cost containment, and redesigning systems to make appropriate use of new information technology. Academia is, by definition, concerned with changes in practice, and there is no school of nursing not concerned about mounting curricular and program initiatives to better meet today's challenge to do more with less.

The more you are involved in strategic planning, the more likely it is that you will be working closely with others in different fields. Whereas before you were interacting largely with other nurses, and doing your part to strengthen nursing, now you may be tackling an institutional challenge that requires a new kind of interdisciplinary collaboration and you are one of the few nurses involved in planning this effort. This means that you cannot rely on nurse jargon to convey ideas but must learn to be careful to use examples that resonate across disciplines.

An engagement in strategic planning requires political savvy. You spend the early part of your career learning what to do, only to spend more time at this career stage in trying to figure out how to get the buy-in for what needs to be done. I have found that many of us have a self-righteous streak, believing that what needs to be done should just be done, and, therefore, regard the need to be politically savvy with scorn (shouldn't be necessary; just takes precious time). However, politics aren't immaterial; they are essential. The reality is that we live in complex diverse systems, and the belief that anything should be self-evident to everyone is misguided. We can see ourselves as on the side of the angels, but what we forget is that not everyone believes in (or even likes) angels. Knowing what to do is not the same thing as getting it done, and leadership involves valuing both, because leadership, like politics, involves making what is possible happen.

Development of the home setting need not mean holding a formal administrative position, though all administrators should be ready to wrestle with the developmental challenges of this stage. Even if you do not have an administrative title, all senior clinicians and senior faculty have an obligation to develop the institutions where they work. Mentoring is important at this stage, too, but it now takes the form of someone with experience at this level sharing successes, failures, and tips.

Because a mentor at this stage is needed to provide feedback regarding strategy, such a person is often referred to as a coach (Kowalski & Casper, 2007). That word is more in keeping with the nondirective questioning that enables the person at this career stage to reflect, analyze, and find solutions to problems. In working with the protégé, the coach really gets to know that person's strengths and achievements. Aware of how the person is building her own expertise in developing others, the coach is often in a position to recommend the protégé for an honor or for additional preparation for leadership, for example, the Robert Wood

Johnson Foundation's Health Policy Program (RWJF, 2010) or Nurse Executive Program.

The area where most nurses need some mentoring at this career stage is knowing how to delegate previously held responsibilities to others, while also providing the mentoring that will enable them to handle their new assignments. It's not that you haven't done considerable delegation in the past; for example, monitoring how the work of nurses' aides and licensed practical nurses contributes to the overall nursing team. However, this is the stage when your responsibilities increase and you cannot continue to do everything that you once did yourself. Where before you were the one to see all the patients on a particular service, now you supervise other RNs and spend your time helping them develop their clinical savvy rather than showing off your own. Where before you were either the one who collected all the research data or oversaw that the RAs did it right, now you are juggling more than one grant and have to hire a grants manager whom you have to develop so that person can be responsible for the coordination you previously handled.

Development of the home setting means being concerned about the organization's image, infrastructure, and resources. You can complain publicly about how inadequate the organization is in the first two career stages (when perhaps you needed to do so to prove to yourself how discerning you were), but that ceases to be an option in this stage, because you have a role to play in correcting any deficiencies and moving the institution forward. Given that all organizations have problems, what steps are you taking to address the ones in your setting? What are you doing to convey a sufficiently positive view to make others want to join the organization? If there is a lack of resources, human and otherwise, what are you going to do in working with others to get new ones and strengthen the workforce?

I do not think that you can develop real expertise without addressing the challenges of this career stage. You can become proficient in your area of nursing with experience, but it is in confronting the system issues that shape practice, education, and research that you move to a higher level of ability yourself. It is in teaching that you learn the subject matter at a deeper level; it is in developing the institution that you fully understand all that is involved in realizing the aspirational goals of a practice profession; it is in working on committees with colleagues in other fields that you develop a more complicated sense of the issues facing health care and higher education. Determining whether your organization promotes and supports best practices also makes you ready for the next career stage.

Development of Field/Health Care

This is the career stage at which you move beyond your home setting and take a more active role in shaping the profession and health care in general. Once you get known as someone who has improved their own institution or as an expert in a particular area, opportunities become available elsewhere. A local official puts together an expert panel to examine "A 2020 View of Health Care" and you are invited to join the group. A professional organization invites you to serve on a committee to develop new leadership opportunities for nurses in your specialty. Such opportunities provide you with occasions to exercise the power of your authority in creating a vision for the future.

While in the previous stage you moved from focusing solely on the here and now to being more concerned about the future, you now have even more opportunities to shape the future as a consultant in the area of your expertise. You may be asked to serve as an advisor to various efforts and organizations or to assume a leadership role in some organization, for example, serving on an editorial board, running for office, writing a think piece for the field, or participating in a consensus conference devoted to figuring out which research findings should shape practice guidelines. Any speaking or writing you did in the past would have focused on your own expertise; now you may be asked to create a vision of the future that requires you to analyze broadly the work of many others in your field. You may be asked to speak out about the issues of the day and propose an agenda for the future that stimulates debate and discussion.

Because your opinion is valued, you are increasingly asked to serve as a reference, for example, recommending nurses for posted positions or evaluating a faculty dossier for tenure and promotion at another university (McBride & Lovejoy, 1995). You continue to mentor but increasingly find yourself coaching leaders at other institutions who are trying to develop their organizations and want to know how you handled similar situations. You are now at the level where what you know is valued, and so is your sense of strategy. As you share your strategic savvy with others, you are forced to analyze anew what you believe, and these reflections often propel your thinking to another level of conceptual complexity.

You still need mentoring, but what you need is to have senior colleagues recommend you for special opportunities that you might not consider without some coaxing. For example, a colleague might urge you to consider applying for the position of Chief Informatics Officer after serving successfully as the head of nursing informatics. Such senior colleagues may serve as references for you and may sponsor you for major honors—for example, fellowship in the American Academy of Nursing—providing you with wise counsel about how to shape the application to make a successful case for the regional or national impact of your work. You still need help at this point, but what you need to know is typically information that is not taught formally, for example, how to describe the impact of your work in 300 words or less, how to function effectively on a board, and how to testify before a legislative committee.

In this stage you often have more opportunities than ever before, partly because others know of you and partly because your boundary-spanning activities reveal more possibilities to you. There are many clinical and academic positions that do not belong to any one field—for example, serving as Chief Operating Officer (COO) or Provost—and you may be considered for them once you have demonstrated excellence in your own profession and home institution (more about this in chapter 13). All of these possibilities further change what you want, reenergizing you, one may hope, in the process. If you have had a full career, you may approach your Medicare years with some longing for more control over your time but also some trepidation about whether there's still a professional role for you to play. That brings us to the final career stage.

The Gadfly Period

Once you are no longer constrained by institutional obligations—that is, you have reached the age when most peers are retired and you are thinking of doing the same—there can be new career opportunities. Although some nurses dream of this time as an opportunity to finally clean out closets and others envision never-ending rounds of golf or babysitting grandchildren, this can be a period that is uniquely gratifying and important professionally. I realized the importance of this stage in watching what Virginia Henderson accomplished at an age when most would be thinking of retirement. Much of what we know her best for—*The Nature of Nursing* (1966), which defined nursing internationally, and the *Nursing Studies Index* (1972), which redirected nursing research—was published when she was already collecting social security (at ages 69 and 75 years, respectively). Although few of us will do such grand things in our later years, her career makes the point that this may be a period when we have considerable impact, because we have blocks of time to devote to a pet project and we are readier than ever before to speak our minds without having to worry about consequences for our career or our institution.

"Gadfly" may seem an unusual word to describe this career stage, because the usual meaning of the word has the connotation of a pest or irritant. I am using the word, however, in the same sense that Plato did in his *Apology* when he has Socrates describe himself as sort of a gadfly who asks the questions that stir others into life (Jowett, 1937, pp. 413–414). The gadfly in this instance is a truth teller who helps others to confront what they might prefer to ignore but need to tackle lest they be lulled into complacency. Moreover, health care certainly has a need for such truth telling.

I remember participating in the 1980s in the development of a women's mental health research agenda at the National Institute of Mental Health (NIMH). Having written the position paper for psychiatric-mental health nursing, I joined others who had done the same for psychiatry, social work, and psychology to hammer out an interdisciplinary plan. The first morning that we all were together was unproductive in that the emphasis was on all that had been accomplished to date by the agency instead of what must be done to meet unaddressed needs. By lunchtime, those of us charged with this task were upset with the lack of progress, and the impasse was resolved when the most chronologically gifted of us, a retired microbiologist, began the afternoon session by saying, "Let's cut the crap; there's a great deal that we're not doing that needs to be addressed." I now see that none of the rest of us could have said that, because we all wanted to be invited back. This professor emerita could be outspoken because she didn't care if she ever served again on another NIMH committee, which gave her a freedom to speak out that none of the rest of us had. Of course, her outspokenness guaranteed that she would be invited back to serve a similar purpose in the future, but it took me a few more years to be wise enough to comprehend that point.

The postinstitutional-retirement years can be an important professional period when you take on special assignments, serve as a consultant, coach current leaders, and challenge younger colleagues to new ways of thinking. After I retired from university teaching, I wanted to continue to be of service, but I also wanted better control over my schedule, so I could do more fun things. It was a relief to me to become "Angela" again after years of having been "The Dean," because the former was more outspoken than the latter could be. No one really wants an opinionated dean; they want someone who will facilitate others and the institution.

Without a title and an institutional position, I was free to reclaim my edge and be more provocative (and arguably more interesting).

Free to be forthright, the seasoned nurse can force important head-on discussions. The former nurse manager can be outspoken at a professional meeting about some aspect of patient safety in a way that might have earlier embarrassed an employer, and the resulting candor may prod others to take the matter more seriously. The former faculty member may be able to admit more readily to what academia isn't handling well and open up an important area for honest discussion and improvement.

Mentoring continues to be important at this career stage, because the person entering this period needs to be encouraged to rethink the so-called retirement years in less stereotyped fashion. This career stage is not a matter of working or not working but of imagining ways in which you can make a contribution, in keeping with your education, experience, and energy. For some, this stage may mean close to full-time work doing consultation and special projects. For some, this stage will involve meaningful part-time work, for example, the experienced critical-care nurse who now spends two days a week staffing the e-ICU, where she can make full use of her expertise and do it sitting down and off her aching feet. For others, this stage will involve committee work that enables them to continue to socialize with interesting people while addressing a significant problem.

Too often, nurses approach this stage worn out by all the responsibilities that they have borne over the years and full of fantasies about the glories of never having to set an alarm clock again. However, the large number of nurses who keep up their licensure well into old age tells another story. Large numbers of nurses want to keep up their professional identity in some fashion, even if they would rather not work as many hours as they once did.

In summary, leadership for me means orchestrating a career, not just doing a job well. It means moving over time from promise to momentum to harvest (Shirey, 2009). Once you have developed some modicum of personal proficiency, you branch out and become more engaged in moving your home institution forward, in advancing the profession, and, most of all, in changing health care for the better. The careerist sees getting older not as moving into decline but as having the advantage of reaping the fruits of one's labors. When you were young, you were limited by what you personally knew or could do; now your sphere of influence is broad because it is built on a mighty collegial network that you can harness as needed for the greater good.

Key Take-Away Points

- A career is a long-term commitment through which self-realization and service to others are both achieved.
- The advantage of a career framework with multiple stages is that one doesn't start out expecting to be fully developed at the beginning.
- Mentoring is needed throughout a career, not just at the start.
- Mentoring over the course of a career takes many forms—guiding, advising, protecting, sponsoring, challenging, coaching, recommending, facilitating, and so forth.
- There are five career stages whereby the individual moves from (1) becoming prepared, to (2) demonstrating the ability to work independently and interdependently in achieving professional goals, then (3) developing others and the home institution, and (4) advancing the profession and health care, eventually (5) daring to be a truth teller.
- Exerting leadership presupposes complete career development, that is, going through all five career stages.

REFERENCES

Benner, P. (1984). *From novice to expert: Excellence and power in clinical nursing practice* (pp. 13–34). Menlo Park, CA: Addison-Wesley.

Bureau of Health Professions. (2004). *A comparison of changes in the professional practice of nurse practitioners, physician assistants, and certified nurse midwives: 1992 and 2000.* Retrieved June 7, 2008, from http://bhpr.hrsa.gov/healthworkforce/reports/scope/scope1-2.htm

Bureau of Health Professions. (2010). *The registered nurse population. Initial findings from the 2008 National Sample Survey of Registered Nurses.* Retrieved March 20, 2010, from http://bhpr.hrsa.gov/healthworkforce/rnsurvey/initialfindings2008.pdf

Care, N. S. (1984). Career choice. *Ethics, 94,* 283–302.

Chandler, D. E., & Kram, K. E. (2007). Mentoring and developmental networks in the new career context. In H. Gunz & M. Peiperl (Eds.), *Handbook of career studies* (pp. 241–267). Thousand Oaks, CA: Sage Publications.

Coffield, F. (Ed.). (2000). *The necessity of informal learning.* Bristol, UK: The Policy Press.

Cohen, J. A., Palumbo, M. V., Rambur, B., & Mongeon, J. (2004). Middle school students' perceptions of an ideal career and a career in nursing. *Journal of Professional Nursing, 20,* 202–210.

Dalton, G. W., Thompson, P. H., & Price, R. L. (1977). The four stages of professional careers: A new look at performance by professionals. *Organizational Dynamics, 6,* 19–42.

Flexner, A. (1910). *Medical education in the United States and Canada: A report to the Carnegie Foundation for the Advancement of Teaching.* New York: Carnegie Foundation for the Advancement of Teaching.

Goleman, D., Boyatzis, R. E., & McKee, A. (2004). *Primal leadership: Learning to lead with emotional intelligence.* Cambridge, MA: Harvard Business School Press.

Henderson, V. (1966). *The nature of nursing: A definition and its implications for practice, research, and education.* New York: Macmillan.

Henderson, V. (1972). *Nursing studies index.* Philadelphia, PA: Lippincott Williams & Wilkins.

Jinks, A. M., & Bradley, E. (2004). Angels, handmaiden, battleaxe or whore? A study which examines changes in newly recruited student nurses' attitudes to gender and nursing stereotypes. *Nurse Education Today, 24,* 121–127.

Jowett, M. A. (Trans.). (1937). *The dialogues of Plato* (Vol. 1). New York: Random House.

Kalisch, P. A., & Kalisch, B. J. (1987). *The changing image of the nurse.* Menlo Park, CA: Addison-Wesley.

Kowalski, K., & Casper, C. (2007). The coaching process: An effective tool for professional development. *Nursing Administration Quarterly, 31,* 171–179.

Mayer, J. D., & Salovey, P. (1995). Emotional intelligence and the constitution and regulation of feelings. *Applied and Preventive Psychology, 4,* 197–208.

McBride, A. B. (2007). Beyond gendered health professions. In M. Hager (Ed.), *Women and medicine* (pp. 109–145). New York: Josiah Macy, Jr. Foundation.

McBride, A. B., & Lovejoy, K. B. (1995). Requesting and writing effective letters of recommendation: Some guidelines for candidates and sponsors. *Journal of Nursing Education, 34*(2), 95–96.

Pellegrino, E. D. (2002). Professionalism, profession and the virtues of the good physician. *The Mount Sinai Journal of Medicine, 69,* 378–384.

Pellico, L. H., Brewer, C. S., & Kovner, C. T. (2009). What newly licensed registered nurses have to say about their first experience. *Nursing Outlook, 57,* 194–203.

Robert Wood Johnson Foundation. (2010). *Healthy Policy Fellows.* Retrieved August 31, 2010, from http://healthypolicyfellows.org/aboutus.php

Salovey, P., & Mayer, J. M. (1990). Emotional intelligence. *Imagination, Cognition, and Personality, 9,* 189–191, 193, 195, 198–200.

Schorr, T. M. (1981a). Editorial: Getting our act together. *American Journal of Nursing, 81,* 719.

Schorr, T. M. (1981b). Editorial: Yes, Virginia, nursing is a profession. *American Journal of Nursing, 81,* 959.

Shirey, M. R. (2009). Building an extraordinary career in nursing: Promise, momentum and harvest. *The Journal of Continuing Education in Nursing, 40,* 394–400.

Sternberg, R. J. & Horvath, J. A. (Eds.) (1999). *Tacit knowledge in professional practice: Researcher and practitioner perspectives.* Mahwah, NJ: Lawrence Erlbaum.

Part II

Leadership as Achieving Organizational Goals

Chapter 5

Naming What We Do

This chapter switches gears, away from pondering what leadership means from the viewpoint of personal qualities to the perspective of what you need to do to achieve the values and goals of your workplace. The previous chapters of this book focused on self-understanding as a prerequisite to leadership—necessary but not sufficient—and now the focus is on leadership as the ability to effect desired change in an organization. No matter how charismatic a person is, real effectiveness isn't determined simply by personality but by whether you can work with others to achieve the organization's mission and values. Do you know how to put processes in place that encourage commitment, role clarity, high morale, job satisfaction, good citizenship, and innovation? Do you know how to achieve a range of organizational outcomes, be they safety, quality care, stakeholder satisfaction, low staff turnover, growth in market share, or new services?

There has long been the assumption that the person who "stands out" as special or is approved of by supervisors and peers alike is likely to be able to build teams that produce results over time, but the threads of connection between personal success and group achievement have been implied more than proven (Kaiser, Hogan, & Craig, 2008). Career success defined in terms of reputation, salary, and status is not the same thing as achieving organizational effectiveness. Some even cynically think that getting ahead personally may depend more on looking good and not rocking the boat than on leading effectively (Sayles, 1993), though there is growing appreciation for leadership that maximizes organizational performance, particularly in the aftermath of the recent financial debacle when arrogant CEOs lost sight of the good of the whole.

The author of the bestseller *Good to Great* has published a follow-up monograph in which he discusses the particular situation of not-for-profit organizations like hospitals and universities that cannot be run merely as businesses because they are by definition always concerned with more than the bottom line, going beyond what is currently known (Collins, 2005). Such organizations, where the overwhelming majority of nurses work, need personnel capable of five different levels of leadership: (1) highly competent individuals who are knowledgeable, skilled, and organized in completing their assignments, (2) contributing team members who work well with others and help achieve group objectives, (3) capable managers who know how to organize people and other resources to achieve existing goals, (4) effective persons capable of inspiring commitment to and pursuit of a vision that encourages higher performance, and (5) executives who transform their organizations by building enduring excellence and creatively meeting the challenges of their day.

As a nurse, I can ponder that leadership hierarchy and feel good about the extent to which my profession is peopled by individuals capable of delivering at those performance levels. The first four levels of performance are visible to each one of us on a daily basis; they describe what you expect of the staff nurse, faculty member, unit manager, and CNO. I regularly encounter nurses who know how to use their caregiving skills to help patients and their families get through a difficult situation with dignity, who work with colleagues on a curriculum committee to update courses in light of new accreditation standards, who mount new efforts to eliminate "never" events such as third- and fourth-degree pressure ulcers, and who urge colleagues to tackle new challenges such as achieving Magnet hospital status.

At the highest level of performance, I can name many names, some famous and some unknown beyond their agency's walls. Joyce Clifford revamped nursing services at Boston's Beth Israel Hospital, challenging all nurses to achieve the highest levels of professional practice (Clifford & Horvath, 1990). In the process, she created an environment that was so attractive to nurses that there was a waiting list of those eager to join the organization even in the midst of nursing shortages elsewhere. When she became dean, Claire Fagin transformed the University of Pennsylvania School of Nursing into a research-intensive environment, then went on to become the first woman (interim) president of that Ivy League university. As Commissioner of the Social Security Administration in President Clinton's first term, Shirley Chater overhauled that agency, making it more customer minded (she's responsible for the periodic updates all American workers now receive describing benefits to date). She forged 65,000 employees and a budget that exceeded $480 billion into an organization that received the highest ranking of success for customer service when compared with ten companies, including Nordstrom, AT&T, JC Penney, and so forth. Rebecca Rimel joined the Pew Charitable Trusts in 1983 as health program manager and is now President and CEO of that foundation dedicated to solving today's most challenging problems.

I can also name nurses whose leadership contribution is the development of new organizational structures. For example, Greg Mortenson, who coauthored the bestseller *Three Cups of Tea: One Man's Mission to Promote Peace . . . One School at a Time* (Mortenson & Relin, 2006) and *Stones into Schools: Promoting Peace with Books, Not Bombs, in Afghanistan and Pakistan* (Mortenson & Bryan, 2009). He co founded and serves as Executive Director of the Central Asia Institute and founded Pennies for Peace; the former is a nonprofit organization to promote and support community-based education, particularly for girls in rural Afghanistan and Pakistan, and the latter engages American children in the education of these children in other countries.

I can name many names, but I am not so sure the general public equates nursing with such leadership. There is a tendency to assume that leadership at remarkable levels means that the person no longer is a "real" nurse. Physicians who leave direct patient care and become university officers, hospital CEOs, heads of government agencies, and foundation presidents are more likely to be seen as extending their MD expertise into non-traditional areas in need of their skills, but nurses who do so are more likely to be asked, "Why did you leave nursing?" This is the case because the image of the nurse cross-culturally has historically been of someone active and good but relatively powerless (Austin, Champion, & Tzeng, 1985; Champion, Austin, & Tzeng, 1987).

Beyond Gendered Views of Nursing

Stereotyped views of nursing, as the opposite of what we think of as leadership, abound even in the 21st century. The Healthcare Group of JWT (J. Walter Thompson) Specialized Communications completed research for a campaign later undertaken by Sigma Theta Tau International, the honor society of nursing, to recruit the next generation of nurses; 1,800 students in 10 U.S. cities who were entering grades 2 through 10 were interviewed. The memo summarizing findings noted that most students received their impression of nursing from the television program *ER*, and that they perceived no compelling reason to become a nurse. The students were clear about what was positive about medicine as a career option, but described nursing as "more like shop," "doing the same job for 40 years," and "a girl's job." Most boys did not even think nursing was an option for them (Sherman, 2000).

Because hospital nurses have 24-hour responsibility for patients, they work collectively as a team. This cooperative approach tends to make what each person individually contributes less discernible. Nurses have been socialized "into the old religious notion that they are part of a mass, and should not, therefore, highlight their individual contributions to either the patient or the health care team" (Gordon, 2005, p. 215); but this approach contributes to the invisibility of the work, making it seem more like good housekeeping, only noticed in its absence. Valuing the integrative nature of nursing is further complicated by the premium long placed on discrete billable services rendered. In hospital budgets, nursing is typically treated as a huge unavoidable expense rather than as a contribution to the bottom line, but that is changing as the connection between quality and nursing is increasingly made (more about that in the last third of this book).

The multitasking that is nursing at its best is much more complicated than adding up a series of discrete tasks would suggest. The nurse may be performing a relatively simple task, such as a dressing change, and simultaneously conducting a mental status examination, checking for drug side effects, and providing tips about wound care after discharge. The patient may describe a nurse who stops in to ask questions as personable, but not understand that the exchange has more to do with surveillance and assessment, rather than pleasant personality (Gordon, 1997). Because nurses persist in being regarded as implementers rather than decision makers, it is no wonder that they are assigned (and assign themselves) day-to-day responsibility for patient safety, but may be excluded from leadership meetings planning change. However, if their insights don't inform the change process, new strategies to improve patient care are not likely to have the desired effects.

The central theme of de Beauvoir's masterpiece, *The Second Sex* (1952), is that women have historically been defined as "other" in relation to men, and that conceptualization helps explain the problem that nurses face too. Historically, "he" is sovereign and "she" is liege, just as the physician is described as captain of the ship and nurses as crew. As the focus of attention, he plays his part "through exploits or projects that serve as a mode of transcendence" (p. xxviii) while she is doomed to "immanence," bearing responsibility for the maintenance work of holding together family and home. Though enormous cultural change has taken place since de Beauvoir first wrote of these distinctions (e.g., she is often a physician and he is increasingly a nurse), her notion that the healthy adult is synonymous with being male, with the female relegated to "other" status, can still be found in some clinical judgments of professionals and the attitudes of medical students (Phillips & Ferguson, 1999).

Considerable effort has been devoted to addressing this stereotype, but not as much attention has been paid to the extent to which the "doing vs. helping" distinctions that hold between men and women also hold between medicine and the other health professions, particularly nursing. What nurses actually do attracts relatively little attention and admiration once it is described as helping physicians, and the work of the latter becomes even more exalted if all "other" health care workers are organized to help them. To the extent that the nurse is largely thought of as a helpmeet, physicians and nurses value different things in their interactions with each other, and those differences can get in the way of effective collaboration.

MDs tend to see a good nurse as one who helps them. RNs, by contrast, want to be appreciated principally for what they contribute to patient care, not to the physician's well-being and effectiveness (Back & Arnold, 2005; Prescott & Bowen, 1985). Many a time, I have listened to physicians praise "*my* nurse" for "all she did to help *me* avoid mistakes" and wondered if the nurse in question really saw the praise as a compliment. Who is the nurse nursing—the physician or the patient?

The reality is that nurses and physicians do not know much about each other since they are socialized in separate silos. In an attempt to change that, medical students and senior-level baccalaureate nursing students at Indiana University participated in a clinical simulation exercise. In the debriefing, both groups were surprised about what each other knew. The medical students had previously thought of nurses as largely helpful in finding something; the nursing students had been taught that if they had a question they should go to their instructors who would, if need be, report a problem to the nurse in charge, who would then speak to the medical student/physician. When they discussed the shared case, they were surprised to find that each field brought important information to the discussion (Reese, Jeffries, & Engum, 2010). And that appreciation is just what you need for meaningful teamwork in life after graduation.

Why do the health professions remain so gendered, with physicians seen as doers and nurses relegated to the status of helpers? No doubt the very word *nurse* conjures up images of female nurturance that centuries of men in nursing, including the founding of a number of religious communities responsible for looking after the sick and Walt Whitman's nursing during the Civil War, have not expunged from our collective consciousness. Obviously, there is no easy answer to the persistence of these doing vs. helping distinctions, but some insights are available if we analyze the first two waves of the Women's Movement.

The suffragettes used natural-law language—women are inherently more virtuous than men—to put forward arguments for why women should get the vote. During this period, nursing, teaching (K-12), and social work were encouraged as career options that dovetailed nicely with what were considered to be the real goals for women, that is, getting married and raising children. Described as extensions of women's roles within the family, such work was valued. The down side, of course, was that the prevailing ideological stance prevented people from noticing that Florence Nightingale did not just apply cold compresses to fevered brows but was an accomplished author and effective administrator (Neuhauser, 2003).

With the vote in hand and ample experience in every work sector during World War II, it is not surprising that women later began to focus their energies on equal opportunity and full entry into the workforce and public life. Being seen as virtuous—selfless, obedient, kind, and devoted—seemed a poor substitute for being regarded as competent in a time of rapid technological and scientific development. This second wave of the Women's Movement focused on girls and women getting access to advantages and opportunities previously only available to boys and men, and those in the vanguard tended to keep their distance from perceived "female ghettos like nursing" (Valentine, 1996, p. 105). The growing emphasis on career opportunities had the consequence of making motherhood seem incompatible with feminist values and the traditionally female professions seem old-fashioned (McBride, 1973, 1977).

The daughters and sons of these feminists have rejected the notion that parenthood is incompatible with working outside the home, though society still has not fully confronted the infrastructure supports that need to be in place for this to happen (Friedan, 1998). What has also not happened is a revaluing of the traditionally female professions based on what they offer in the 21st century to patients and careerists alike. To move in that direction, however, requires that additional thought be given to the persistence and insidious nature of stereotype.

Even though most people have become sensitive about typecasting others, still aren't all that concerned about discriminating based on gender (Czopp & Monteith, 2003). Once a profession has been sex-typed, perceptions of that field are difficult to change (Crompton, 1987). Glick and Fiske (2001) have suggested that stereotypes are particularly likely to be accepted if negative depictions are also accompanied by positive representations, thus possibly explaining why perceptions of nurses as comparatively low in power but full of integrity persist. ("Nurses top list," 2006; Robert Wood Johnson Foundation [RWJF], 2010).

How nurses fare is further affected by organizational climate (Johnson & McIntyre, 1998). Acker (1990) has criticized the notion that organizations are gender neutral; indeed there is a line of studies that analyzes the gendered nature of jobs and their reward structure (Mumby & Ashcraft, 2006). Hospitals and universities, where the majority of nurses work, are examples of gendered organizations because both still tend to be peopled at the highest levels—top positions and members of the board—by men, with women expected to maintain the day-to-day workings of the organization—providing meals, cleaning the buildings, running the various laboratories, keeping track of records, staffing offices, and managing a range of services (Hochschild, 1983).

Both institutions are known for putting women into situations in which they may have the responsibility of coverage without corresponding authority to change what is provided. Complicated responsibilities assumed by nurses do not necessarily raise their status because such activities may still be regarded as proceeding from physician authority, even though nurses are already legally accountable for both their independent roles (e.g., surveillance and environmental safety) and their interdependent roles (e.g., implementation of medical treatment).

It may seem a stretch to begin this chapter by arguing in favor of defining leadership as organizational effectiveness and then tackling how undervalued nursing is and the persistence of stereotype, but I think our field can only achieve all levels of leadership if each one of us doesn't succumb to underestimating what we contribute to organizations even if others still do. I know I didn't start out thinking of what I could add institutionally. Early on, I wanted skills to earn a living and work that was gratifying. I liked being able to make patients and their families feel better about their situations.

I remember undergraduate classes on "Is nursing a profession?" but I heard those discussions as preparing me to have pre-emptive answers in case anyone might think that nursing is only task-oriented rather than learned. I didn't think much then about leadership; I thought about providing a service that reflected my values. Truth be told, I was of two minds in my outlook—I absorbed the notion that nurses should be change agents but I also was nervous about being in charge. Like many women of my generation, I was reluctant to take charge unless I was convinced that I could handle every contingency, but that view, of course, means that you are likely to shy away from ultimate accountability until you believe that you are mistake-proof. That approach keeps you focused on whether you are up to the task at hand rather than on how you can use your talents to make a difference.

It is not surprising that I felt this way because this was a period when girls/women felt that they had to be twice as good to be any good. If you didn't handle every challenge perfectly, then you were open to the criticism that women weren't meant to do that kind of thing. You would be complimented when you were effective, "You're smart enough to be a doctor," and you took pleasure in being considered exceptional even as you heard the insult behind the compliment that kept you feeling on guard. This was also a period when you were prepared academically to function in a staff role, and there wasn't much context provided about how that role would, with experience, lead to other responsibilities even if you stayed working in the same setting, or about how nursing fit into the overall health care system.

When I think about it now, I'm not sure I knew what possibilities existed over the course of a full career or how nurses uniquely contributed to organizations. I knew what different kinds of patients needed. I knew about health promotion and disease prevention. I knew what it meant to act professionally, and to speak up proudly about what it meant to be a nurse. I knew that RN licensure meant that I had mastered the basics to practice safely. I was a sponge absorbing many ought-tos, but I did not have the bearing of a leader.

If I thought something could be done better, I was more likely to be critical of how others organized matters than to consider that this was an opportunity for me to make things better. That ostrich-in-the-sand approach to larger issues was reinforced by the custom at the time of dividing up the profession into clinical leadership and administrative leadership, technological nursing and professional nursing, and basic RN practice and advanced practice. That carving up of responsibilities meant that organizational effectiveness was the sole province of administrators, not staff nurses, and advanced practice was equated with functioning autonomously rather than the performance of the team. The emphasis was on getting various increments of education to allow you to do different things, rather than on exerting leadership no matter where you are planted.

I mentioned this before, but I cannot overstate the difference that getting a master's degree at Yale made to my career. Because this Ivy League university had a long tradition of preparing leaders, the emphasis in the School of Nursing was on making a difference. Once admitted, the focus wasn't on constantly proving that you were worthy to be in the program, but on deciding what you were going to do with your configuration of talents. These messages had the effect of making me less self-conscious about whether I was "any good," and made me confront what I wanted to do to make a difference. Instead of jumping through hoops to prove worthiness, I was encouraged to move toward something. Yale had confidence in my abilities, so I had more confidence in my ideas, making me more daring and willing to try new approaches.

I am not alone in being so affected. In the summer of 2008, I canvassed a few Yale graduates who had been elected to fellowship in the American Academy of Nursing. I was curious to know how their experience at Yale shaped their subsequent leadership, since leadership was the theme of the keynote I was about to deliver at the next reunion. Frankly, I was surprised by the similarity of the points made by alumnae of multiple generations. They noted that the school of nursing had strengthened their conviction that they could change the system, their commitment to social justice and interdisciplinary collaboration, their professional passion, and their inventiveness. Essentials, I would argue, for leadership to be exerted (McBride, 2009).

Operating at an Organizational Level

Confronting whether you can make system-level differences is inextricably tied to organizational effectiveness. For years, I taught a graduate course in which I asked students, "Do you know what your supervisor/ your institution needs from you?" I was always surprised at how taken aback the students were by that question. Many said that they had never thought about that question. Some thought the question implied that you should be a sycophant and kowtow to your employer, giving him what he wanted rather than what was best. The reason I posed the question had nothing to do with flattering the boss. Over time, I had formed the opinion that you would not be taken seriously simply by telling others how important nursing is to the organization, and, instead, needed to figure out what the corporate goals were, thereafter describing all you did as a nurse as achieving the institutional mission. I had become convinced of the importance of this strategy, in part, because the students to whom I posed the question frequently told me that they acted differently once they started making the connection between what the institution needed from them and what they did, and found themselves taken more seriously by others as a result.

CEOs of hospitals, presidents/chancellors of universities, and heads of government agencies aren't really interested in the disciplinary aspirations of any profession. If anything, they are worried that support of any one group will only lead all the other groups to make new demands. They do, however, all want quality outcomes, skills development, satisfied customers, interdisciplinary collaboration, prudent leveraging of resources, cooperative partnerships, and cutting-edge work affirmed by external official recognition. When you describe what you do as a nurse as meeting the goals of the institution, you also come off as less self-serving in your remarks. The more you frame what you are doing within a unit or a department in terms of the goals of the larger organization, the easier it is to get your team to work together to achieve outcomes, be they productivity, revenue, or satisfaction goals, because that conceptualization forces them to think outside themselves.

What I am advocating is not unlike the moral of a story told about two stonemasons in the Middle Ages who were each asked what they were doing. One said, "I'm cutting these blocks." The other replied, "I'm building a cathedral." This anecdote was supposed to illustrate the difference between the person who focuses only on the here-and-now and one who sees the big picture. I would argue that there is a comparable difference between nurses who describe their work as taking care of a certain number of patients and those who describe their work as achieving the mission and values of the clinical facility.

In recent decades, nursing has been more oriented to process than to outcomes, largely because the nursing process—consisting of assessment, diagnosis, planning, implementation, and evaluation—has been described as the common thread uniting all nurses (American Nurses Association, 2009). Relationship-centered care emphasized nursing process, teaching process, and family process with some unintended consequences. Though laudable in its intentions, stressing these concepts mistakenly conveyed, I think, the impression that nursing was always in flux, never quite getting anywhere. It is not that nurses weren't concerned with outcomes; they are always part of planning and evaluation, but outcomes weren't center stage the way they are if your focus is on how nurses work to achieve institutional goals. If you think in terms of process, your focus is on whether you are doing the right thing; if you think in terms of outcomes, your focus is on whether what you are doing is effective in achieving desired results.

The emphasis on nursing process was also meant to underscore the autonomous abilities of the nurse. As professional problem-solvers, nurses, it was argued, had a self-governing expertise not unlike the other health care professionals who were independent agents seemingly less constrained by institutional structures. This desire for professional fulfillment made independent practice seem attractive and subtly focused attention away from how you might effect organizational change. The best way to deal with organizations that didn't support your professional development sometimes seemed to be just getting out of the organization and putting up your own shingle.

What was insufficiently stressed in process-oriented approaches is that all patient-provider or student–teacher relationships not only have consequences for the affected individuals, but in the aggregate they must also meet the larger institutional mission. You can take good care of someone struggling with bipolar illness, but you have to be simultaneously concerned about how that person's experience interfaces with reimbursement and readmission guidelines. As a faculty member, you are concerned with the learning of your clinical group, but also have to be concerned about how students' overall performance affects the school's accreditation status.

Being able to name what we do in terms of clear-cut outcomes is important if others are to appreciate the contributions of our profession and if we are to deliver results proportional to the pride behind our rhetoric. There are several very significant attempts within the field that seek to strengthen movement in this direction. One approach is development of professional practice models that spell out the organizational authority and responsibility of nurses in terms of scope of practice and professional standards, thereby empowering the decision making of nurses who operate under these statutory and professional expectations (O'Rourke, 2003). Complementing those models is usually some sustained development of structures that encourage the full participation of nurses in the work of the organization (Caramanica, 2004). Shared governance can take many forms, but at its best it means that nurses are represented on all appropriate teams and councils that are moving the work of the organization forward. The more nurses are visible in such interdisciplinary groups, the more others "see" what they do, and the more nurses understand how what they do fits into the big picture.

The Magnet Hospital Recognition Program has been developed by the American Nurses Credentialing Center (2009) to recognize organizations that support nursing excellence. The intention of this program was to showcase the interrelationship between best professional practice and the achievement of organizational goals. Nurses in hospitals that have achieved that designation describe greater control over their practice and increased recognition, status, and prestige as a result (Kramer & Schmalenberg, 2003). What is more, those organizations have demonstrably better outcomes (Havens & Aiken, 1999; Scott, Sochalski, & Aiken, 1999).

It is also worth mentioning that administrators in such organizations will not be effective if they continue to cling to the old command-and-control view of leadership, because their task now isn't so much to make all the decisions, but to encourage all nurses to make a difference by hiring and developing managers who can encourage wise decision making in others. Although traditionally the emphasis was on hiring skilled nurses to do right by their patients, the emphasis now is on developing skilled nurses who are continuously innovative as they seek to achieve evolving standards of care.

Something similar has happened in schools of nursing as they have moved over time away from being largely concerned about workforce production to performing well on all university indicators of success including student performance, innovative teaching, community part-nerships, philanthropic support, externally funded research, faculty rec-ognition, and national rankings. Like the Magnet Hospital Recognition Program, the National League for Nursing has created ways to recog-nize excellence and innovation in nursing education (2009). Nursing is increasingly represented on a full range of university committees, and school of nursing administrators who operate as Mother Superior are not likely to be effective, because "Mother (or Daddy), may I?" styles of governance do not encourage the desired innovation.

Being able to name what we do doesn't seem at first glance to be a revolutionary tactic. Nurses have long known what they do, and, if any-thing, have been annoyed that others didn't understand what they did. Because most nurses were women, however, they were prone to inter-mix gender roles and nursing roles emphasizing the responsive nature of both. As both a woman and a nurse, you were less likely to start with a plan of action, but developed your approach in response to the needs of others. There is nothing inherently wrong with this strategy. Indeed, assessment should always precede action. But a predisposition to be responsive can get in the way of moving forward the overall values and goals of the enterprise, which is what leaders do.

There is another predisposition that interferes with our being able to identify what we do, and it is another consequence of so much emphasis within the profession on nursing process. Nurses as a group tend to name everything they do as nursing. If they take care of patients who improve, what they did is described as nursing. If they develop an intervention that is proven to be efficacious in a random controlled trial, that intervention is likely to be described as nursing and published in a nursing journal.

One understands how this tendency came to pass. If you want to be seen as professional by others, then it makes sense to brand all that you do as part of what it means to be a nurse, but there are unintended consequences here also. Health care professionals not in the field are less likely to see what you do as relevant to them. Quite simply, when all you did over time is bundled and labeled as "nursing," the underlying complicated principles and actions at play remain invisible. As other health care professionals have become more interested in palliative care and patient self-management, I have heard complaints from nurses who grumble that both have long been around; only historically they were called nursing and thus not appreciated. Alas, a review of those subjects may not locate nursing's body of work in the interdisciplinary literature if they were always described as falling under the umbrella term of "nursing."

The point of naming what you do, other than using the code word of "nursing," is for others to see what you do. Naming what you do to meet the values and mission of the institution places the work in a larger context; forcing inclusion of the profession in the decision making of the larger environment. And the more others see the range of what nurses do, the more you cannot represent the profession through one person only; for example, the CNO or dean, because the breadth of professional knowledge in nursing is broader and deeper than what any person can master.

When our academic health center joined with another major hospital to become a new hospital network, I was appointed to the new structure's Medical Education Committee. The committee consisted of at least 18 physicians, representing the range of medical specialties, but only one person each from allied health and nursing, the respective deans. When the physicians wanted to add yet one more physician to the committee so that another subspecialty could be represented, I balked. I told them that they needed to add another nurse more than they needed another physician because nursing is complicated, too big and complex to be represented by only one person. Interestingly enough, they heard my protestations as a statement of personal inadequacy, and proceeded to reassure me that I was doing a fine job of representing nursing. I told them that I knew I was doing a good job. My point was that all of nursing could no more be represented by one person than all of medicine could be represented by one person. They did add another nurse to the committee *and* another physician, but I'm not sure they ever understood my point.

When all of what our field does is described as nursing, then one person can be thought to represent that discipline, and usually people ask the person in charge to serve that function. The person in that boundary-spanning role usually enjoys performing that service because you get to know lots of important and interesting people. Knowing what is going on adds to one's sense of self-importance because information is a kind of power that you can use for good or ill. Being the source of information for all in your discipline can be a privileged position, not easily relinquished, but holding on to being the point person for all progress means something else: that all advancement will be limited by your time, interests, and abilities. Authorize others to represent nursing, and the public view of nursing will expand, enriched by the range of expertise on display. What is more, each nurse develops leadership potential, making successor preparation easier than it has been in the past.

The more nurses are represented on all councils and committees according to their experience and skills, the more the person in charge of nursing for the organization has to play a different role, not personally going from meeting to meeting, but insinuating the appropriate nursing expertise into each group and preparing those nurses to function effectively and move others in that direction. You get so much more in the long run, if there are many nurse leaders rather than one, but it can seem like a loss as you begin to move in this direction. That is why the subject matter in the first third of this book is important. If you are still very insecure, you might be reluctant to give up being center stage in every forum, not understanding that both the CNO and the entire discipline will truly look impressive when the richness of the field can no longer be personified by one face.

The "look" of nursing must be wide ranging. Diversity in nursing is important for many reasons, but most especially in order to have other professionals and the public alike understand how complex and varied our profession is. When nurses look and sound different—in terms of gender, race, age, education, specialty, expertise, functioning, experience— then the overall view of nursing is bound to be dynamic and far from stereotyped. Nursing doesn't contribute to the goals of the organization in one way, but in many ways, and we need to explain what we do to meet all of our organizations' goals, not just the ones with which we have been traditionally identified. Staff nurses give care and coordinate the care given by others; nurse managers are involved in more boundary-spanning activities getting nurse teams and other health professionals to move organizational and population-based initiatives; some nurse experts assume hospital- or network-wide responsibility for quality initiatives, regulatory compliance, informatics solutions, and the like; the CNO works with the executive leadership to set hospital or network-wide initiatives; the nurse on the board monitors organizational progress and participates in planning for an uncertain future.

Regardless of where you sit, leadership is exercised in service to the organization's mission and values. Using the language of organizational service is more likely to strengthen the perception of nursing as important than talking about the importance of nursing is likely to improve the position of our field. Explaining what you do each and every day in service to organizational initiatives means that you have countless opportunities to make those connections in the minds of others, and over time those associations will increasingly be made by others. And the more nurses see different kinds of nursing leadership, the more they will have a sense of the range of exciting possibilities before them.

Key Take-Away Points

- Leadership is increasingly defined as the ability to work successfully with others to achieve the organization's values and mission.
- There is a leadership hierarchy in nursing that ranges from individual performance and productive teamwork to inspiring higher performance and creating enduring excellence.
- Stereotyped views of nursing stress virtue and busyness but not strength and innovation, thus reinforcing the notion that nurses are helpers, not leaders.
- The longstanding emphasis on nursing process has had the unintended consequence of making processes seem more important than outcomes when the converse is the case.
- A new wave of the Women's Movement is needed, one that revalues for men and women what the traditionally female professions actually have to offer in the 21st century to patients and careerists alike.
- The point of naming what you do is for others to see what you do and how you contribute to the organization as a whole.
- The more others see the contributions of nurses to the organization, the more nurses will be included in key decision-making forums.
- The more all nurses are expected to be leaders, the more nurse leaders cannot operate from a command-and-control framework but must lead by developing the leadership of others.

REFERENCES

Acker, J. (1990). Hierarchies, jobs, bodies: A theory of gendered organizations. *Gender and Society, 4,* 139–158.

American Nurses Association. (2009). *The nursing process: A common thread amongst all nurses.* Retrieved May 22, 2009, from http://www.nursingworld .org/EspeciallyForYou/StudentNurses/Thenursingprocess.aspx

American Nurses Credentialing Center. (2009). *Magnet program overview.* Retrieved May 23, 2009, from http://www.nursecredentialing.org/Magnet/ProgramOverview.aspx

Austin, J. K., Champion, V. L., & Tzeng, O. C. S. (1985). Cross-cultural comparison on nursing image. *International Journal of Nursing Studies, 22,* 231–239.

Back, A. L., & Arnold, R. M. (2005). Dealing with conflict in caring for the seriously ill. *Journal of the American Medical Association, 293,* 1374–1381.

Caramanica, L. (2004). Shared governance: Hartford Hospital's experience. *Online Journal of Issues in Nursing, 9*(1), Manuscript 2. Retrieved May 23, 2009, from http://www.nursingworld.org/MainMenuCategories/ANAMarketplace/ANAPeriodicals/OJIN/TableofContents/Volume92004/No1Jan04/HartfordHospitalsExperience.aspx

Champion, V. L., Austin, J. K., & Tzeng, O. C. S. (1987). Cross-cultural comparison of images of nurses and physicians. *International Nursing Review, 34,* 43–48.

Clifford, J. C., & Horvath, K. (Eds.). (1990). *Advancing professional nursing practice: Innovations at Boston's Beth Israel Hospital.* New York: Springer Publishing.

Collins, J. (2005). *Good to great and the social sectors.* Boulder, CO: Author.

Crompton, R. (1987). Gender, status and professionalism. *Sociology, 21,* 413–428.

Czopp, A. M., & Monteith, M. J. (2003). Confronting prejudice (literally): Reaction to confrontations of racial and gender bias. *Personality and Social Psychology Bulletin, 29,* 532–544.

de Beauvoir, S. (1952). *The second sex* (H. M. Parshley, Trans.). New York: Bantam Books.

Friedan, B. (1998). *The second stage.* Cambridge, MA: Harvard University Press.

Glick, P., & Fiske, S. (2001). An ambivalent alliance: Hostile and benevolent sexism as complementary justifications for gender inequality. *American Psychologist, 56,* 109–118.

Gordon, S. (1997). *Life support. Three nurses on the front lines.* Boston: Little, Brown.

Gordon, S. (2005). *Nursing against the odds: How health care cost cutting, media stereotypes, and medical hubris undermine nurses and patient care.* Ithaca, NY: ILR Press/Cornell University Press.

Havens, D. S., & Aiken, L. H. (1999). Shaping systems to promote desired outcomes: The magnet hospital model. *Journal of Nursing Administration, 29*(2), 14–20.

Hochschild, A. (1983). *The managed heart: Commercialization of human feeling.* Berkeley, CA: University of California Press.

Johnson, J. J., & McIntyre, C. L. (1998). Organizational culture and climate correlates of job satisfaction. *Psychological Reports, 82,* 843–850.

Kaiser, R. B., Hogan, R., & Craig, S. B. (2008). Leadership and the fate of organizations. *American Psychologist, 63,* 96–110.

Kramer, M., & Schmalenberg, C. E. (2003). Magnet hospital nurses describe control over nursing practice. *Western Journal of Nursing Research, 25,* 434–452.

McBride, A. B. (1973). *The growth and development of mothers*. New York: Harper & Row.

McBride, A. B. (1977). *Living with contradictions. A married feminist*. New York: Harper Colophon Books.

McBride, A. B. (2009). Truth of the matter. What are you going to do with your considerable gifts? *Yale Nursing Matters, 9*(2), 21.

Mortenson, G., & Bryan, M. (2009). *Stones into schools: Promoting peace with books, not bombs, in Afghanistan and Pakistan*. New York: Viking Books.

Mortenson, G. & Relin, D. O. (2006). *Three cups of tea. One man's mission to promote peace . . . one school at a time*. New York: Viking Books.

Mumby, D. K., & Ashcraft, K. L. (2006). Organizational communication studies and gendered organization: A response to Martin and Collinson. *Gender, Work, and Organization, 13*, 68–90.

National League for Nursing. (2009). *Excellence initiatives*. Retrieved May 25, 2009, from http://www.nln.org/excellence/index.htm

Neuhauser, D. (2003). Florence Nightingale gets no respect: As a statistician, that is. *British Medical Journal, 12*, 317.

Nurses top list in honesty and ethics again in Gallup poll. (2006, February–April). *ISNA Bulletin, 32*, 1.

O'Rourke, M. W. (2003). Rebuilding a professional practice model: The return of role-based practice accountability. *Nursing Administration Quarterly, 27*(2), 95–105.

Phillips, S. P., & Ferguson, K. E. (1999). Do students' attitudes toward women change during medical school? *Canadian Medical Journal, 160*, 357–361.

Prescott, P. A., & Bowen, S. A. (1985). Physician-nurse relationships. *Annals of Internal Medicine, 103*, 127–133.

Reese, C. E., Jeffries, P. R., & Engum, S. A. (2010). Learning together: Using simulations to develop nursing and medical student collaboration. *Nursing Education Perspectives, 31*(1), 33–37.

Robert Wood Johnson Foundation. (2010, January 20). *Nursing leadership from bedside to boardroom: Opinion leaders' perceptions*. Retrieved April 8, 2010, from http://www.rwjf.org/humancapital/product.jsp?id=54491

Sayles, L. R. (1993). *The working leader: The triumph of high performance over conventional management principles*. New York: McGraw-Hill.

Scott, J. G., Sochalski, J., & Aiken, L. H. (1999). Review of magnet hospital research: Findings and implications for professional nursing practice. *Journal of Nursing Administration, 29*(1), 9–19.

Sherman, G. (2000, August 28). *Nurses for a healthier tomorrow coalition members*. Retrieved May 18, 2009, from http://nursingadvocacy.org/research/lit/jwt_memo1.html

Valentine, P. E. B. (1996). Nursing: A ghettoized profession relegated to women's sphere. *International Journal of Nursing Studies, 33*, 98–106.

Chapter 6

Telling Others What to Do/ What You Do

Naming what we do is important in exerting leadership, but so is clearly telling others what needs doing and why that is the case. I am not endorsing a command-and-control approach, but because my own approach leans toward being nonautocratic I have often failed to be explicit about matters, thus adding to the confusion. Not wanting to appear to order people around, I frequently erred on the side of being vague about next steps and then was disappointed that events did not unfold as I would have wished. I confused being authoritarian (demanding but not responsive) with being authoritative (clear expectations but responsive) in the same way that these approaches have been talked about in other discussions of what encourages competence (Baumrind, 1991). Looking back on my entire career, I would say that the subject of this chapter is one that I appreciate even more in hindsight. Much of what I discuss may appear rather simplistic or self-evident on first hearing, but the underlying message about the importance of clarity is central to organizational effectiveness.

I read in *The New Yorker* that "a common mistake of very smart people is to assume that other people's minds work in the same way that theirs do" (Lanchester, 2009, p. 86). Though the piece was about the foibles of high finance, I think the sentiment has broad application even if you're uncomfortable with describing yourself as "very smart." If you think something is obvious then you assume others do too. If you know what should be done, there's the inclination to believe that every intelligent person knows what to do too. Moreover, if they don't, as far as you are concerned it's prima facie evidence that they are not intelligent! If you don't need the obvious spelled out for you to proceed, there's the tendency to believe that others regard the same things as self-evident, and, like you, think that spelling out the patently obvious is vaguely demeaning. Some physicians, for example, deride protocols as "cookbook medicine," but these materials have been found to be useful aids in standardizing processes among different kinds of health professionals and wringing out unnecessary variation (Gittell, 1998).

Another reason some of us resist the notion of spelling out what seems obvious to us is that it smacks of the mechanical more than the professional. However, clarity should not be confused with being stilted. You can remind colleagues of where they've been and where they're going without repeatedly using the same words and sounding like a broken record. I once had to deal with a chancellor on a regional campus who was a street fighter at heart. He didn't like to negotiate and always wanted to trounce his debating partner. His tactics unnerved me, which he of course thoroughly enjoyed. I used to prepare for my visits on that campus with some centering exercises, reminding myself that I was capable of repeating my position over and over again using different words. By staying on message, I was able to keep him on message too and not get diverted from what I wanted to achieve. His was an extreme case, but thanks to him I did hone my ability to keep on message and realized the value of saying the same thing in different ways to reinforce my central point.

In the spirit of servant leadership, there are ways of checking out understandings as if they are being raised for the greater good (which they are): "Let's pause before we proceed, to see if everyone is on the same page" . . . "Before we end this meeting, let's take five minutes to summarize next steps so we each know what our assignments for the next month are" . . . "We talked a great deal about what we want to accomplish, so let's make sure we're in agreement about what needs doing first, second, and third." Another way of doing the same thing is to send colleagues an e-mail right after a meeting, in which you thank them for spending time with you and summarize understandings. Not only are these summarizing actions useful if minutes are being taken but also you've precluded future misunderstandings. In the case of the confirmatory e-mail or letter, you now have a record that can be referred back to in case of later forgetfulness on either side.

I said at the beginning that I had a hard time telling others what to do and that's because I've always been sensitive about being bossy, an allegation long hurled at women taking charge and one that continues to shape female behavior to this day (Bennett, Ellison, & Ball, 2010). The possibility that others would see me as bossy had a chilling effect on my willingness to offer to do some things. Self-conscious about being bossy, I developed an ambivalent attitude toward being the boss. However, that kind of defensive posture keeps you focused on yourself more than on facilitating others. If you just focus on being helpful to others, making

sure that they are clear about how to proceed, you come off as supportive rather than domineering, and that's important to keep in mind.

Sense Making—A Responsibility of Leaders

It took me a while to understand that clarity about expectations, next
steps, processes, and directions are integral to leadership no matter
the kind of position held. Before I fully understood the responsibility
of the leader to be clear, I was defensively prone to thinking that "they
should just know," so I was more likely to get annoyed when others
didn't proceed as expected than to examine my assumptions. When
I did examine my behavior, I realized that I was guilty of expecting
colleagues to be mind readers, and that is both a silly and an unproductive expectation.

De Pree (1989) believed that defining reality is the first responsibility of leaders, a viewpoint later underscored in Sigma Theta Tau
International's resource paper on leadership (2005). Most people in an
organization are totally comfortable interacting with only those whom
they see every day. In every organization, people on the fourth floor are
suspicious of people on the first floor; even those who work on the same
floor may be wary of those in the southeast wing if they reside in the
northwest corridor. Individuals may know what their responsibilities
are, but they do not know much about what others do. Leaders by definition have interests, duties, and a purview that span boundaries, thus
making them knowledgeable about how different tasks fit within the
organization. It is, therefore, their responsibility to explain how the different pieces fit together. Therefore, when I emphasize the importance
of telling others what to do, I'm really underscoring the value of taking
responsibility for such sense making.

I think people work more effectively if they understand how the
pieces fit together, but many in leadership positions fail to recognize both
how much they know and how much others don't know. I have heard
deans bemoan the datedness of their faculty's views, not remembering
that administrators generally attend more external meetings than their
colleagues; therefore, it is not surprising that they have a better sense of
trends. The faculty's preference for the traditional may have little to do
with whether they are venturesome and more to do with limited information. I have listened to unit managers complain that staff nurses are not
committed to moving toward paperless record keeping, forgetting that

the directors weren't enthusiastic about the electronic changes planned when they first heard of them much earlier. In this case, reluctance does not necessarily mean obstinacy; it may mean being personally worried about learning how to do things differently. Providing supports for new learning might make all the difference in attitude.

When you bypass the step of explaining why an action is necessary, that's when telling others what to do does appear high-handed to employees and they are likely to take on the fatalistic attitude of workers dealing with a toy-soldier boss. They think that you are going off on a tangent because they do not understand what is driving you and why needed next steps are important to the organization and their own careers. I think that a number of individuals in leadership positions still have a "Do it because I'm the boss" mentality—not unlike "I'm your mother, that's why"—that has more to do with wanting one's own authority to be acknowledged than it does with what's needed in the situation. Explaining why something is important is not a sign of weakness; it is being savvy about the situation.

Sense making, as a leadership activity, means regularly taking responsibility for providing a context for needed actions. It means beginning a discussion of the need for an initiative by explaining why the hospital, agency, or university is moving in a certain direction. It means taking a moment before asking for any vote to remind all who will be making choices about options previously weighed and fact-finding that preceded this final decision making. I learned that there was a big difference in how groups supported change depending on whether I took the time to recall steps already taken to move in a particular direction. Providing a context for those in attendance made them less likely to think that administration was going off half cocked and, therefore, they were less likely to be negative. As the one in charge of moving an action forward, I was typically the one who understood best what had brought us to this point in time, so it made sense for me to take responsibility for clarifying the situation. And, of course, you can perform this function without being the one who does all the talking; instead you can be the one who lines up all who will do the talking and use the occasion to thank all concerned for their work to date.

In a similar vein, I found that it made a big difference if I provided a context when making new hires. Whenever I interviewed anyone for a position, I would begin the interview by summarizing where I thought the institution was and where it was going, so the applicant would be aware that all hiring was embedded in some sense of fit between person and place. In the process, I invited candidates to do the same, that is, think through whether this was a place that would enable them to blossom. Over time, this strategy bore results, because all new hires shared a common sense of where we were and where we were going, so they didn't have to be convinced to move in a new direction. Their collective orientation then reinforced a sense of communal direction, and there is something very powerful about a group of people who tell the same story about where an organization is headed. As a group, they attract the attention and interest of others similarly inclined, which further reinforces the central message.

Providing a context so the work ahead makes sense also means explaining what you do in your leadership position. I know people who equate being a charge nurse with paper shuffling or the computer equivalent; they do not appreciate the dozens of ways that person shapes quality care by creating an environment in which others can do their best. I have dealt with people who think that all faculty do is teach a few hours a week, because all they see is the time spent in the classroom; they never see the class preparation, time spent counseling, hours working on a grant application, and professional service. I know people who think that deans have an easy job because they see them most of the time in social situations, so they equate being a dean with dressing up and going to receptions. They do not understand what such administrators do behind the scenes and that receptions are prime occasions for letting stakeholders know what everyone in the school is doing; such friend making is part of fund-raising.

Once you are in a leadership position, you tend to think that colleagues who hold such simplistic views must be naïve because you know firsthand how complicated those positions really are. The truth of the matter is that all of us hold simplistic views about the complexities of any position if we are not directly involved in the day-to-day living out of those roles. I've come to believe that the issue is not that kind of thinking but whether leaders assume responsibility to help nurses at one level of operations really understand what those at other levels do. When all of us look at the positions others hold, we see only a small portion of what others actually do, so it is no wonder that we have a skewed notion of their complexities. I see working on these understandings as necessary in engaging colleagues to move forward, whatever tasks are at hand, but I also see such explanations as important to successor planning. If others fully understand what's involved in leadership roles, then those positions may seem more interesting and exciting.

When I stopped serving as Department Chair, I had a sabbatical leave to do some serious writing. A month after I returned from this leave, a faculty member said, "I now know what you did as chairperson; when you were in that position not too many bad things happened." Her comment gave me an opening to discuss how invisible averted problems are, but avoiding problems is as important as concretely achieving desired outcomes. It was a gratifying conversation, because it's always special when what you do and take pride in is appreciated, and this discussion did pique this person's interest in administration. Before, she had seen administration more as shuffling papers; now she began to see it more as an interesting game of strategy.

No matter what kind of leadership position you hold, there are three areas in which being clear about expectations, next steps, and direction is important to achieving organizational goals: (a) having job descriptions that accurately reflect current sensibilities, (b) using meetings to maximum advantage, and (c) touching base meaningfully with those who report to you. In all three areas, you have to be clear about how you want others to proceed and how you hope others see your role as interfacing with their own.

Evolving Job Descriptions

Mention job descriptions and eyes glaze over. Most of us think in terms of postings on job-openings sites—formal documents but not necessarily interesting ones. I used to think that such documents were deadly dull until I started reading some descriptions where there was a big gap between the formal requirements and what I thought the job included. One year into being a dean, I reread with a fresh eye the job description for that position and was struck by the fact that at least half of what I did wasn't even hinted at in the document. What was emphasized was the role of the dean in shaping academic programs. Little attention was paid to the dean's responsibilities either in helping the school achieve the university's mission with respect to research or in relating to practice. Although academic programs are the base business of any school of nursing, I believed that faculty shaped curriculum more than administrators. I thought my job consisted of two major parts: the inside part was helping faculty, staff, students, and the administrators who reported to me become as effective as possible in their roles and prepare for the future; the outside part was interfacing with the many stakeholders important to the development of the school and leveraging their support to meet the school's mission. (By the way, I think those two functions could, with some editing, describe what is required in any leadership position.)

Realizing how dated the job description was led me to rewrite it with my administrative council. I didn't want to be held accountable for what I didn't think I should be doing, and I wanted to be credited with addressing what I thought I should be doing. The review process was a useful one for all concerned because it provided an opportunity for us to reflect on what a dean at this point in time should achieve. When the school had a small faculty and few academic programs, the dean used to be more concerned with daily operations within the school of nursing's building. Now there were many faculty and academic programs (four different undergraduate options, many master's specialties, a PhD program, and postdoctoral research training) and a research-practice mission. As a result, today's dean needed to work with others to strengthen their capabilities, and that required more of a developmental than a command-and-control orientation. Where once deans did not leave their buildings that much, today's dean needed to be out and about building the school's image and reputation through strategic alliances within the profession, university, community, and state.

The more we talked about what a dean should do, the more we discussed what a department chair or assistant/associate dean should pursue. Did they need to manage all daily operations themselves or to set up processes, many of which could be handled by judicious use of clerical and professional staff? This give-and-take led all concerned to think more creatively about the mix between maintaining and changing and between managing the present and preparing for the future. In the process, I was able to shift the focus of those who reported to me, away from bringing the dean problems that she was then expected to solve, and on to each administrator's generating "solutions" that we could then discuss in terms of their feasibility and completeness. As these conversations progressed, expectations for every position were reviewed, and the school substantially increased use of professional staff because the faculty and nurse administrators needed to be free to do what they could do best, using professional staff for what they do best.

That move in our school to greater use of professional staff mirrors a major shift in the field. During the decades when nursing was most concerned with proving that it was truly professional, there was a tendency to have all the work for which nurses were responsible carried out by nurses. If RNs were responsible for the running of a clinical unit, then only RNs were to be hired to carry out that function, so the logic went. If it was a school of nursing, then all teaching, advising, marketing, and fund-raising was done by nurses. These days the profession has less to prove and is clearer about how it contributes to the health of the nation; consequently, nurses are free to think more creatively about what they need to do themselves and what they take responsibility for managing but others carry out. This shift means, I think, that nurses are more prepared to exert leadership, which of its very nature implies designing new processes and using people to advantage, rather than doing everything yourself.

Job descriptions, because they are meant to summarize key values and responsibilities, are an excellent starting point for telling others what needs doing. I know of situations where each job description is reviewed yearly at the same time when annual evaluations take place. The idea is to monitor how the job is changing so as to ensure that the description captures shifting sensibilities. With advances in information and communication technology, it becomes particularly important to use such occasions to review evolving notions of whether one does things directly or puts in place electronic processes whereby things get done.

I remember when each worker within our school of nursing finally got a personal computer and printer and the training on how to use these tools. After that major shift, we had to rethink faculty and clerical staff roles because the latter no longer spent their days typing, so they now could take on some higher-level communication responsibilities that had previously been performed by faculty. Once all faculty members had their own computers and printers, publication expectations increased. You could now make editorial improvements without weighing each suggested change as to whether it was important enough to merit retyping the whole paper, so the writing/rewriting process was less laborious.

Job descriptions should reflect the culture. The more complex the organization, the more leadership means shaping organizational culture and then developing processes, systems, and structures that reinforce the values (Kotter, 1996; Schein, 2004). If you simply increase the controls proportionate to the complexity of the organization in the hope that such formalities will cope with the complexity, then you run the risk of creating a convoluted bureaucracy. This is particularly true when employees are highly educated professionals and prepared to function independently (Pepper, 2003). They resist micromanagement because it makes them feel that they are not being appreciated for their expertise. If you take as your task shaping organizational culture, then job descriptions should affirm the organization's overall values commitment, all the while reminding everyone that they are encouraged to be innovative in service to the mission (Goleman, 2000).

One of the most transformational changes in job descriptions that I participated in took place in our hospital network, Clarian Health. Inspired by the Institute of Medicine's various quality reports, the organization sought to establish a culture of quality and safety. Units set quality-improvement goals appropriate to their specialty, and the board, seeking to strengthen policy in this direction, voted to revise every job description and incorporate into each role—from housekeeper to CEO—a responsibility for quality and safety. Over a two-year period, every job description was rewritten in that direction, and the orientation for every new employee included some discussion of these responsibilities. This move was paralleled by doing the same for every student, resident, and fellow who had clinical experience within the system. This attempt to shape the overall culture was one of many initiatives with the same aim. Over time, the concerted effort changed staff satisfaction for the better—in part, I think, because an important organizational goal was concretely described as belonging to one and all and constantly reaffirmed by all concerned.

Job descriptions are an important starting point in articulating the essential leadership skills required of all nurses in complex organizations. For example, I am of the opinion that all job descriptions need to underscore the importance of successfully functioning teams in creating a positive culture (Kalisch, Curley, & Stefanow, 2007). Nurses at all organizational levels need to act as if their contributions to various groups are critical to the larger organization's success. That sensibility is all-important in using to advantage all the meetings that are the lifeblood of any organization.

Effective Meetings—The Lifeblood of Any Organization

Anyone knowing me over the years might be laughing now about the preceding sentence. Like many before me, I started off scorning meetings as time wasters. I had had my share of meetings that rambled and didn't go anywhere. Mention some committee assignments, and a feeling of dread would flood my being; too many meetings were more of an exercise in dysfunctional behavior than anything positive. In fact, I used to think that meetings were less a means to important ends and more a penance for my sins; Lencioni understood such an outlook when he wrote *Death by Meeting* (2004). Now I can admit that I had a rotten attitude: thinking that the fault belonged to others, imagining that good meetings "just happened" (though they didn't happen to me), and accepting disruptive or apathetic behavior as if it were inevitable. Over the course of many decades, my attitude changed 180 degrees, and I came to believe the following:

- In today's complex organizations where most nurses work—clinical/community agencies, universities, governmental structures—all services are provided through well-functioning teams, and governance is exercised through committees of various sorts. Therefore, group work isn't an extra or an annoyance; it is the principal pathway by which the collaborative work of the organization is accomplished.
- Team leaders, committee chairs, and members of these structures are rarely taught the principles for successful collaboration in such circumstances, and they need to be educated to exert both good leadership and good followership—get the right (diverse) stakeholders to the table; set ground rules for behavior (no BlackBerry use, no ad hominem attacks, no knitting); make sure everyone knows what purpose the group serves; have an agenda with clearly defined realistic goals; start and end on time; expect people to come prepared; don't allow the opinionated to dominate; and end the meeting by summarizing outcomes and next steps.
- Meetings work best if they are a time for responding to data collected or fact-finding completed, rather than a time for doing fundamental work, so they need preparation beforehand and follow-up to be of maximum benefit. Like teaching, meetings require much more groundwork and effort than the time actually spent together. To get such fact-finding accomplished expeditiously, consider small subcommittees; in this commuting age when so much work is exchanged online, don't hesitate to give away work to one person who might be able to accomplish more between in-person meetings if he or she does not have to arrange yet another sit-down meeting with other people.
- The follow-up portion of minutes is not just a column to be filled in for tidy recordkeeping; it is important to be specific about what is to be done next and by whom so that progress can be checked and reported on at the next meeting. Over the course of a year, all the follow-up sections should collectively facilitate the write-up of annual reports. It is easy to "lose" initiatives when other pressing matters take precedence, but it is important to keep track of them

until they have been declared completed or incorporated into business as usual.

- Make sure the silent are encouraged to voice their opinions so their passivity isn't erroneously assumed to signify agreement. Don't let the group confuse consensus (general agreement) with unanimity (agreed on by everyone); the latter isn't necessary to move something important forward. A bogus sense of democracy can also lead to endless meetings. What is important is that all the stakeholders have a voice rather than the deciding say.

Committee work is another area in which being clear about what is to be done and how this work interfaces with other parts of the organization are important aspects of leadership (Copp, 1996). One of the best committee chairs I ever worked with is Dr. Robert Graham, who currently holds an Endowed Chair in Family Medicine at the University of Cincinnati, having held a number of federal positions, including that of Assistant Surgeon General. Until recently, he chaired the selection committee for the Robert Wood Johnson Foundation's Health Policy Fellows Program and was masterful in getting committee members of various disciplines to reach consensus. He was particularly clear about processes, believing that if you are very precise about how you plan to proceed, then committee members will not only make good decisions but will also feel good about the process even if not every choice is one for which they voted. He thinks that a good committee chair is not like a quarterback who gives signals that others follow but is like an orchestra conductor who gets a group of talented people to work together and accomplish more than they could separately. It is an interesting perspective, because the emphasis doesn't begin with getting the right conclusion—it begins with setting in place transparent processes that have an integrity that is likely to beget the best conclusion.

I think the nursing profession has a love–hate relationship with committees. Too often they are regarded as a distraction from the main work of caring for patients or conducting research, and supervisors even counsel that one not take on any committee assignments before getting one's sea legs as a clinician or scholar. It is true that committee work can eat your time, if you do not know how to clarify expectations at the start. But committees can be the first important step in moving away from self-absorption and absorption with your own work and learning how to function in, and to affect, the larger organization, a step that will enable you to have more insights into how your work fits into and can thrive in the organization. The focus shouldn't be on avoiding committee work but on making sure that the organization values and encourages good meeting behavior in any career ladder. I have served as an external advisor to schools of nursing in Hong Kong and have been impressed with the extent to which committee work is equated with leadership there. They are particularly good at giving each person on the committee responsibility for moving forward a specific aspect of the work to be completed, so each person is responsible for a piece of the final product.

Committee work can be much more creative than we sometimes think, particularly if we don't assume that the way things are done currently has to limit what we can do. Most of the work of professional organizations gets done through committee structures, and most executive directors are pleased when members come to the table with new initiatives. I have contributed to committees by not only following through on what was asked of me but by also using them for an array of professional purposes. For example, I have served on some committees just so I would get to know the major figures at our academic health center and be better plugged into what was happening.

When I chaired Sigma Theta Tau International's Program Committee, I used that position to lobby for a research day at the biennial meeting; before that time, research was advanced in preconvention and postconvention workshops rather than being an integral part of the convention. I used my position on the Policy Committee of the Society for Research in Child Development to get them to devote one of their policy reports to an analysis of the establishment of the National Center for Nursing Research (McBride, 1987). When I was on the National Advisory Mental Health Council of the Alcohol, Drug Abuse, and Mental Health Administration, I partnered with the nurse who staffed that group to write about research opportunities at the National Institute of Mental Health (McBride & Friedenberg, 1989). That article made NIMH leadership more open to developing some additional opportunities just for nurses, and we publicized those new opportunities both to inform nurses about their options and to show our appreciation publicly (McBride, Friedenberg, Babich, & Bush, 1992). Not all committee work leads to publications, but committee work can lead to outcomes well beyond whatever the initial task of the group is. Particularly when you serve on interdisciplinary committees, there is always an opportunity to be of help *and* to change how other fields see nursing.

The Robert Wood Johnson Foundation has supported the Center to Champion Nursing in America (2010), which is charged with increasing the role of nurses in decision making about care delivery and management. One of the major initiatives of this effort is to get more nurses on boards (Feeg, 2009). There are many factors that go into board selection—professional reputation, specific expertise, cultural competence, previous connections with key stakeholders—but knowing how to function on interdisciplinary committees is crucial. Of course, performance in one forum leads to requests for you to do the same in another situation. Mary Wakefield, who was named administrator of the Health Resources Services Administration (HRSA) by President Barack Obama on February 20, 2009, is a perfect example. There are many reasons for her attaining her new position, but one has to be her stellar service in developing four of the major quality reports issued early on by the Institute of Medicine. Not all of us will go from committee assignments to a major position in government, but those who achieve major positions have invariably learned to work well with others through committee work.

Relationship Building

Being clear about job descriptions and how committees will proceed is important. It is also important to be in contact regularly with those who report to you and to whom you report in order to clarify evolving expectations. Most of us are good about discussing role expectations when relationships begin, but there is some inclination to talk less as the relationship progresses, particularly if the behavior is adequate to the task. Both sides get busy, and you know each other well enough to have a good sense of what each other is like. You may meet once a year formally for an annual evaluation, but even that special time might be rushed or formulaic.

I think it is important to have some regular time to discuss current problems, the progress of projects in development, and the change in environment. Even in high-level positions, I've had bosses who didn't go out of their way to see me or anyone else regularly; they expected you to touch base if there were problems. The trouble with this approach is that if you see only some people when there are problems, there's some tendency to begin to see them as problems. I always wanted my boss to think that I was competent almost all the time, and that if I had a problem we needed to bring in the Marines, because this must be a grave situation if I was at a loss. Meeting regularly not only gives the supervisor a sense of the employee's overall abilities, but it gives the employee a better sense of how the boss thinks. One of the things I learned along the way when I decided to set regular meetings with one of my bosses is how much his decision making was shaped by larger issues that I didn't think much about, and I started thinking about them so I could shape my approach with him accordingly. It was important learning for me as I contemplated moving to another level of leadership.

Administrators are forced to meet with low performers. Working with human relations officers, they document their ineffectiveness, attempts to get them to improve, and what resulted from these actions. The colleagues we often meet less with are high performers, because they are self-starters and know where they are going. That is the group, though, that the organization most needs to develop. Their very competence may leave them and others believing that they are doing just fine, and that they are meeting current expectations, but these individuals are most likely to profit from regularly being encouraged to stretch in new directions.

Studer's work on hardwiring excellence emphasizes working closely with high performers—thanking them for their contributions; telling them where the organization is headed; outlining why they are important to the institution's future; and asking what resources they need to move their part of the institution forward (2003, p. 124). The idea is to work closely with high performers in order to fuel their engagement further because they are already good at connecting the dots, and when energized they will, hopefully, go on to do something similar with those individuals who report directly to them. Since high performers are personally productive, we do tend to think that they can get others to do the same, but that may not be the case. They minimally need some coaching in how they can bring out the best when those who report to them vary in their performance levels: Do they know how to work with people whose behavior is different from their own? Do they tend to compete with up-and-coming high performers? Do they know how to bring out the best in others?

It is hoped that middle performers will be inspired by the high performers, but they may need more of an exchange of ideas about where the organization is headed and how they can make their mark in moving forward, because they may not have the same intuitive grasp of these matters and their role in facilitating progress. Repeatedly interacting with them and restating future directions should help them see how they fit into the organization and enable them to develop an expanded sense of their capabilities. Because they are not as quick to make connections, this is the group that may need particular help in figuring out how they can build on existing strengths.

Nurses make good organizational leaders because they have historically valued investing in relationships, seeing the nurse–patient relationship as of therapeutic benefit—but we haven't always understood how important it is to keep talking with one another all the time. There can be no end point to the continuing conversation because there is no end to the challenges we face in the 21st century. There is, however, growing recognition that routines that force interaction, develop boundary spanners—supervisors, department chairs, case managers, and the like, who integrate the work of other people—and promote team meetings collectively work to strengthen relational coordination, and those many opportunities for interaction among participants increase effectiveness, assuming added significance under conditions of uncertainty (Gittell, 2002).

This chapter is titled somewhat provocatively, equating leadership with telling others what to do. The words are meant to be an attention-grabber: "Is she advocating high-handed behavior?" I quickly dismiss that autocratic straw man, only to highlight how important it is for leaders to be straightforward in clearly explaining expectations, next steps, processes, and direction—and doing all of this while constantly reminding colleagues of how the context (of care, teaching, and science) is changing. Urging clarity by constantly clarifying the issues may sound deceptively simple, but being clear is never simple. You keep aiming in that direction, hoping that all you are doing to communicate a consistent message has the effect of making all concerned hear the central message and see themselves as engaged in the important work of the organization.

Key Take-Away Points

- You cannot expect others to be mind readers, so you cannot expect others to do what you want done without telling them.
- Being able to be clear with others about expectations, next steps, processes, and direction is integral to leadership, no matter the position held.
- Leaders have interests, responsibilities, and a purview that span boundaries, making them knowledgeable about how the pieces fit within the organization; therefore, they have a responsibility for making sense of why a course of action is necessary.
- Providing a context so the work ahead makes sense also means explaining what you do in your leadership position to support the efforts of others and further institutional goals.
- All of us hold simplistic views about the complexities of any position if we are not directly involved in the day-to-day living of these

roles, so nurse leaders must help nurses at one level of operations understand what those at other levels do.

- Job descriptions should reflect current organizational sensibilities. Most leadership positions require you to (a) help those individuals who report to you directly to be effective in their roles and get prepared for the future and to (b) interface with key stakeholders so as to leverage their support to meet the institution's mission.
- Successfully functioning teams and committee work are the lifeblood of complex organizations, so all nurses need high-level meeting-management skills.
- It is important to be in contact regularly with those who report to you, so they know where the organization is going and their role in the institution's future.

REFERENCES

Baumrind, D. (1991). The influence of parenting style on adolescent competence and substance use. *Journal of Early Adolescence, 11*(1), 56–95.

Bennett, J., Ellison, J., & Ball, S. (2010, March 29). Are we there yet? *Newsweek*, 42–46.

Center to Champion Nursing in America. (2010). *Leadership*. Retrieved August 31, 2010, from http://championnursing.org/category/topics/23/overview

Copp, L. A. (1996). Meetings and the irresponsible use of time. *Journal of Professional Nursing, 12*, 261–263.

De Pree, M. (1989). *Leadership is an art.* New York: Dell Publishing.

Feeg, V. D. (2009). An interview with Thomas W. Chapman, EdD, MPH. President and chief executive for the HSC Foundation. *Nursing Economics, 27*, 229–232.

Gittell, J. H. (1998). Beth Israel Deaconess Medical Center: Coordinating patient care. *Harvard Business School Case*, 899–213.

Gittell, J. H. (2002). Coordinating mechanisms in care provider groups: Relational coordination as a mediator and input uncertainty as a moderator of performance effects. *Management Science, 48*, 1408–1426.

Goleman, D. (2000). Leadership that gets results. *Harvard Business Review, 78*(2), 78–93.

Kalisch, B. J., Curley, M., & Stefanow, S. (2007). An intervention to enhance nursing staff teamwork and engagement. *Journal of Nursing Administration, 37*(2), 77–84.

Kotter, J. P. (1996). *Leading change.* Boston: Harvard Business School Press.

Lanchester, J. (2009, June 1). Outsmarted: High finance vs. human nature. *The New Yorker*, 83–87.

Lencioni, P. (2004). *Death by meeting.* San Francisco: Jossey-Bass.

McBride, A. B. (1987). The National Center for Nursing Research. *Social Policy Report* (a publication of the Society for Research in Child Development), 2(2), 1–11.

McBride, A. B., & Friedenberg, E. (1989). Research opportunities at the National Institute of Mental Health. *Image: Journal of Nursing Scholarship, 21,* 251–253.

McBride, A. B., Friedenberg, E. C., Babich, K., & Bush, C. (1992). Nursing research at NIMH: An update. *Archives of Psychiatric Nursing, 6,* 138–141.

National Institute of Standards and Technology. (2001). *Baldridge National Quality Program.* Retrieved July 10, 2009, from http://www.baldridge.nist.gov/Improvement_Act.htm

Pepper, A. (2003). Leading professionals: A science, a philosophy and a way of working. *Journal of Change Management, 3,* 349–360.

Schein, E. H. (2004). *Organizational culture and leadership* (3rd ed.). San Francisco: Jossey-Bass.

Sigma Theta Tau International. (2005). *Resource paper and position statement on: Leadership and leadership development priorities.* Retrieved July 10, 2009, from http://www.nursingsociety.org/aboutus/PositionPapers/Documents/position_leadership.doc

Studer, Q. (2003). *Hardwiring excellence.* Gulf Breeze, FL: Fire Starter Publishing.

Chapter 7

It's All About Communication

There is no leadership article or book, in or out of nursing, that doesn't stress the importance of interpersonal and communication effectiveness in achieving organizational goals. Working with others to realize an organization's values and mission is by definition all about communication— empathic understanding, motivating others, team dynamics, making sense of environmental demands, networking, negotiations, conflict management, presenting your case, building in feedback loops, and creating a learning culture that values constant quality improvement.

It is all about communication. Apply for a position, and your résumé or curriculum vitae (CV) serves the purpose of communicating your learning, experience, and leadership potential. Any time major clinical mistakes are made, chances are that faulty communication was either the primary problem or a contributing factor (Maxfield, Granny, McMillan, Patterson, & Switzler, 2005). In recruiting for students or patients, you are always concerned with marketing a certain image so as to attract customers.

The main message of this chapter is that a professional career requires continued development in interpersonal and communication effectiveness. If you thought that the course on public speaking that you had to take in college would not help you all that much if you went into nursing, then you may be pleasantly surprised by how useful that experience was in preparing you to go before an assortment of groups and make a convincing case for a course of action. If you hated to write term papers and thought you were finished with such writing in life after graduation, then you may be unprepared for all the writing you have to do thereafter—letters of recommendation, grant submissions, progress reports, columns for newsletters, and so forth. If you are already good at managing nursing groups with short-term goals, then you may underestimate the new communication skills that you have to develop to function effectively in interdisciplinary groups with complicated long-term goals.

There is no way that this chapter can summarize all of the communication skills a leader uses over the course of a career, and some have already been covered in other chapters (e.g., the skills involved in running effective meetings). Undergraduate and graduate courses are full of needed information about communication—spoken, written, visual, electronic, and so forth. Instead of trying to summarize the communication essentials that nurse leaders should have acquired along the way and will need to develop additionally over time, I focus on some communication skills important to goal achievement that I learned to appreciate more with experience. They fall under the following headings: (a) courtesies, (b) self-presentation, (c) negotiations, (d) the importance of data arrays and publication, and (e) the value of understanding the viewpoint of others.

Courtesies

Remembering what your mother said about good manners would seem not to need repeating in a book on leadership, but decorum has fallen into disrepute in our increasingly casual culture; etiquette can advance your career (Pagana, 2008). For me courtesy is code for understanding how to behave appropriately in an array of social situations. Do you know certain meet-and-greet behaviors? I used to make fun of the way businessmen at Rotary meetings go around the room shaking hands with one and all—it struck me as canned behavior—but I came to realize how important a warm welcome is when you come into a meeting room and reconnect with colleagues. Do you know how to make sure that everyone attending a reception feels at ease? If you are a leader in an organization, then you need to make sure that important guests are not lost in the crowd. Do you realize that cursing in public is unseemly in a professional even if you are experiencing the most just of angers?

Protocol can be a problem for people like me who grew up in families who didn't entertain much, though my mother was very good about teaching the basics—please, thank you, knowing what fork or spoon to choose if confronted with an abundance of cutlery (use the ones farthest from the plate for earlier courses). I know I'm not alone in feeling uncomfortable in formal situations, because I know of at least one hospital with a distinguished foreign clientele where the chief nurse officer has provided a version of "diplomatic" training for the nursing staff so they would feel less self-conscious about interacting with statesmen or celebrity guests.

There is no courtesy, I think, more important than the "thank you." It can take many forms—sending a card, an e-mail acknowledgment, a handwritten note, a phone call, a bouquet of flowers—but you never go wrong recognizing that others have helped you. I didn't always think that way and I am not uniformly good in this department, but the more experienced I've become, the more I have come to realize that all those appreciations build threads of connection. Reinforced for one good action, people consider another one in your direction, for example, taking your phone call even if they are busy.

I'm inclined to agree with Thoreau, that "most men [and women] lead lives of quiet desperation," meaning that they are not sure that anyone notices or cares what happens in their lives. That is why people appreciate notes of goodwill on important occasions—engagements, weddings, the birth of a child, birthdays, hospitalizations, promotions, and bereavements. When you are younger, I think you tend to assume that these things don't matter all that much: Why would you care that I noticed? However, you do notice courtesies and count people who remember you as special. And if that person is an important person in the organization where you work, it matters even more.

The more I traveled to other countries, the more I came to appreciate formalities. Being decorous doesn't have to be stiff; it means appreciating prevailing customs. In American culture, one might jump to a work-related issue right away in the name of efficiency, but in Asian culture, there are certain social niceties that need to be observed beforehand. The advantage of such niceties is that it gives you something to do, while you are still sizing up the people and the situation, so you don't have to worry as much about what to say first because greeting behaviors are somewhat scripted. Gift-giving is important in many leader-to-leader situations (remember President Obama's first visit to the United Kingdom and the brouhaha in the British newspapers about whether his gift to the Prime Minister was special enough to reflect the special relationship between the two countries). When confronted with such situations, I learned to ask ahead of time about expectations and found that most workplaces have gifts suitable for such occasions in the development or communications office. When I asked for help in this direction, I think I also changed the impression they had of the School of Nursing; before, they had not thought about our school in statesman terms.

I feel awkward writing about the importance of courtesies in the development of leadership, because I am all too aware of my failings.

If you are pressed for time, you forget to do some of the things you know to do. You can overcome this limitation by instructing your staff to help you remember or by programming your electronic calendar and task list, but that can go only so far. The most important advice that I can give about courtesy is that you keep trying to act appropriately even when you want to act out with a string of expletives. It is the constant attempt to be considerate that counts more than 100% performance. Courtesies are not trivial; they are a manifestation of overall self-mastery, and self-mastery is connected to becoming masterful.

Self-Presentation

Almost all leadership programs cover self-presentation at some point. The subject matter can vary from reminding you to practice the basics of good grooming—be clean, no garlic or cigarette smoke on the breath, don't overdo makeup or cologne—to media training. Not everyone understands the importance of the basics. Some assume that the right they have socially to please themselves and flaunt their individuality—long hair, lots of jewelry, tattoos, various body piercings—should hold for the work setting too. But I have seen a supercompetent woman in another field wear flowing brightly colored garments to a job interview, and the flamboyance of her style was interpreted by a largely male interview committee as not having the proper demeanor for the elevated position. She didn't get the promotion, even though she answered all the questions asked with wit and wisdom. You can argue that her dress shouldn't have counted against her, but it did. Hillary Clinton and Nancy Pelosi may be kidded a great deal about their pantsuit uniforms, but their tailored-yet-feminine appearance reinforces the notion that their substance is more important than their style.

Nurses as a group have lost an agreed-upon professional look with the disappearance of a set uniform and cap (Houweling, 2004). Scrubs have become the de facto uniform in many hospitals, but they don't communicate capability as much as they do a rumpled approach to life (Seabrook, 2002). I understand the appeal of comfort and practicality, but I believe that professional nurses should look professional whether that involves lab coats embroidered with the name of the hospital, distinctive name tags or patches that make clear who is an RN, and/or the use of business cards (Mason & Buhler-Wilkerson, 2004). I also think that the smarter you look in the classroom, the more you look prepared for difficult questions.

I have long wished that appearance didn't matter, because I have been overweight all my life and don't look like a model for physical fitness, but the reality is that appearance does communicate a first impression. No matter what your shape, you minimally have to look professional enough to be taken seriously. What that means will vary with the work setting and your responsibilities, but if you don't wear a uniform that already conveys a sense of authority, then you all the more have to ask yourself if your appearance and demeanor do communicate how seriously you wish to be treated.

These days, it isn't just personal appearance that sets a tone, but the look of one's workspace and Facebook page. If your work requires you to do a lot of driving and colleagues regularly accompany you in the car, then leftover soda cans and chewed baby toys aren't likely to convince any passengers that you are prepared for the day. A chaotic or messy office doesn't instill confidence that the person at the desk gets things done. There are some geniuses who get by with clutter all around, but most of us do not have an international reputation to fall back on. Facebook pages with inappropriate partying photographs or negative comments about the boss can do serious damage to one's professional reputation. Twitter something off the cuff and you may live to regret your spontaneity. You cannot take a shoot-from-the-hip remark back, so it is better to err on the side of caution. I have learned this the hard way.

Concerned that nurses are viewed in stereotyped terms, many leadership programs focus on media training so that the next generation will be better prepared to convey the richness of the field. It is important to know how to describe your work succinctly in jargon-free language so the inherent importance of what you do is evident. I have been videotaped answering questions and found the subsequent critique of my performance to be very helpful: I tend to ramble when answering questions, forgetting to put a period at the end of a complete thought and to come up for air (and the next question). I often nod as others talk, a psychiatric-nurse habit meant to convey "I'm listening to you," but on television that nodding can seem to be agreement with positions I do not hold. When I was less experienced, I used to cringe when asked what I thought was a dumb question, and now I've learned how to deflect the question and speak to one I know how to answer—"What you asked is a good question, but to answer that, you first have to ask . . . ."

I wish I could say that media training transformed me. It didn't, but it did force me to take responsibility for the messages I conveyed to others, one of the points of Goffman's classic *The Presentation of Self in Everyday Life* (1959). Whereas before, I thought the other person was dense not to "get" what I was saying, I now realize, as a leader should, that I have to try to control the messages I send out. The other person can choose not to agree with me, but it is up to me to argue my case as well as possible. Self-monitoring—vigilance about how you are perceived combined with flexibility in your behavioral repertoire—is associated with leadership effectiveness because it is professionally task-oriented (Anderson, 1987). I like to think of self-monitoring as being tactical the way a good chess player is, imagining not just the next move but subsequent ones, so you are not so intent on what you have to say that you don't consider how it will be taken by others. If you want others to take your viewpoint seriously, you have to do your best to stay on message so it can be heard.

Historically, women in general and women nurses in particular have often felt devalued. Alas, feeling unappreciated makes those affected more prone to uncertainty, stress, frustration, and anger (Inzlicht, McKay, & Aronson, 2006; Spencer, Steele, & Quinn, 1999). Hypervigilant because of past grievances, the person may be on the lookout for slights and less able to self-monitor appropriately. For self-protection, the devalued person or group may even discount a certain amount of negative feedback as merely prejudicial because so many comments have a stereotyped flavor, but such discounting runs the risk of missed opportunities for improvement (Aronson & Inzlicht, 2004).

In the ultimate irony, trying hard to manage the impressions that are being formed—"I *am* knowledgeable"—can activate further negative thinking and impair the ability to control and regulate one's actions (Cadinu, Maass, Rosabianca, & Kiesner, 2005; Inzlicht & Ben-Zeev, 2000, 2003). I mention how hypervigilance can affect the ability to self-monitor, because my own self-consciousness in the early career years caused me to discount some accurate feedback I received about my faults as merely prejudiced thinking. Instead of taking the feedback to heart, I stubbornly put off changing because I felt entitled to savor my grievances, and my prickliness, in turn, was off-putting to those who might have wanted to help me improve.

Part of self-presentation is practicing what we preach. We talk about the importance of role modeling good communication skills, but most of us still hope others pay more attention to what we say than to what we do, because acting all the time on one's principles is not easy. I'm thinking here of all those secret-pleasure behaviors that can impede teamwork and culture building in an organization—backbiting, gossip, formation of cliques, and not being respectful of others. Badmouthing someone you don't like can be so appealing, yet every time you pass on hearsay or prattle on about someone else's faults you say less about the person and more about yourself. Others begin to wonder if you aren't a person who will talk about them, too, as soon as they leave the room. Can you be trusted? I noticed over time that there were some nurses who consistently went against the tide, responding to rumor with "That doesn't sound like how she would act" or "Maybe we don't know the whole story," and I wanted to be fair-minded like them. "If you can't say anything good, don't say anything at all" isn't just a matter of civility. Respectful communication is a feature of the best work environments (American Association of Critical-Care Nurses [AACN], 2005; Ulrich et al., 2007).

For professionals, one's CV is an important aspect of self-presentation. Do you keep it up to date? So many nurses I've known don't bother, but if you cannot keep track of what you have done professionally, then who else will? Computers have made it easy to stay current, because you can add information as soon as there's a new development. Most organizations have a set format for such a document, so I won't go into what should be on one, though there are common headings (title[s] a person holds, contact information, education, work history, professional memberships and offices held, honors/awards, consultations, presentations and publications, grant funding, significant committee work, etc.).

There are, however, certain principles that hold across the board. Check spelling and grammar. Too many people don't know the difference between principal investigator (correct) and principle investigator and between the plural (respondents) and the possessive (respondent's), and if someone is considering you for an award, such mistakes on your CV can leave a bad impression. (If you are not good in this area, do make friends with someone who is, because spell check doesn't help in these situations.) Don't pad. Mention an achievement under one category, not the same one under several different headings. Provide full particulars. If you've received an honor, don't just give the name of the award; say something about the purpose, awarding agency, and date of conferral so the reader has a sense of its importance. Don't describe your work in glowing terms. Provide the information that would enable the reader to have a good opinion of you. You wouldn't say, "I was a transformational unit manager," but you might say, "During my tenure as unit manager, quality-improvement efforts were undertaken resulting over a year in a 50% decrease in infections and a 65% decrease in falls."

My experience is that nurses in clinical practice do not take the CV as seriously as their academic counterparts unless they are about to look for another position. However, I think an up-to-date CV is important to all nurses and should be required when annual evaluations are made. What is not yet on your CV, but should be there at this career stage, can be a starting-off point for setting future goals. If you have no presentations on your CV but have been innovative in getting everyone to take hand washing seriously on your unit with significant results, then you should be encouraged to recount that achievement at an appropriate professional meeting.

Over the course of a career, you are likely to develop an assortment of documents describing yourself for different purposes. There should be a full CV that lists all aspects of your career. If you are a researcher, then you will have a description of your research achievements in the format mandated by government agencies. You may also develop a one-page biographical sketch that you use for many purposes, in lieu of a lengthier document, because it summarizes in journalistic fashion the highlights of your career. You may even put together a one-paragraph description of yourself suitable for use as an introduction when you are invited to speak. As my CV got longer over time, I found myself drafting these shorter versions of what I had accomplished because some readers of the full CV picked out idiosyncratic things to say about me that I didn't think captured how I saw myself. Moreover, I decided that I wanted to control how I came across to others.

Image Building

Understanding the importance of self-presentation prepares you for appreciating the importance of building the image of where you work—that is, doing your part as a leader in that organization to convey a positive impression. That doesn't mean you are oblivious to institutional weaknesses and problems. Minimally, it means that you do not contribute to the negative impression by unthinkingly saying things like "Everyone at our place is crazy" or "We're bad at . . ." Maximally, it means that you regularly communicate what is best about where you work. And if you are still working for the organization, there must be something worthy.

One of the things that I have said when describing enterprises with which I am affiliated is, "We are better than we used to be and not as good as we are going to be." Of course, you follow up such a generalization with concrete examples of improvements and place the current improvement efforts within a larger context of a commitment to excellence in an area of benefit to the public. The more you talk about concrete steps to improve and achievements to date, so long as they are based on reality, the more you help fellow workers to feel good about working for the institution at this point in time. We all want to think that we are at a place on the move and that we will look back at this point in our lives saying that was a good time to be at this institution. Seeing the good in current efforts is a promissory statement about what can be accomplished if we set our minds to it.

Institutional image building requires that we ask many of the same questions that you pose when trying to improve self-presentation: Does the place look inviting physically? Do the staff look professional enough to be taken seriously? Does the institution's Web site communicate a good first impression, conveying a rich blending of information and vibrancy? Do we practice what we preach about being respectful of one and all? Are information materials—handouts, brochures, in-house newsletters, magazines—written in clear, jargon-free language? Do we decorate the public corridors with images that describe a vibrant past, our strong committment to diversity, and the range of what we are currently doing (sort of a public CV)? Are we in control of our image? Impressions, both conscious and subliminal, shape subsequent behavior, so they have consequences in satisfaction ratings, morale, return business, and the like.

Negotiations

The topic of negotiations is vast, particularly with regard to dispute resolution. Kritek (2007) is particularly good at discussing how you negotiate at uneven tables where others have greater advantages. I have negotiated in a broad array of situations—hiring new personnel; encouraging someone ineffective to resign; relocating clinical services. Along the way, I've learned a number of things: (a) be respectful of all parties; (b) gather information for comparative purposes so you go into talks knowing what is normative; (c) know the difference between bargaining for yourself (your salary and benefits) and for your profession (institutions understand that new leaders are likely to ask for additional resources when first hired so that they can move their part of the organization forward) and bargain for both; (d) when possible, have someone who reports to you do some initial fact finding so that person can figure out what the other side wants and you have time to figure out a strategy;

(e) don't think of negotiations as arguing over a "fixed pie" but a process by which both sides benefit; and (f) know what advantages you have.

Socialized to have a bit of a "poor me" attitude, I found the aspect of negotiations I had to work most at understanding was the advantages I had in various situations. Like many other nurses, I tended to think that if I didn't have money, which I usually did not have, then I didn't have any advantages. But that is far from the case. Nurses have a number of advantages they don't always see as being of tactical benefit that can be used strategically. In clinical agencies, they can close units if working conditions are not safe and new units cannot be opened if nursing coverage is not available, so they can directly influence the bottom line. In universities, schools of nursing usually provide more community-based services than any other field, and these activities can be an asset whenever town/gown tensions are building. Because nurses have been schooled to be patient advocates, they can use this expertise to give weight to what they have to say—"I am making this point on behalf of all the patients and their families struggling with this problem." Since nurses are trusted by the public, any partnership they make with consumers can be formidable in providing testimony to a legislative committee.

Years ago when I first became a department chair, I needed adjunct faculty to serve as preceptors for graduate students' clinical experiences. Alas, being an adjunct meant "without tenure and remuneration," so I didn't know how I was going to engage the number of clinicians I needed without having anything to offer in return. Being an adjunct faculty member was an official university appointment, so I set off trying to figure out what else that could mean other than a letter for one's files, which is all it had been to date. This involved brainstorming with others in the department to figure out what we had that others wanted. We eventually wound up describing an adjunct position as an opportunity to determine if a position in academia was appealing. In addition, we were able to offer all adjunct faculty the following: library privileges (they really had them already as state taxpayers, but we emphasized this benefit), free parking on the (infrequent) days they attended meetings, a listing in the department's directory, invitations to departmental social events and meetings, plus a reduced registration fee for school-sponsored continuing-education programming. There was little in what we offered that was brand new; it was a matter of finding out what was already possible and packaging all of these possibilities so the total seemed substantive. In addition, we started the tradition of not only formally thanking these preceptors at the end of each school year but also sending a letter of appreciation to their employers.

Hiring these days isn't just a matter of salary and benefits but of enticing individuals with customized packages. If salaries and benefits are more or less comparable across institutions, which they increasingly are in the same geographic area, then the advantage goes to the recruiter who customizes the offer, making clear the unique advantages of the organization. In recruiting faculty, this can mean the support of a research assistant (most schools link such positions to tuition reimbursement so such help is mutually beneficial), needed equipment/software, travel monies to conferences, arranging a courtesy appointment in another department/school, and a listing of all the opportunities that exist at the university for which the person can apply, for example, internal research funding, sabbatical awards, information technology resources, research centers, and the like. In recruiting clinicians, this can mean arranging a joint appointment with a school of nursing, ensuring that the new hire becomes part of an important policy-making committee, and information about foundation monies available to support clinical innovations.

In my examples, I've deliberately stayed away from mentioning perks that cost a great deal of money, because my point is that most of us have resources in our environments that we take for granted and don't describe explicitly when making an offer. Describing the leadership-development opportunities available in the institution can always be a powerful asset in negotiations. Prospective employees do not just want to work for an institution, they want a sense that the organization will facilitate their growth and development over time (recall Care's definition of career in chapter 4), hence the appeal of career ladders and mentoring programs. Partnering with the local Chamber of Commerce to take advantage of all the materials that they have about cultural, sports, shopping, and recreational events is another way to make a move seem more attractive. In my experience, you have an advantage if you are attuned to the special requirements of the individual—a job for the partner, education for a developmentally challenged child, a community that welcomes diversity, and an opportunity to cultivate an avocational interest.

Leaders need to know what advantages they bring to any bargaining session. I have come to clinical tables with data describing the number of our graduates who are now employed within the institution. As I negotiated for preceptors and clinical experiences, I wanted to demonstrate that helping us was really enlightened self-interest, because those placements alleviated their workforce shortages. I have come to university tables with data describing the number of clinical hours contributed by our RN graduate students to area agencies. Since the university had a goal of civic engagement, I wanted to put a number to the time contributed free of charge to the community by these already-licensed professionals (and I costed it out). Universities may not pay property taxes, but they "give" in other ways that can be enumerated and used to advantage in negotiations.

The Importance of Data Arrays and Publication

In negotiations, data are important, and such information is useful in countless situations where you are hoping to exert influence. Florence Nightingale, the first woman elected to fellowship in England's Royal Statistical Society, understood that an effective response to bureaucratic resistance could be data, particularly if displayed in an attractive pie chart (Gill, 2005). Asking for a pay increase for personnel isn't likely to get anyone's attention in a tight economy, but a table showing how average salaries already fall below the 50th percentile for your market is likely to command attention, particularly if you also have data that show how many people were recruited by other institutions as salaries fell in buying power. Add to that an estimate for how much it costs to recruit and orient someone new, and you may have made a persuasive case for some pay increases in a year when others are not getting any.

Early in my career, I thought an appeal to justice or at least parity should carry the day. The reality is that we are all now living in a world that is dubious about generalizations and rhetorical flourishes. Now more than ever, to believe in an argument we demand data that support it. Unlike research where the findings proceed from the design and methods, data for leadership involves collecting an assortment of facts that buttress the case you want to make. In one budget hearing, I wanted to make the case for our school being tops nationally and therefore worthy of additional investment. I put together a table listing indicators of excellence: the top 15 graduate programs according to *U.S. News & World Report* rankings (there were ties, so the top 15 positions could be claimed by 18 schools of nursing), the top 18 schools in NIH funding, all schools with NIH-funded institutional research training grants, and all schools with NIH-supported research centers. I then created a final column, listing all of the schools that had appeared in every other column. There were only eight names in that last column, and our school was one of them, so I argued successfully in the hearings that we were a top school, and thus deserved additional support. You could certainly accuse me of having slanted the data to make my point (for one thing, they were not independent indicators, because columns three and four were also included in column two), but I could also argue that I was using some nationally acceptable success indicators—and we did get additional support.

Until you realize the importance of data, you may not be familiar with where you can get data for purposes of comparison. Professional associations and government agencies are excellent sources for facts and figures. For example, the American Association of Colleges of Nursing does a first-rate job of keeping track regionally and nationally of salary information for faculty and administrators, breaking the information down by public and private universities and whether they are research intensive. The American Association of University Professors has similar data comparing salary information by discipline. Clinical agencies collect an assortment of statistics for accreditation and regulatory purposes. Nurses have historically been involved in data collection for others but have not asked offices concerned with institutional management for much information to serve their own purposes. As the electronic health record becomes the norm, enormous amounts of data will be available to help answer questions of importance for nurses—and the savvy leader will make friends with the office that prepares data arrays. Minimally, all nurses working for clinical agencies should know how they are faring on the nurse-sensitive quality indicators (American Nurses Association [ANA], 2009). I really do mean *all* nurses should be aware of this information, not just administrators, because satisfactory performance is the responsibility of all concerned, and the strategic use of past successes is likewise of common concern in negotiating current challenges.

There was a period in the 1990s when my campus became very involved in information management (Banta et al., 2002). In preparation for budget hearings, binders of data were handed out to all deans and financial officers describing how their schools fared on dozens of indicators of concern to the university, for example, credit hours, number of faculty, alumni perceptions of the worth of their degree, faculty satisfaction, student debt, grant funding, and so forth. I used the data to construct tables showing how the school of nursing fared compared to other schools, and this information proved useful in helping faculty, staff, and other stakeholders develop an accurate picture of current realities. Understanding the situation, the faculty and staff were enormously helpful in brainstorming how we might improve our numbers. I was also able to use the campus data to change the chancellor's image of nursing. There had long been the belief that nursing was a lumbering organization top-heavy with administrators, but a comparison across schools demonstrated that we had the third lowest administrative costs, well under the 15% generally described in business circles as the upper limit for sound administration.

The strategic use of data isn't normally taught as a powerful tool in achieving organizational effectiveness, nor is the importance of publishing. If you are in academia, then you are expected to "publish or perish," but this isn't expected of nurses in other realms. I see publication, however, as vital to impression formation. If you are an engaging teacher or a caring clinician and your student or patient thrives, those are private goods between the parties, important but not necessarily of importance to others. However, if you write up some teaching strategy, clinical innovation, or administrative success, then your work enters the public domain. Once in the public domain, it becomes more real to others. Since someone bothered to publish the idea, then your ideas must be taken more seriously.

When I refer to publication, I mean anything from an op-ed piece in the local newspaper to a story in the organization's newsletter to a think piece in a nursing journal to publishing findings of interdisciplinary interest in the *New England Journal of Medicine*. Once your work is mentioned in print, what you do becomes visible to others, and that visibility lends credence to your viewpoint on the home front. There is something very powerful about giving someone you want to convince to move in a certain direction a copy of an article you've written on the subject or one that has been written about your work. What is more, the very act of writing up what you have done is bound to make you think through the issues more thoroughly than you've done heretofore because you have to be convincing to merit publication (the standard is either saying something new or saying something old in a new way).

I have coauthored for publication the work that was done in adopting the budgetary practices of responsibility-centered management and in adapting our organizational structure to meet the changing needs of the state (McBride, Neiman, & Johnson, 2000; McBride, Yeager, & Farley, 2005). In both instances, the work was prompted by changing conditions and institutional necessities, but publishing what we learned from the experience accomplished several other objectives—there was a written record of what happened for future reference as needed (and we wrote the record); university officials were impressed that what we were doing was of national interest; the publication helped build the reputation of my collaborators; both articles resulted in requests for out-of-state consultation on the topic under consideration. In the process, we took ourselves more seriously and were taken more seriously by significant others, and I think we were energized to innovate in other directions. Not only does publication benefit the authors by enriching the CV, but it draws attention to the organization birthing the work, an important ingredient in upgrading institutional reputations.

Written descriptions of change processes and data arrays illustrating the concrete changes nurses make are manifestations of a growing emphasis on the achievement of measurable outcomes (Trossman, 2009). The focus can be on an illustrative case or the aggregate experience of a specific patient population, but both serve the purpose of making what nurses do concrete and visible, not easily discounted with stereotyped generalizations. Data arrays and publication are important ingredients in building the profession's positive image, and most organizations have offices charged with helping you to communicate what is going on within the organization, if you just ask for their assistance—which nursing hasn't historically done.

The Value of Understanding Others

From the prayer of St. Francis of Assisi (*Grant that I may not so much seek . . . to be understood as to understand*) to Covey's Habit #5 (*Seek first to understand, then to be understood*), understanding is regarded as the key to interpersonal and communication effectiveness. We have also long known that getting patients to talk about their experience can be an intervention in itself (McBride, 1969), but we may not always appreciate the consequences for leadership. In leadership positions, I was often concerned about what I was going to do next to handle a challenge; my focus was so much on my performance that I didn't listen as much as I should have. You try so hard to solve problems, but there are so many that you cannot do much about, so you feel inadequate and just wish the person presenting the problem would go away. Because nurses as a group are action oriented, I think we have particular difficulty when we are confronted with situations that don't lend themselves to obvious solutions, which is of course when you are most in need of leadership.

The mistake that I sometimes made is forgetting that listening is an action; it is not a substitute for action but an important activity in its own right. Listening carefully, you get a better appreciation of the issues. Maybe you realize that there's more to the matter than you first thought or maybe you realize that there is a basic misunderstanding. In listening, you often get ideas about how to proceed that you certainly didn't have beforehand. Even when there are no clear answers to a problem, having your viewpoint appreciated by someone in authority can make a huge difference in how the other person feels about the situation. I learned to say, "I don't know if I can resolve the issue you've raised, but minimally I want you to leave my office convinced that I at least understand your perspective." Before the person left, I would repeat back the theme of the conversation, asking, "Did I state your point of view correctly?— because I want to make sure that I 'got' your perspective."

Part of listening is tolerating silences. I learned this from my younger daughter Kara who is an expert in second-language acquisition. I have often heard her say that too many teachers pose a question and then answer it themselves because they're uncomfortable with silences. The person who isn't clear about what to say or how to say it is going to be halting in his/her speech, and there is a tendency to jump in and finish sentences thinking that you are being helpful. What you say may, however, cause the person to despair that you will ever understand, because you cannot wait to get in the next word. I still am not comfortable with silences, but I have taught myself to say to others, "Take your time saying what you want in the way you want because I care about your point of view."

Not taking time to listen can escalate matters too. If you are feeling defensive and imply that the problem isn't really a problem or are feeling too much the schoolmarm and push a premature solution, the other person is likely to get more upset. It feels to the person as if she or he is being told that her or his point of view doesn't matter. Listen carefully and the emotion behind the situation becomes less explosive, with both sides in a better frame of mind to think about how to proceed. If you listen to others, they are also more likely to listen to what you subsequently have to say, and your viewpoint might provide the person with insights that can trigger constructive next steps.

Most people appreciate that their points of view aren't the only ones that you are hearing. They understand that a leader has to listen to everyone and use that information to come up with the best course of action to meet the values and goals of the organization. Indeed, you are always on sound ground when you don't make differences of opinion personal matters but turn the conversation in the direction of how "we together" can meet the institutional mission—"Together we need to do what is best for our patients and their families." Going back to such basics has a way of clarifying matters, redirecting efforts toward putting first things first so the values and mission of the organization can be realized, and that is what interpersonal and communication effectiveness should be about.

Key Take-Away Points

- Achieving organizational goals is all about communication—clarifying, motivating others, team dynamics, making sense of environmental demands, networking, negotiating, conflict management, presenting your case, building feedback loops, and reinforcing cultural values.
- Knowing how to behave appropriately in an array of social situations is the foundation for good interpersonal relations.
- You have to look and act professional to be taken seriously.
- Self-monitoring, as a leadership ability, means the person seeks to shape how she or he is perceived in order to achieve professional objectives.
- Leaders assume responsibility for building the image of their workplace.
- In negotiations, it is important to know what advantages you bring to the table.
- Measurable outcomes and published results are important in building the image of the profession.
- Communications-wise, you are always on sound ground when you bring conversations back to the realization of institutional values and mission.

REFERENCES

American Association of Critical-Care Nurses. (2005). *AACN standards for establishing and sustaining healthy work environments. A journey to excellence.* Retrieved July 18, 2009, from http://www.aacn.org/WD/HWE/Docs/HWEStandards.pdf

American Nurses Association. (2009). *Nurse-sensitive indicators.* Retrieved July 22, 2009, from http://www.nursingworld.org/MainMenuCategories/ThePracticeofProfessionalNursing/PatientSafetyQuality/Research-Measurement/The-National-Database/Nursing-Sensitive-Indicators_1.aspx

Anderson, L. R. (1987). Self-monitoring and performance in nontraditional occupations. *Basic and Applied Social Psychology, 8*(1 & 2), 85–96.

Aronson, J., & Inzlicht, M. (2004). The ups and downs of attributional ambiguity: Stereotype vulnerability and the academic self-knowledge of African American college students. *Psychological Sciences, 15,* 829–836.

Banta, T. W., et al. (2002). *Building a scholarship of assessment.* San Francisco: Jossey-Bass.

Cadinu, M., Maass, A., Rosabianca, A., & Kiesner, J. (2005). Why do women underperform under stereotype threat? Evidence for the role of negative thinking. *Psychological Science, 16,* 572–578.

Goffman, E. (1959). *The presentation of self in everyday life*. New York: Doubleday.

Houweling, L. (2004). Image, function, and style. A history of the nursing uniform. *American Journal of Nursing, 104*(4), 40–48.

Inzlicht, M., & Ben-Zeev, T. (2000). A threatening intellectual environment: Why females are susceptible to experiencing problem-solving deficits in the presence of males. *Psychological Science, 11*, 365–371.

Inzlicht, M., & Ben-Zeev, T. (2003). Do high-achieving female students underperform in private? The implications of threatening environment on intellectual processing. *Journal of Educational Psychology, 95*, 796–805.

Inzlicht, M., McKay, L., & Aronson, J. (2006). Stigma as ego depletion. How being the target of prejudice affects self-control. *Psychological Science, 17*, 262–269.

Kritek, P. B. (2007). *Negotiating at an uneven table. Developing moral courage in resolving our conflicts* (2nd ed.). San Francisco: Jossey-Bass.

Mason, D. J., & Buhler-Wilkerson, K. (2004). Who's the RN? Identifying nurses simply by the patch. *American Journal of Nursing, 104*(4), 11.

Maxfield, D., Granny, J., McMillan, R., Patterson, K., & Switzler, A. (2005). *Silence kills: The seven crucial conversations for healthcare*. Provo, UT: VitalSmarts.

McBride, M. A. B. (1969). The additive to the analgesic. *American Journal of Nursing, 69*, 974–976.

McBride, A. B., Neiman, S., & Johnson, J. (2000). Responsibility-centered management: A ten-year nursing assessment. *Journal of Professional Nursing, 16*(4), 1–10.

McBride, A. B., Yeager, L., & Farley, S. (2005). Evolving as a university-wide school of nursing. *Journal of Professional Nursing, 21*, 16–22.

Pagana, K. D. (2008). *The nurse's etiquette advantage: How professional etiquette can advance your nursing career*. Indianapolis, IN: Center Nursing Press.

Seabrook, J. (2002, March 18). Annals of style. The white dress. *The New Yorker*, 122–126.

Spencer, S. J., Steele, C. M., & Quinn, D. M. (1999). Stereotype threat and women's math performance. *Journal of Experimental Social Psychology, 35*, 4–28.

Trossman, S. (2009). The proof is in the data. Findings bolster nurses' stance that RN care makes a difference. *The American Nurse, 6*, 13.

Ulrich, B. T., Woods, D., Hart, K. A., Lavandero, R., Leggett, J., & Taylor, D. (2007). Critical care nurses' work environments. Value of excellence in Beacon units and Magnet organizations. *Critical Care Nurse, 27*(3), 68–77.

Chapter 8

Resource Development

It is impossible to achieve organizational goals without resources, so leadership requires that attention be paid to developing them, but I did not always think it was my responsibility. I had a great deal to learn in this respect. I've worked for organizations all my life, and for the first two decades I thought that a good employer is just expected to provide resources—a building to work in, utilities, housekeeping, proper equipment, fair salaries, and benefits. My job as a clinician or educator was to use the resources well, not to get them in the first place or to leverage them for additional resources. I came of age professionally in the 1960s, at a time of expanding opportunities—new universities, new hospitals, and new positions—when growth seemed limitless, and this mindset contributed to my presumptions about resources being "givens."

This way of thinking seems positively antiquated in the 21st century because we've recently experienced the greatest economic downturn since the Great Depression, and just about everyone in our society is aware of the ephemeral nature of funding. But even as we've collectively come to realize how limited our resources are at present, my old belief—that using resources well is noble but actually getting them is grubby—continues to characterize the thinking of too many of us. This old-fashioned thinking is something we have to confront if we expect to exert leadership.

How did my thinking about generating resources change over time? It began to change in the 1980s when I received $25,000 for the Kellogg National Fellowship to support my individual development plan for the three-year period of the grant and learned firsthand that having resources one can direct over time causes one to be very creative in making each dollar stretch as far as possible. Before, I had always worked in settings that were "use it or lose it" by the end of each fiscal year, so I learned to be creative in not giving money back, but until this fellowship I hadn't learned how to leverage what I have to get additional resources. Concurrent with this fellowship, I chaired a department where I didn't have any budget under my control. All expenses were paid centrally and there wasn't any funding available to cover what I thought was important, so the only way I could get resources for some needed faculty development was to sell the best coffee in the building. These twin experiences taught me how infantilized one feels if one believes that one has the responsibility for strengthening faculty and staff capabilities but has not one cent under his or her control and that even small amounts of entrepreneurial money can make a difference.

But my big "ah-ha" moment came when I was an officer of Sigma Theta Tau International. In the 1980s, the organization had forged an innovative Ten-Year Plan focused on the development of nurse leadership through three major goals—knowledge development, knowledge dissemination, and knowledge utilization—that culminated in the building of the International Center for Nursing Scholarship. As members of the organization sought to construct a headquarters that would serve the profession, we realized that resource development needed to be added as a fourth goal or we wouldn't be able to achieve the other three (Watts, 1997, p. 37). You can talk all you want about nurses as knowledge workers, but you won't be able to accomplish much without the proper supports, financial and otherwise.

In the ensuing years, I learned many other lessons about developing, managing, and leveraging resources: Resource development takes many forms other than money, but money is important . . . Like so many other aspects of leadership, you cannot just hold those with administrative titles responsible for resource development; it is a responsibility that belongs in some sense to everyone . . . There is a power in knowing how much things actually cost, using that knowledge to make reasonable decisions, and involving others in doing the same . . . You don't have to be wealthy to be a philanthropist, but being a philanthropist is part of becoming a leader.

Understanding the Resource Base

To achieve organizational goals, you need to deploy resources strategically, but many of us have not been taught to think in those terms. Economics isn't normally part of our undergraduate or graduate programs. (I was recently at a meeting of nurse leaders and when asked what they all needed to know more about, the majority wished they had had more of an economics background.) The nursing process is concerned with assessment, intervention, and evaluation but not resource development per se. I was taught to identify all of a patient's needs and meet as many as I could, rather than to triage in all circumstances. That aiming for the ideal, noble as the intentions were, left many of us ill-prepared to distinguish between what's possible given the constraints on time and other resources and what's not, a talent you need in deploying resources strategically. The reality is that triaging is an everyday requirement of life because you face resource limitations on a daily basis and have to be strategic about where you are going to direct your time, talent, and treasure.

On the whole, we nurses see ourselves as deserving, therefore entitled to resources, so we may get annoyed when they are not provided and we do not know how to change the situation for ourselves. Nurse researchers are encouraged to get grants, but they may not fully understand the importance of that revenue stream and the value of peer review in confirming what good ideas should be pursued. Administrators are taught to read and prepare budgets, but that functional skill isn't the same thing as broadly understanding the various revenue streams available, knowing how to deploy resources strategically to achieve the most important institutional goals, recognizing growth areas amenable to new initiatives, and figuring out incentives that encourage moving in an innovative and important direction.

When you fully realize that you cannot just take resources for granted, you begin to recognize the importance of understanding the structure of the resource base so that you can begin to manipulate it to support your goals. If you understand how various programs reimburse for care, then you are in a better position to figure out how to organize services to maximize reimbursement. For example, our hospital network's contract with the leading insurance provider in our state stipulates that we have to achieve the highest level of quality care to obtain the highest level of reimbursement, and the difference is a seven-figure sum. Nurses who understand how they contribute directly to these quality goals are in a better position to value their services in various negotiations. I have seen effective nurse leaders argue successfully that the orientation of every new nurse costs the organization thousands of dollars, so unit managers should be entitled to those monies for other career-ladder activities if they can save that expenditure with improved retention.

I used to think that because I worked for a public university my school was state supported, and it was, but not at the level I first thought. Over my tenure as dean, the percentage of state support dropped dramatically as government revenues were either diverted to other priorities (K-12 education and jails) or (more recently) declined. And when you did the economic modeling to see how much tuition and various other fees really covered, you realized that it was only a fraction of total instructional costs, with the gap much larger in educating graduate students where student–teacher ratios are smaller. Knowing what the real instructional costs were led me to argue for a different tuition structure, one that was more mindful of how expensive professional education is and one more in keeping with what was already the case in all the other professional schools.

What you learn about financing will vary depending on the setting where you work, but the more you know about such matters, the more you can learn to argue on behalf of what is important to you. My education was geared toward clinical and research excellence, not resource management, but I learned that organizations can be very helpful in educating you to learn about these matters if you express interest. When I first became a dean, I asked the chief financial officer of the campus to help me in understanding how we could make better use of resources, and he offered to put together a three-person task force to assist me in assessing management processes and fiscal controls. The team he convened made many suggestions and over time I implemented the majority of them. What I also got from them was their continuing interest in the school. As we improved our bottom line, I thanked them repeatedly for their part in making this happen, and they continued to be helpful to us.

My point is that you do not have to be a financial whiz to deploy resources strategically, but you cannot be an effective leader if you don't at least try to appreciate your area's assets and liabilities and those of the organization in which you operate. Not only have I used university experts to take a look at our state of affairs, but I have also asked savvy members of our board of advisors to provide feedback in their areas of expertise. Most people are willing to be helpful, and I find that you learn a great deal by asking several people for advice. Listening to the advice you receive from the first person helps you phrase the questions better when you ask the second or third person for suggestions, and the answers collectively point you usually in a looked-for direction.

Part of understanding the resource base for what you do is recognizing how your organization makes available additional resources. Is there some rule of thumb for dispensing discretionary monies based on how well the market is doing? One of the hospitals where I have worked has made a commitment to become a center of excellence in critical care, and foundation support is only likely to be given to projects that move that major goal forward, so you would be wise to propose only new initiatives that focus in that direction. There were some years when my campus had discretionary funding to encourage partnerships only in set areas (e.g., informatics), so the school of nursing worked to develop initiatives in those areas of shared concern. To move schools in certain directions—for example, in the development of web-based courses or electronic portfolios—the campus also would have to make some resources available for demonstration projects. If I thought we would all have to move eventually in these directions, I was eager to take the lead because the school profited from having both new monies for a pilot program and the goodwill of central administration for being venturesome.

Resources Take Many Forms

Resource development takes many forms besides someone presenting you with a check. Short (1997) studied the resources that administrators of schools of nursing thought they needed to achieve their goals, and the top 10 resources mentioned in descending order were communication skills, interpersonal skills, creativity in thinking, ability to mobilize groups, intellectual ability, academic credentials, willingness to take risks, credibility within the profession, innovativeness, and collegial support. Access to economic resources was surprisingly ranked only 14th. What may be more telling than the findings per se is that the 24-item questionnaire used in this study had only one item concerned with economic matters per se, either suggesting that the researchers involved over time in this line of inquiry (Kinsey, 1986; Short, 1997; Vance, 1977) prized intangibles over tangibles or assuming that you need the former to parlay them into the latter, which you do.

The most obvious nonmonetary resource is development of people, and you don't always need additional dollars to improve the situation of your constituents. You can help them develop new skills by taking advantage of the opportunities that already exist within the organization through human resources, marketing, and other departments; for example, I have encouraged novice managers to attend university minicourses on how to supervise others. You can create interest groups so that like-minded individuals already working for the organization can use each other to improve their tracking of policy or writing skills. You can ease entry into the setting through big brother–sister and little brother–sister pairings. You can build an advisory board to forge new connections with valued stakeholders; what board members contribute at organized meetings is often less important than having easy access to them for individual consultation when you need help in their areas of expertise.

If you work in a clinical setting, then increasing the number of patients who prefer to come to your setting is an aspect of resource development because more business usually translates later on into more money and clinical clout. If you work in an academic setting, you may consider expanding your resource base by figuring out how to repackage courses and sections of existing courses as certificate programs or how to tie together continuing-education offerings so that they add up to course credit that's a "come-on" for the next degree. Cultivating alumni and retirees is a valuable asset because both groups may be willing and experienced volunteers. Not only is the goodwill of these constituents important, but also their appreciation that may translate into philanthropic donations at a later time.

Part of resource development may include working with state legislators and your congressional delegation to develop new programs in support of nursing and health care. Lobbying for workforce supports at the local or national level can make a big difference in the number of nurses entering the field or the number of faculty available to teach them. Sometimes resource development means working with elected officials to include an earmark for a special project in pending legislation. Another strategy that can be advantageous is to seek waivers of existing regulations so that a new way of using nurses to manage care can be tried and reimbursed without rules changing permanently before the innovation is proven successful.

In this day and age, resource development must include collaboration and strategic partnerships. Instead of developing a new course when you don't have the faculty expertise, you can sometimes achieve the same goal by adopting one that's suitable and already on the books in another school. Collaboration is most likely to be successful if all parties make financial or in-kind contributions to the overall enterprise, recognizing that the total is so much more than each could have mustered separately. The Robert Wood Johnson Foundation (2004) has come to require such leveraging of resources in many of their grant awards. For example, their *Colleagues in Caring* Project required participating partners to amass a certain amount of resources just for an application to be competitive initially. Of the 23 statewide and multicounty consortiums created, the ones that were most successful had collaborators highly invested in the partnership. In my experience, it is better to work out in detail how any collaboration will work before there are any profits to divide; in the beginning all partners have hopes and are most likely to be even-handed about how to proceed.

The point I'm making about resource development is that you have to be creative in recognizing what is a resource and in parlaying small resources into something more substantial. The Biblical parable of the loaves and fishes is a lesson in leadership: You always begin with less than you need to achieve your aspirational goals, so you have to either reconfigure or expand the resource base to move in the desired direction. Once you get over thinking that resources are "not my problem" and realize that creative wheeling and dealing can be generative, then you can unleash your ingenuity. Not every idea is going to work; that's why you need trusted colleagues to dampen your enthusiasm appropriately. But once you take on the identity that you have to be *resourceful* to accomplish your goals and realize your values, then thinking that way can actually be fun.

A Shared Responsibility

Thinking about how you can be resourceful is certainly preferable to believing that you cannot do anything if others don't provide you with all the resources you need to do a good job; the latter approach only leaves you paralyzed. Believing in resourcefulness as a component of leadership means that the burden of finding resources doesn't have to fall just on the designated top administrator's shoulders. It is a shared responsibility. All who claim to be leaders, whether or not they have an administrative title, have some obligation to be resourceful. Not only does this mean coming up with ideas yourself, but it also means getting others to begin to think that way, too.

Not everyone even "sees" resources, so I think a leader needs to assist others in doing so. I have observed departments where the university was willing to make a spousal hire and the faculty treated this offer as an imposition—being pushed to hire someone they didn't want to hire—instead of as an additional resource. The person was qualified, but people wanted to hold out for the "best person impossible" and in the process lost an opportunity that would not come that way again. I've known people who resisted being sent to a summer leadership program, all expenses paid, because it would be time consuming. In both cases, I believe that the opportunities were not presented as wonderful resources, so the individuals concerned saw them only as impositions.

In a world that is increasingly driven by the need for cost-effective outcomes, it behooves all of us who expect to exert leadership to be able to say how we contribute to the resource base of our institutions. Do we bring in a portion of our salaries through grants, credit hours taught, new efficiencies, the cost savings created by a reduction of infections and falls, partnerships made, a practice plan, entrepreneurial ventures, or fund-raising? I am not saying that each person needs to raise enough resources to pay his or her salaries and benefits, but the world is quickly moving in that direction, and we have to get ready for that eventuality. I am convinced that nurses have to be identified as revenue producers to be valued (Stepura & Miller, 1989), and seeing yourself that way puts a spring in your step because you do feel valuable and you begin to talk differently about what you contribute to the organization. The more you can articulate the added value you provide, the more you have avoided having anyone else dismiss you as merely a cost and not a benefit.

Understanding how each of us contribute to the resource base of our institutions is one part of the equation, and knowing something about the real costs of doing business is the essential other half. I grew up in a family where my father always gave my mother his paycheck for her to manage the home. She did a wonderful job of making the most of his salary, but she regularly claimed to get almost everything on sale. She would bring home new purchases and immediately cut off the tags, so he wouldn't know the real price and argue with her about whether the items were needed. When she died, he really was at a disadvantage in that he didn't know what things actually cost. I think you can manage reality better if you understand what you get for your money and forgo magical thinking about nonexistent bargains.

The broader truth of this approach was proven to me when our university adopted responsibility-centered management. A financial philosophy that places accountability with the decision makers at the least centralized point possible provides strong incentives for income generation and encourages a longer planning horizon because you can save money for a big project without losing it (Barr, 2002; Stocum & Rooney, 1997). Yes, it's a system with a number of flaws. However, I feel about it the way Churchill did when he said, "Democracy is the worst form of government except for all those others that have been tried." What I liked about the system was that it put the school' leadership in control of school of nursing finances—you got all the revenues, you paid all the bills, and you paid taxes in support of centralized services (e.g., library, maintenance, utilities, and president's office). What I disliked was that we all had to give up any residual fantasies that we clung to about someone else saving us from having to keep resources and expenses in balance.

Even when I had sizable budget shortfalls, which I did early on, I found that I preferred being responsible for figuring out next steps, rather than being micromanaged by someone in central administration.

In the process, we all learned a great deal. This kind of system works best if there is an information-rich environment, so I sent out annual financial letters describing our situation with appropriate graphs and tables, making the community more engaged as a whole in using resources wisely (McBride, Neiman, & Johnson, 2000). For example, as faculty became more familiar with the variability in course costs, some took to heart trying to figure out what made some more cost effective than others, and understanding these differences led to positive changes. In this kind of system, you are more likely to audit your success in using resources to meet academic goals than when you are just concerned with a financial audit. As a result of the overall transparency that the approach encouraged, we all became savvier about shaping our future, certainly more so than we had been when we didn't know much about these kinds of things. I knew attitudes were changing when a longtime faculty member on our Budgetary Affairs Committee, who did not suffer fools lightly, proudly recounted how she had told colleagues elsewhere on campus that they weren't as careful in managing their resources as the school of nursing was!

An organization that encourages entrepreneurial behavior supports the creativity and innovation that have long been associated with leadership, and it helps if you have incentives in place to promote such inventiveness. Some clinical units are beginning to consider a reward structure for achieving quality-improvement goals that translate into dollars saved. I know of schools of nursing where you can increase your salary by a set percentage for the duration of an externally funded grant/contract. At my school, I developed a formula whereby grants/contracts benefitted both principal investigators and their departments, so individual success in grant writing had positive consequences for one and all.

To reward excellence and encourage productivity, I did away with across-the-board salary increases for faculty and staff and made salary increases much more merit based than they had been. All concerned could apply for merit consideration, and there were three different levels of merit possible to reward a range of achievements in teaching, research, and professional/university service. The applications were peer reviewed, with administration stipulating how much money was available and monitoring the process to ensure even-handedness. Some merit was given out in base-pay increases—when your base pay is increased, it becomes the gift that keeps on giving over the years because one jump in pay changes the base for the next increase—and some in one-time bonuses, thus providing more ways to reward different performance levels. We even gave some bonus money out to reward high performance over more than a year. Not everyone was pleased with the process, but the majority believed it to be fair. And from my point of view, our limited resources were deployed in a way that encouraged innovation and productivity.

When resource development is a shared responsibility, you truly begin to think differently. It's not just the chief nurse officer or school of nursing dean who is concerned about the deployment and leveraging of resources. Everyone is expected to take the matter personally. Scientists understand how their grants and contracts contribute to the school. Master teachers take on the problem of meeting the need for specialty education without simultaneously multiplying the number of unaffordable small classes. Managers take seriously bargaining with vendors for services. A staff person tells you about a wealthy person she knows through church who might be interested in contributing to a fund-raising campaign. The advantage of embracing a *village* approach to resource development is that you get many, many more good ideas than any one person can envision. You need to think creatively about resource development now that we are living in a period in which government has empty coffers because growth isn't likely to come from the public sector.

One caveat is in order if all concerned are going to be involved in resource development, particularly in this time of recessionary forces. You won't get others involved if they believe that you only talk shared responsibility but have amassed a disproportionate share of the resources yourself. It is important that others believe belt tightening affects you, too. For example, our hospital network has weathered the latest round of financial troubles with morale relatively high, in part because the top administrators took a 10% decrease in salary before other fiscal measures were implemented. During one of my first rounds of cost-cutting as a new dean, I sold the company car that deans had historically driven; the amount of savings was modest, but the gesture got me an enormous amount of goodwill.

Philanthropy and Philanthropists

I talked earlier in this chapter about the many forms that resource development can take—redeploying cost savings, grants/contracts, forging partnerships, repackaging products to capture another market, and lobbying for new earmarks—but the one where I had the most to learn was going after philanthropic dollars. The thought of asking people for money struck me as venal and unprofessional, and I was not a money-grubbing person. My thinking was profoundly changed by a couple of things. First, I was on the board of Sigma Theta Tau International starting from the time we first considered building a headquarters through the time we dedicated the completed structure (1983–1989), and I saw what nursing collectively achieved with philanthropic dollars. Second, the more I understood the financing of my school and even the financing of the hospital, the more I came to appreciate the need for philanthropic dollars to support initiatives that were impossible to realize in other ways. Let me elaborate on both these influences.

When we first conducted a feasibility study to see if we could raise enough money to build what became the International Center for Nursing Scholarship, the results were sobering. We needed to raise about $4 million, and findings suggested that the figure was higher than we could raise. The estimate of what we could raise was conservative because organized nursing had little experience with fund-raising in the 1980s, and those interviewed for the feasibility study didn't know if nurses would contribute to a campaign and if non-nurses would be supportive. The board at the time decided to go forward with the campaign believing that there would be more support than could be predicted. By the time the mortgage was paid off in 1991, over $5 million had been raised (Watts, 1997, p. 88). About half was given by non-nurses interested in civic development—individuals and foundations/companies wanting to encourage locating the headquarters in Indianapolis. The other half was donated by individual nurses and Sigma Theta Tau chapters. Individuals made donations of varying sizes in part so that their names or those of special others could be engraved for posterity on columns, windows, and bricks. Chapters held fund-raisers so that their division of Sigma Theta Tau International would be part of building this "home" for nursing. Virginia Woolf wrote about women needing "A Room of One's Own," and nurses began to talk about a home of their own. This campaign taught me that big things can be accomplished by banding together and that non-nurses can care deeply about the development of nursing.

When I became the dean of a public university, I realized anew the importance of philanthropy as a revenue stream. Philanthropy was the way to get discretionary dollars for new initiatives (DeLellis, Kardos, & Langston, 1999). For example, the monies available for faculty salaries weren't enough to recruit a high-powered researcher so we could develop expertise in an important specialty, but raising money for an endowed professorship or chair allowed us to move in that direction. The fact that it was an endowed professorship lent prestige to the position, whereas the monies associated with the endowment, when combined with what was already in the budget, added up to enough to afford a senior person.

Philanthropy has been particularly important in raising monies for a new building or the refurbishing of an old one, as evidenced by Sigma Theta Tau International's experience and that of many hospitals. In schools of nursing, the funding of endowed professorships and chairs has been an important vehicle to support the senior scientists capable of building programs of scholarship. For example, the number of endowed professorships and chairs in the United States climbed from 20 in 1984 to 262 in 2004, and the number continues to grow (Fitzpatrick, Fitzpatrick, & Dressler, 2005).

Just as others have, I learned that fund-raising for nursing requires you to explain the nature of nursing to many different stakeholders, lining up the values of our profession with what they value (Fitzpatrick, 2000; Fitzpatrick & Deller, 2000). You find out what they value by reading about the missions of foundations, learning about what corporations have donated to in the past, and finding out about their interests. If people do not understand how nursing brings to fruition what is important to them, then you have to point out the connection. Doing this can be upsetting when you find out that many people think nursing is under medicine and not a discipline in its own right. But doing this can be uplifting, as when you find out how grateful a family is because a nurse once made a difference in their lives.

An external advisory board can be helpful in connecting you with non-nurses in the community (Appel, Campbell, Lynch, & Novotny, 2007), introducing you both to individuals who might be interested eventually in helping you and to the way such connections are made in the community. For example, the chair of my school's advisory board, Marge Tarplee, suggested that she sponsor me for membership in Rotary International so that I could begin to mingle with business influentials. She also recommended other members of the board who were either known philanthropists or CEOs of community foundations. When you get into fund-raising, you realize that it is first and foremost about building relationships, "friend raising," something nurses know how to do as part of their stock and trade.

As with all relationship-based approaches, there is no quick fix. You have to build a relationship before someone wants to make an investment in you. The thing is that you never know what relationship will convert into major financial support. I have asked well-to-do individuals for support without success, only to receive a five-figure check or a bequest from someone I'd never met who hadn't before made a contribution larger than $100. I have lobbied an estate-planning lawyer for support of nursing; he never varied in his support of medicine, but he was once asked, by another lawyer, which school of nursing his wealthy client should support, and he recommended our school. This connection eventually led to a multimillion-dollar gift. What is true of day-to-day nursing practice is also true of nursing philanthropy: You need to treat everyone with respect and kindness because you never know what long-term difference your actions will make.

In my fund-raising experience, I learned a number of things:

- You have to "look alive" for people to want to invest in you; that is why telling the story of what you are doing in brochures, magazines, Web sites, radio/television interviews, and the like is important.
- Good stewardship—public recognition of contributors, invitations to participate in interesting events, thank-you notes and calls from those benefitting from funding, and honoring benefactors—is a good investment because satisfied supporters are the group most likely to make repeat contributions.
- You need to bake philanthropy into the culture—encouraging graduation and reunion classes to make a group gift, honoring retirees with contributions to scholarships in their name, and recognizing extraordinary personnel with monies that they can distribute to support philanthropy within the institution.

Most of all, I learned how important it is to create an appealing mission statement that asserted our values, described what prevented realization of those values, outlined what ought to be done to change the situation, and affirmed that we had the ability to move in that direction. To my great fortune, my university established a Center on Philanthropy to increase understanding of philanthropy and improve its practice (http://www.philanthropy.iupui.edu), and that Center's Fund Raising School provided classes to help deans understand how to make the case statement for needed resources more clearly and forcefully than in the past. In learning to write this case statement, what we really wound up doing was to take a fresh look at where we were and where we were going, aka strategic planning. The resulting statement helped establish agreement inside the organization, provided a backdrop for developing fund-raising materials, and created a basis for priority setting and institutional evaluation. The point is that you need to know where you are headed and why you want to go there before you can convince anyone to join forces with you. If you are excited about the prospects ahead, that is to the good, because your own enthusiasm can engage others.

Fund-raising didn't come easy to me because I still remember when the Ivy League universities went coed at the end of the 1960s and there was a great deal of talk about whether the future husbands of these coeds would contribute to their wives' alma maters. The assumption was that women wouldn't have the money to give in their own right. The world has changed dramatically since then and we have learned many things which are particularly relevant to a profession still largely peopled by women:

- Female employment is not only up but paying better than ever before.
- Women's longevity also makes them more likely to end up in control of their husbands' assets.
- Women are particularly drawn to philanthropic activities that provide a way to forge community and socialize; they also feel a strong responsibility to help those who have less.
- Volunteering is a predictor of women's giving.
- There is evidence that women are more generous than men, particularly to educational causes (Krotz, 2009; Shaw & Taylor, 1995).

In my own dealings with women nurses, I have found that some of us do continue to think of ourselves as not likely to be philanthropists for a variety of reasons—we may still feel poor even after that is really no longer the case or we may believe that we already "gave at the office," for our life of professional service is a gift of sorts. After years of growing up in modest circumstances, it took me a while to think of myself as a philanthropist, but over time, I found the notion of joining forces with others to accomplish something bigger than we could do otherwise increasingly attractive, so I began to see such giving as another aspect of leadership.

My personal philanthropic investment deepened as I came to serve on various community boards; Pesut (2007) talks about something similar happening to men in nursing. Leadership on boards brings with it the expectation, stated or unstated, of financial support. At the onset, I thought I could "get away" with imparting my wisdom, rather than parting with my money, but I soon realized that if you want to be viewed as a leader, then you have to act the way other community leaders do. Over time, I even agreed to do some extra paid consultation just so I could get additional resources to give away to my favorite causes. In hindsight, I am convinced that my board-level support of a hospital foundation eventually played a role in my being asked to join the board of their consolidated hospital network, a policy position of the first order.

This chapter stresses that you have to play a role in resource development if you wish to play a larger role in shaping an organization. If you want to be influential, you cannot hide behind arguing that it's your job only to use resources wisely rather than being the person to get them in the first place. How much you take on of resource development will vary depending on setting and inclination, but minimally you have to become familiar with how your institution's resource base is managed and deployed so that you can figure out how your work fits into these processes. Creativity in this day and age requires not only good ideas but some thought as to how these ideas can be actualized with resources. Nurses in hospitals, universities, and other settings should play an active role in any fund-raising campaigns mounted by their institutions to ensure that their priorities are front and center as the public is engaged.

Key Take-Away Points

- Nurses have to be *resourceful* to accomplish their goals and realize their values.
- Resource development is essential to organizational effectiveness, so it must be an expectation of professional leadership and not just a responsibility of those with administrative titles. You won't, however, get others involved in resource development if they believe that you only talk shared responsibility but have a disproportionate share of the resources.
- It is important to understand the resource base of the organization where you work so you know how to direct time, talent, and treasure in support of your goals.
- Resource development can take many forms, from helping others take advantage of opportunities already in place and developing strategic partnerships to lobbying for new programs and fund-raising.
- An organization that encourages entrepreneurial behavior supports creativity, and it helps if you have incentives in place to reward innovation.
- Fund-raising requires you to explain the nature of nursing to stakeholders, lining up the values of our profession with what others value.
- You don't have to be wealthy to be a philanthropist, but being one is part of becoming a leader because board members are expected to support the organizations where they provide leadership.

REFERENCES

Appel, N., Campbell, S. H., Lynch, N., & Novotny, J. M. (2007). Creating effective external advisory boards for schools of nursing. *Journal of Professional Nursing, 23,* 343–350.

Barr, M. J. (2002). *The Jossey-Bass academic administrator's guide to budgets and financial management.* San Francisco: Jossey-Bass.

DeLellis, A. J., Kardos, E. G., & Langston, N. F. (1999). Development in schools of nursing. Fund-raising to further long-range strategic plans. *Nurse Educator, 24*(3), 29–34.

Fitzpatrick, J. J. (2000). Private support for nursing. What is the philanthropic appeal. In A. B. McBride (Comp.). *Nursing and philanthropy. An energizing metaphor for the 21st century* (pp. 65–77). Indianapolis, IN: Center Nursing Press.

Fitzpatrick, J. J., & Deller, S. S. (2000). *Fundraising skills for health care executives.* New York: Springer Publishing.

Fitzpatrick, J. J., Fitzpatrick, M. L., & Dressler, M. B. (2005). Endowed chairs and professorships in schools of nursing: A 2004 update. *Journal of Professional Nursing, 21,* 244–252.

Kinsey, D. C. (1986). The new nurse influentials. *Nursing Outlook, 34,* 238–240.

Krotz, J. L. (2009). *Making philanthropy count: How women are changing the world.* Indianapolis, IN: Women's Philanthropy Institute at the Center on Philanthropy at Indiana University.

McBride, A. B., Neiman, S., & Johnson, J. (2000). Responsibility-centered management: A ten-year nursing assessment. *Journal of Professional Nursing, 16*(4), 1–10.

Pesut, D. J. (2007). Leadership: How to achieve success in nursing organizations. In C. E. O'Lynn & R. E. Tranbarger (Eds.), *Men in nursing. History, challenges and opportunities* (pp. 153–168). New York: Springer Publishing.

Robert Wood Johnson Foundation. (2004). *Colleagues in Caring: Regional Collaboratives for Nursing Work Force Development.* Retrieved August 13, 2009, from http://www.rwjf.org/reports/npreports/colleagues.htm

Shaw, S. C., & Taylor, M. A. (1995). *Reinventing fundraising: Realizing the potential of women's philanthropy.* San Francisco: Jossey-Bass.

Short, J. D. (1997). Profile of administrators of schools of nursing, Part I: Resources for goal achievement. *Journal of Professional Nursing, 13*(1), 7–12.

Stepura, B. A., & Miller, K. (1989). Financial management series. Converting nursing care cost to revenue. *Journal of Nursing Management, 19*(5), 18–22.

Stocum, D. L., & Rooney, P. M. (1997). Responding to resource constraints: A departmentally based system of responsibility center management. *Change, 29*(5), 50–57.

Vance, C. N. (1977). A group profile of contemporary influentials in American nursing. *Dissertation Abstracts International 38,* 473B. (UMI No. DA7804472).

Watts, N. J. (1997). *The adventurous years: Leaders in action 1973–1993.* Indianapolis, IN: Center Nursing Press.

Chapter 9

Appreciating Others

There is no aspect of leadership that I enjoy more than helping others reach their potential. It is rewarding in a way that other things aren't because any investment in people pays dividends forevermore. And if your motivation is inclined to be more monetary, it is wise to remember that personnel cost is by far the biggest item in any service organization's budget, so maximizing the potential of employees is the best way to deliver value on investment. Help individuals achieve their career goals, and they tend to reciprocate, wanting to do their best for the institution. For me, appreciating others includes a broad range of behaviors—valuing the contributions of different kinds of people (from administrators and professionals to clerical staff and maintenance workers; from aides and LPNs to nurse administrators and nurse educators), all of whom contribute to achieving the institutional mission; developing some kind of clinical or academic career ladder so all concerned can continue to grow and develop throughout their careers; understanding that any investment in people can have a ripple effect because most people who have been helped to achieve their potential understand the obligation to "pay it forward" and mentor subsequent generations; and helping others be honored for what they are good at is enlightened self-interest because the reputation of individuals builds the reputation of the organization as a whole and our profession.

Sometimes when you are working hard to be professional yourself, you do not fully appreciate how important others are to the functioning of the organization. You may underestimate the skill and effort involved in cleaning a room full of equipment and people in a short period of time, the stress a secretary feels when one person is supposed to meet the clerical needs of two dozen faculty, or the complexities of getting billing right. Even if you are in the same profession as someone else, you tend unconsciously to value what you do in your position over what someone else does. And if someone is in a profession other than your own and you only see the person at meetings, you may start thinking that all they do is go to meetings, when you have a more complicated view of yourself even though you go to the same meetings. The reality is that most of us are sufficiently self-absorbed that we don't really appreciate all that others contribute to the organization, even when we wish we were more appreciated ourselves for what we do. All this is normal, but those who would be leaders need to rise above these tendencies. Being a leader means that you understand generally how the pieces fit together, so you can then work to maximize their functioning. If you don't understand how different people contribute to meeting the institutional mission, then you are rather indifferent to the issue of how they can be helped to do their jobs better.

Increasingly, the focus in service settings of all kinds (hospitals, clinics, community colleges, universities, government agencies, etc.) is on displaying the hallmarks of a learning organization—a spirit of inquiry undergirds a community-wide commitment to continuous quality improvement; all concerned are provided needed supports and feedback so that they can get better over time (Institute of Medicine [IOM], 2004, 2007). Service settings are aspiring in this direction because communities of learning tend to do better on key parameters, as is evidenced in the Magnet Hospital movement. Becoming a community of learning means that the leadership is involved in informing everyone about key initiatives and ways they will be asked to contribute, providing forums to find out about learning needs, encouraging additional education that allows the person to grow in the current position or move to one with more responsibility, and giving feedback that reinforces positive performance and encourages tackling the next level of development.

Many larger institutions have a tradition of paying for formal education that benefits the organization, and most have in-house learning opportunities to help staff master the complexities of new equipment, information technology systems, OSHA requirements, and other regulations. I think, however, that opportunities are too often mentioned in a scattershot fashion and not integrated into some overarching view of a community of learning that leaders might draw on in facilitating employees and in reaffirming appreciation for their efforts. Some institutions do make a point of using their house newsletter to share information about opportunities systematically, confirming in the process how important individual development is to the enterprise.

In my own experience, I tried to increase the number of developmental opportunities available to staff and faculty alike—creating a staff council so that clerical and professional staff could begin to articulate their needs (we already had a faculty council); sponsoring programs that help staff, faculty, and administrators build their skills; giving every faculty member some professional development monies to attend relevant conferences; allotting staff development monies to meet group concerns; and establishing awards that recognize staff and faculty excellence in key areas. We were limited financially in what we could do, but I learned in the process that everything you did to make people more effective and feel appreciated had a long-term effect in creating a caring (and productive) culture.

There were two relatively small things that I did in the spirit of building a community of learning that helped set the tone. First, I tried to reinforce that we were a community, and this meant that we appreciated everyone in the building, not just the faculty. I created a Person of the Month award open to everyone who worked there; the prize was lunch for two at our campus restaurant. There were some who thought the idea smacked too much of supermarket-style management, but I remember with special fondness what it meant to the housekeeper who donned her Sunday clothes and took her husband out to lunch where she worked and the faculty member who did the same with her son (she was very distinguished but a free lunch impressed her teenage son more than any other recognition had).

The other thing that I think was important in developing a sense of community had to do with explaining to different groups why the work of other people was important. That didn't mean that I made up something good to say about everyone, but I did try to help those who valued one set of abilities see the worth in others who were good at very different things. My paternal grandmother was widowed early and had to raise seven children (ages 2–16 years) on her own. Alas, she was so needy herself that she tended to invite confidences from her children by telling each one of them at various times what another sibling had said that was negative about him/her. As I watched her make herself the center of the family and saw how poorly her children got along with each other, I decided that I would try to spread either positive comments—"Just the other day, she was saying how gifted you are"—or at least accuracy.

In the spirit of appreciation, I tried to do all I could to thank colleagues who had made a difference in the life of the organization, for example, making the rounds after an accreditation visit to thank everyone personally for their contributions. In my office, I had a big drawer full of small things that I could whip out every time something special happened—"congratulations" banners to decorate someone's office after being notified that a grant application had been funded, individual packets of bath salts with names like "tranquility" or "serenity" to present to someone who had demonstrated aplomb in handling something difficult, pieces of chocolate labeled "euphoria" and "ecstasy" to accompany a note saying how happy I was at a contribution made, and so forth. Don't get me wrong, I didn't do this all the time in a way that others would find silly, but I did try to personalize my appreciation of others and found that even very distinguished colleagues appreciated little star earrings recognizing their stardom.

Probably the most substantive move made to appreciate faculty involved adoption in our promotion/tenure guidelines of Boyer's (1997) notion that the priorities of the professoriate should reflect the range of what faculties do. You shouldn't just value the scholarship of discovery, NIH-funded research, but should also value the scholarship of integration, the scholarship of application, and the scholarship of teaching. Concurrently, we affirmed that scholarship of any kind has to be judged by the same criteria, including use of appropriate methods, the achievement of significant results, communication of findings through refereed presentations and publications, and the ability to respond constructively to criticism (Glassick, 1997). What this move did was to demonstrate an appreciation of the range of faculty work, while holding each person responsible for meeting current performance expectations.

When I entered nursing, the focus wasn't on appreciation. It was a world more given to judgments than development. I would like to say that the world has changed dramatically since then, but new nurses still tell stories about how unwelcoming beginnings can be (Pellico, Brewer, & Kovner, 2009). Seasoned nurses can be harsh and cruel in their criticism of new nurses; it is often said that we "eat our young." Nurse managers may overlook such behavior for fear that any reprimands will only cause the experienced to leave; perhaps they do not have supervisors urging them to exert leadership rather than to maintain the status quo. There is still some sense of "if I had to go through this, then you do too," rather than an understanding of the fact that our collective professional aspirations will only be achieved when we confront the complexities of practice and proceed from a realistic view of what nurses need, if they are going to complete successfully the journey from novice to expert as either clinicians or academicians. Minimally, they need help with career transitions—moving from student to newly licensed RN, to individual contributor, to frontline manager, to manager of managers, to senior executive, or moving from graduate student to postdoc, to junior faculty, to senior faculty, and possibly, department chair or dean.

In all transitions, mentors are important in helping to negotiate changing situations and responsibilities (Vance & Olson, 1998).

Mentoring has been primarily associated with specialty preparation (Barker, 2006; Hayes, 2005) and research training (Byrne & Keefe, 2002; Maas et al., 2006). Unlike a classroom teacher who is charged with conveying specific knowledge and overseeing formal tests of ability, the mentor role is more amorphous, providing more personal help in understanding context, processes, and demand requirements. Mentor in Greek mythology was the wise advisor who helped Odysseus' son in the father's absence, but Mentor was also the form of Athena, goddess of wisdom, assumed to handle this assignment (Ragins & Kram, 2007). The androgynous nature of Mentor makes this figure a universal symbol of the help needed by all of us as we address new challenges: the mentor provides needed support by being available, being appreciative of individual differences, asking questions that clarify matters, telling you what you may not want to hear but doing it in such a way that you feel heard, facilitating skills development and networking, and celebrating achievements great and small (Lee, Dennis, & Campbell, 2007).

When I was growing up professionally, there wasn't much talk about mentors; sink or swim was the order of the day. There were times when I was expected to perform beyond my abilities, and it was a matter of either figure it out or have patients go without. As the profession began to confront the need for mentoring, the accent was on developing a special coaching relationship across the generations based on similarities— "I see in you what I was like when I was starting out and want to help you"—which comes to an end when the protégé becomes her/his own person. Early descriptions of the mentor stressed generosity rather than professional obligation; in some sense the senior person was doing you a favor. The notion that similarities brought you together and energized the relationship raised questions for many about how individuals of a different gender, culture, race, religion, generation, social class, or lifestyle fared in getting help (Manson, 2009; Toth, 1997). The emphasis on a time-limited relationship early in one's career disregarded the help needed at later transition points.

This is all changing, though not fast enough to suit me. I think we still haven't fully come to terms with the help professionals need in life after graduation in order to reach their full potential. We still think that the new graduate—whether the undergraduate entering the first professional position or the graduate student entering specialty practice or an academic career—should be capable of hitting the ground running without additional help. The more we think this way, the more we don't do anything systematic to change the situation and the more we have dispirited RNs leaving the profession burned out (Hill, 2009). If we take seriously the developmental needs already educated individuals continue to have, then we create institutional plans that provide what will assist their advancement because their continued growth and development means the same for the institution (Foley et al., 2003). Create a "development culture" and you are more likely to grow leaders in your own backyard (Meyers, 2007).

Mentoring has to be seen as a professional obligation all incur, not a nicety. There shouldn't be just one mentor in your life because you need to draw on a range of perspectives and abilities to understand and manage the complexities professionals now face (see Table 4.1 in chapter 4). Indeed, one of the major things a mentor does is to introduce you to others who can be of assistance. The time of intense connection will vary, with those helping you in getting a degree or special training occupying a special place because they welcomed you into the field or specialty, but all the connections made become part of your extended professional family and often can be accessed again and again as needed. Some mentors do, indeed, need to be "like you" because they have firsthand experience in dealing with challenges you may meet and their successes in the face of barriers suggest that you too can succeed. Some mentors need to be deliberately not "like you" so that you can be challenged by different perspectives to stretch goals and move beyond your comfort zone.

Bickel and Brown (2005) have written about the often overlooked generational differences that shape the mentor–mentee relationship, leading both sides to have different and sometimes conflicting expectations. Boomers (1945–1962) respect authority and believe in paying dues; Generation Xers (1963–1981) question authority and don't think that paying dues is relevant. The former may still view mentoring as a kindness, whereas the latter regard mentoring as a right, not a privilege; the former may be uncomfortable providing the frequent, frank feedback that the latter prefer. This can lead older professionals to go on about how unappreciative the younger generation is—"they don't make them like they used to"—with mutual withdrawal as the consequence instead of a generative relationship. Talking through expectations at the start can make all the difference, with both sides discussing expected outcomes and not getting bogged down in one set way to achieve these results.

It's important to target your mentoring style, so that you bring out the strengths of the younger generation who generally want to work *with* you as opposed to *for* you. Boomer mentors may even have difficulty appreciating what subsequent generations find relatively unproblematic; for example, Generation Xers accept diversity and use technology, and their successors, the Millennium Generation, celebrate diversity and assume technology (Thiefoldt & Scheef, 2004). The savvy mentor will take advantage of how comfortable these generations are with negotiating differences and virtualities.

As mentoring has evolved in importance, there has been increasing emphasis on linking it to an individual development plan (IDP) or personal development plan (PDP) as a way to get both mentor and mentee focusing on the same questions: What are the goals for the coming year or two? What actions will have to be undertaken to achieve these goals? What is the time frame for completion of various activities? What resources are needed to move the goals forward? What are the expected outcomes? Using the IDP, the mentoring relationship exists to realize desired outcomes of benefit both to the participants and to the organization in which they work.

The IDP has been used broadly to promote leadership in practice settings (University of Virginia Health System [UVAHS] Professional Nursing Staff Organization, 2008), universities (University of California, San Francisco [UCSF] Academic Affairs, 2009), government (Jacobson, 2008), professional organizations (International Council of Nurses [ICN], 2009), and professional programs (McBride, 2009). In the United Kingdom, all staff are required to have PDPs, and they have been found to work best when appraisal of learning needs is linked to additional development that is actually implemented (Berridge, Kelly, & Gould, 2007). Not surprisingly, they do not work as well if time isn't allocated for either the appraisal or the developmental follow-through because this implies that the institution doesn't see these activities as essential to its core business.

In the United States, postbaccalaureate nurse residency programs have proven to be useful in helping new graduates negotiate the first year of practice with less stress, more satisfaction, and improved organization and prioritization of care (Goode, Lynn, Krsek, & Bednash, 2009; Krugman et al., 2006). These programs include a number of features that build confidence and skills, including an ongoing relationship with a clinical coach. The Robert Wood Johnson Foundation (2009) has implemented something similar to help junior nursing faculty as they establish their programs of research and develop into master teachers. That Nurse Faculty Scholars Program requires each scholar to have an IDP and three mentors—a school of nursing mentor who assists the scholar in meeting the tripartite responsibilities of academia (teaching, research, and professional/institutional service) in a particular university; a university mentor not in nursing who helps the scholar develop an externally funded program of research and make interdisciplinary connections on campus; and a senior nurse elsewhere in the same (or a related) specialty who is expected to serve as a resource in enabling the scholar's line of inquiry to take shape and facilitate big-picture thinking.

One-on-one coaching is increasingly valued, but there is also more stress being placed institutionally on building mentoring structures that tackle generic problems. If all beginners have problems juggling priorities, how about starting a support group aimed at addressing the matter and exchanging helpful tips? If all doctoral students need to keep up with the literature and have their critical abilities honed, then it makes sense to begin a journal club. If a number of junior faculty are interested in improving their teaching, why not institute brown-bag lunches so the like-minded can share pedagogical techniques? The advantage of such groups is that each person is alternately both a resource and a recipient, learning from doing both. Problems that were once thought to be personal become normalized when you realize that everyone else is troubled by the same challenges and insecurities.

Structures that reinforce how each person is simultaneously a resource and a recipient are important because they counteract any notion that you have to be fully prepared before you can be of assistance to anyone else. Senior baccalaureate students can mentor first-year undergraduates; doctoral students nearing completion can provide tips to those starting out. One of the best presentations I ever heard on how to study came from a very pregnant undergraduate who started out saying, "I am about to have my third child and my oldest hasn't yet turned three, so I have to read and remember key facts, because I don't have the time to go back." Not only were her suggestions very pragmatic and helpful, but she also brought to the discussion an authority that no faculty member could.

This growing appreciation for the role of mentoring in professional development has led more enlightened institutions to establish not only mentoring structures but also mentoring policies and resources. For example, the University of Pennsylvania School of Nursing (2007) is clear in its faculty manual that mentoring is a "top priority" and one with relevance to all career stages. The Institute for Clinical Research Education at the University of Pittsburgh (2009) has established a mentoring resources web site that speaks about commonplace concerns with helpful suggestions, for example, how to give feedback. The Johns Hopkins University School of Nursing has tackled the problem of measuring the effectiveness of mentoring (Berk, Berg, Mortimer, Walton-Moss, & Yeo, 2005). In the aggregate, we are beginning to see wide-scale institutional recognition of the importance of providing for lifelong learning if professionals are going to develop the abilities expected of them in this day and age.

A significant number of institutional managers, however, still prefer to bemoan how unprepared their personnel are rather than to do something about the state of affairs. They think assuming institutional responsibility for the fact that people cannot hit the ground running is just the slippery slope to having to provide released time and resources for these developmental purposes. This is where leadership comes in as opposed to mere management. It takes leadership to fashion new approaches, and then measure the consequences, all the while believing that the situation can be improved to everyone's satisfaction. Thankfully, most institutions are realizing that keeping personnel who only get better with experience through mentoring is cost-effective because replacement costs may be even higher than developmental costs.

Although there is growing buy-in regarding the importance of mentoring when individuals are beginning their careers, there is less agreement about the developmental needs of senior clinicians and faculty. The more high ranking people become, the more self-conscious they may be about admitting developmental needs. Mentoring programs favor the young because any investment is likely to pay off in the long run. By the time individuals have been in an institution for a while, there may even be some sense that their personalities are encased in stone and they are not likely to change further even with investment.

This kind of thinking can be problematic because nursing has been a profession with constantly changing expectations, so there are long-standing employees who have watched as their institutions developed supports for new graduates, supports that weren't available to them when they started, and they feel cheated. I have had people complain to me about how much better off they would be if only they had had such opportunities, and I haven't always been sympathetic to their complaints because I wondered if they weren't just rationalizing their limited productivity. Although some of my initial thoughts were crotchety, I've had to admit that they had a point. I eventually came to think that it was worthwhile to ask them, "What do you need that maybe I can see about providing?" For those who had definite ideas about what to do, this strategy has paid off. One faculty member who hadn't been able to get a fundable score for her research grant said she regretted that no one at our institution was good in her area, so no wonder she hadn't been successful in obtaining external funding. I asked her whom she would like as a mentor, and in the spirit of Mundt's (2001) approach, we contracted with that person at another institution to provide mentoring over the next year, with impressive success. What is more, that triumph proved energizing, and the person began to assume more institutional responsibility for facilitating the development of others.

There are some opportunities for mid-career and senior clinicians and faculty to learn how to move to the next level of leadership development. The Institute of Medicine (2009) manages the Robert Wood Johnson Foundation's Health Policy Fellows Program, meant to provide mid-career health professionals with an opportunity to learn more about health policy. The Robert Wood Johnson Foundation's Executive Nurse Fellows Program is an advanced leadership opportunity for nurses in senior executive roles who aspire to shape the health care system of the future (Morjikian & Bellack, 2005). For over a quarter century, Johnson & Johnson has partnered with the Wharton School of Business (2009) in offering a program that encourages nurse executives "to think strategically and hone their leadership abilities." Harvard's Graduate School of Education (2009) offers various summer programs that provide senior administrators in academia with the leadership skills needed to foster meaningful institutional change.

Appreciating others includes giving feedback that is customized to the person. There is growing evidence that indiscriminate praise doesn't change behavior positively, particularly if the commendation is for something relatively immutable like being smart (Bronson & Merryman, 2009; Mueller & Dweck, 1998). An intelligent person repeatedly complimented for being smart might actually decide that it is wise not to be venturesome lest the next undertaking "bomb," demonstrating lack of common sense. What is effective is explicitly commenting on what people do well that is under their control, for example, effort, approach, and preparation. You don't say, "Yesterday's meeting went well; you were terrific," but you say, "I liked the way you handled yesterday's meeting, always bringing people back to the main issue and not allowing anyone to dominate the conversation."

Speak in generalities and a person starts discounting the compliment as hyperbole, cotton-candy enthusiasm. Notice the specific behavior that worked, and you've reaffirmed that you are aware of what makes that person special. The opposite is true too, I think. Overgeneralize in a negative direction and you just sound negative yourself. Say something about one issue that needs a different approach, and the person is likely to take the point seriously, particularly because you are not discounting everything else that person does. Studer (2003) recommends a 3:1 ratio of compliments to criticisms pointing out behavior in need of improvement.

I've said this before, but I think all of us want to be appreciated for what we are good at, so noticing specifics has much more meaning than an enthusiasm that could be gushingly generated about every nurse. And the more you are sensitive to particulars, the better prepared you are for writing letters of recommendation—a major leadership task (McBride & Lovejoy, 1995). The more senior you become, the more you are asked for your opinion, especially in the form of letters of reference, but many nurses do not know how to handle this task. Too many people just regurgitate facts already on the resume and don't add any opinions of value, so what they have to say isn't taken seriously. A good letter is one where you can tell something about how the person handled a situation that is illuminating about that person's character, commitment, sense of responsibility, decision making, focus, determination, compassion, and/or respectful demeanor. The anecdote recounted informs the reader about how special the individual is and complements the condensed information available on the CV about educational preparation, positions held, grant funding, and the like.

I have long believed that one of the obligations of leaders in our field is to actively help deserving colleagues be recognized for their accomplishments. To the extent that our profession has not always been appreciated for its contributions to health care and the world of ideas, I have regarded it as my responsibility to remedy the situation by highlighting excellence in my backyard. In thinking this way, I was very influenced by a talk that psychologist Sandra Lipsitz Bem (1983) gave at a long-ago meeting of the American Academy of Nursing. The theme was "Image-Making in Nursing," and she discussed how women's accomplishments often are undervalued in comparison to the identical performance of men, but that prejudice disappears if the woman is described as "a winner." Her advice was to work to get nurses to be perceived as "blue-ribbon" quality.

This advice made sense to me because what she said generally about women holds for nursing even now that the number of men in nursing has increased exponentially. If a nurse is recognized for clinical excellence, then the person nominating him has to describe what he has done in some detail. This depiction makes the work visible within the institution when the honor is noted in the house newsletter and within the community when mention is made in the local newspaper. The person so recognized is pleased to be appreciated, and colleagues in the institution feel proud to be in the company of an award-winning associate. Academic institutions are particularly mindful of the importance of award-winning faculty members because their successes adds directly to the reputation of the university.

There are people who are genuinely embarrassed to be singled out for praise, but they have to understand that the recognition isn't just personal. I regularly asked those who reported to me directly what award I might nominate them for, and I can remember a department chair saying to me, "I don't care about such things," to which I replied à la Rhett Butler in the movie version of *Gone with The Wind*, "Frankly, my dear, I don't give a damn; what I care about is that our institution is full of award-winning people." Obviously, I was being glib because I do care that my colleagues feel good about their personal career successes, but I also wanted to make the larger point, which even a modest person can understand.

I've never nominated anyone for an honor that I didn't believe he/she deserved. I do not make up things that aren't true, and not telling the truth is a sure way to lose one's own reputation. But there is an art to assembling facts in such a way that they tell a powerful story about the impact a person has had. I also found that working with colleagues as we assembled a convincing application served the developmental purpose of helping them to understand better the connections in the work they'd completed. In articulating what they had accomplished, they were able to see links that hadn't been obvious before, enabling them to have a better sense of logical next steps. In the spirit of chapter 5, they were able to name their contributions, making them clearer about where they were headed.

Whatever skill I've developed in this respect is largely thanks to Doris Merritt, the first acting director of what is now the National Institute of Nursing Research, who successfully nominated me to become a distinguished professor of the university. I had been nominated previously by nurse colleagues but never found out how the dossier fared because it was a secret university committee and you didn't even know who the members were. As an associate dean in our School of Medicine (after retiring from NIH) and someone with decades of political savvy, Dr. Merritt was able to find out that my application was found lacking in certain respects.

Over a number of weeks, she then helped me learn how to present my work in women's health so that it sounded more scholarly and less ideological. She urged me to get external letters of support from colleagues in other fields who valued my work, not just from nurses. My eyes teared up more than once as she helped me describe my work in words that countered prevailing stereotypes about women's studies as frothy science. I was angry that I had to accommodate to the prejudices of others (not looking like a feminist), but all her advice was excellent even when I didn't want to hear it. I benefitted from the fact that this highly respected physician was willing to help me tell my story in words that others could hear, and the application was successful. I told her that I could never thank her enough for what she had done for me, but I would certainly "pass on" the favor. And I have; three other nurse colleagues went on to become distinguished professors.

Because part of appreciating others is appreciating those who helped you advance, I am pleased to say that I went on to nominate Dr. Merritt for several honors that she richly deserved. One of the things I did within the School of Nursing was to establish the Doris Merritt Award to recognize someone, not in our field, who has contributed to the realization of the values of our profession. This proved to be a very sought-after award because she was highly respected in the community. It gave me a great deal of pleasure to tell a couple of physician colleagues who asked how you get that award, "You have to be nicer to nurses than you have been thus far, but this can be one of your career goals."

During the years when I was an officer of Sigma Theta Tau International, I learned how important it is to have awards that recognize the range of what nurses do—awards recognizing clinical excellence, research prowess, leadership abilities, masterful teaching, technological advancements, writing skill, mentoring, and so forth. In having a range of awards, you affirm that the field is varied, offering career opportunities in different areas. A national or international organization should have ways to recognize excellence in the areas promoted by the professional association, but so should local or regional organizations. The more that different aspects of nursing are honored, and the more nurses are nominated and win interdisciplinary honors, the more perceptions of our field by others will be updated steadily in a positive direction.

To accomplish what I've talked about in this chapter however, requires all of us to get over any residual feelings we might harbor about losing ground when others are recognized. Envy is a dangerous emotion because it breeds resentment. Someone else is described in glowing terms and you feel empty. I think you have to feel appreciated enough so that you don't begrudge others praise, otherwise it seeps out when you least expect, leaving you inclined to be spiteful. Leaders have to get over inclinations in this direction because the success of others doesn't mean you are less successful. If those who work with you thrive in the process, then it only builds your reputation as a leader.

Because not all of us are saints capable of giving without some reciprocity, I do think it behooves all of us to remember to thank our mentors (and bosses) in meaningful ways—seeing that they are nominated for appropriate honors, recognizing their contributions when we are honored, and dedicating something to them. I do believe that helping others is a professional obligation and not something you should do only out of kindness, but it is reinforcing when the recipient of mentoring appreciates the kindness that has gone into the process. Appreciation of those who helped you along the way doesn't make what you have accomplished any less your own; expressions of gratitude only prove that you are a leader yourself. You have reached the point where you can identify the specifics of what a senior person did that proved helpful.

Key Take-Away Points

- Appreciating others includes a broad range of behaviors—valuing the contributions of different kinds of people, developing some kind of career ladder so all continue to grow and develop throughout their careers, understanding that investments in people have a ripple effect because those who have been helped tend to "pay it forward" and mentor others, and honoring colleagues in a way that builds the reputation of the organization as a whole and our profession.
- Service settings are increasingly expected to display the hallmarks of a learning organization—the culture reinforces a community-wide commitment to continuous quality improvement; hence, all are provided with needed support and specific feedback so that they can get better over time.
- Mentoring is important at all career transitions. The mentor provides needed support by being available, appreciating individual differences, asking questions that clarify issues, telling you what you may not want to hear but doing it in such a way that you feel heard, facilitating development and networking, and celebrating achievements.
- Mentoring is a professional obligation, not a nicety, and institutional policies should support the development of mentoring structures.
- Even as a person seeks support to handle the next developmental challenge, that person should be serving as a mentor to others less educated and less experienced.
- Women's accomplishments have often been undervalued in comparison to the identical performance of men, but this tendency disappears when a woman is described as a "winner." This phenomenon suggests that it is important to recommend colleagues for appropriate honors to reinforce that nurses are of "blue-ribbon" quality.

- If those who work with you thrive and are recognized for their excellence, it builds your reputation as a leader.
- Appreciating others also means valuing what your seniors have done to help your advancement and building a "development culture."

REFERENCES

Barker, E. R. (2006). Mentoring—A complex relationship. *Journal of the American Academy of Nurse Practitioners, 18,* 56–61.

Bem, S. L. (1983). The making of images: A psychological perspective. In C. A. Williams (Ed.), *Image-making in nursing* (pp. 39–45). Kansas City, MO: American Nurses' Association.

Berk, R. A., Berg, J., Mortimer, R., Walton-Moss, B., & Yeo, T. R. (2005). Measuring the effectiveness of faculty mentoring relationships. *Academic Medicine, 80,* 66–71.

Berridge, E.-J., Kelly, D., & Gould, D. (2007). Staff appraisal and continuing professional development. *Journal of Research in Nursing, 12*(1), 57–70.

Bickel, J., & Brown, A. J. (2005). Generation X: Implications for faculty recruitment and development in academic health centers. *Academic Medicine, 80,* 205–210.

Boyer, E. L. (1997). *Scholarship reconsidered: Priorities of the professoriate.* San Francisco: Jossey-Bass.

Bronson, P., & Merryman, A. (2009). *NurtureShock: New thinking about children.* New York: Hachette Book Group.

Byrne, M. W., & Keefe, M. R. (2002). Building research competence in nursing through mentoring. *Journal of Nursing Scholarship, 34,* 391–396.

Foley, B. J., Redman, R. W., Horn, E. V., Davis, G. T., Neal, E. M., & Van Riper, M. L. (2003). Determining nursing faculty development needs. *Nursing Outlook, 51,* 227–232.

Glassick, C. E. (1997, January 18). *Scholarship assessed.* Retrieved September 7, 2009, from http://www.ugc.edu.hk/eng/doc/ugc/publication/prog/rae/180106.pdf

Goode, C. J., Lynn, M. R., Krsek, C., & Bednash, G. D. (2009). Nurse residency programs: An essential requirement for nursing. *Nursing Economics, 27,* 142–147, 159.

Harvard Graduate School of Education. (2009). *Institute for Educational Management.* Retrieved September 5, 2009, from http://www.gse.harvard.edu/~ppe/highered/programs/iem.html

Hayes, E. F. (2005). Approaches to mentoring: How to mentor and be mentored. *Journal of the American Academy of Nurse Practitioners, 17,* 442–445.

Hill, K. S. (2009, August 30). Why do good nurses leave nursing? *Reflections on Nursing Leadership, 35*(3). Article available to members of Sigma Theta Tau International at http://www.reflectionsonnursingleadership.org/Pages/vol35_3_hill.aspx

Institute of Medicine. (2004). Maximizing workforce capability. In A. Page (Ed.), *Keeping patients safe. Transforming the work environment of nurses* (pp. 162–225). Washington, DC: The National Academies Press.

Institute of Medicine. (2007). *The learning healthcare system: Workshop summary (IOM Roundtable on Evidence-Based Medicine)*. Washington, DC: The National Academies Press.

Institute of Medicine. (2009). *Robert Wood Johnson Foundation Health Policy Fellows Program*. Retrieved September 5, 2009, from http://www.iom.edu/?id=19187

International Council of Nurses. (2009). *Leadership for change*. Retrieved September 3, 2009, from http://www.icn.ch/leadchange.htm

Jacobson, D. (2008). *Using IDPs to leverage strengths*. Retrieved September 3, 2009, from http://govleaders.org/idp.htm

Johnson & Johnson/Wharton. (2009). *Fellows program in management for nurse executives*. Retrieved September 4, 2009, from http://www.executivefellows.net/resource/Program%20Fact%20Sheet%202009.pdf

Krugman, M., Bretschneider, J., Horn, P. B., Krsek, C. A., Moutafis, R. A., & Smith, M. O. (2006). The national post-baccalaureate graduate nurse residency program: A model for excellence in transition to practice. *Journal for Nurses in Staff Development, 22,* 196–205.

Lee, A., Dennis, C., & Campbell, P. (2007). Nature's guide for mentors. *Nature, 447,* 791–797.

Maas, M. L., Strumpf, N. E., Beck, C., Jennings, D., Messecar, D., & Swanson, E. (2006). Mentoring geriatric nurse scientists, educators, clinicians, and leaders in the John A. Hartford Foundation Centers for Geriatric Nursing Excellence. *Nursing Outlook, 54,* 183–188.

Manson, S. M. (2009). Personal journeys, professional paths: Persistence in navigating the crossroads of a research career. *American Journal of Public Health, 99,* S20–S25.

McBride, A. B. (2009). *Individual development plan*. Retrieved September 3, 2009, from http://www.geriatricnursing.org/leadership/docs/IDPworksheet.pdf

McBride, A. B., & Lovejoy, K. B. (1995). Requesting and writing effective letters of recommendation: Some guidelines for candidates and sponsors. *Journal of Nursing Education, 34*(2), 95–96.

Meyers, S. (2007). Growing leaders in your own backyard. *Trustee, 60*(6), 8–11.

Morjikian, R., & Bellack, J. (2005). The Robert Wood Johnson Foundation Executive Nurse Fellows Program, Part 1: Leading change. *Journal of Nursing Administration, 35,* 431–438.

Mueller, C. M., & Dweck, C. S. (1998). Praise for intelligence can undermine children's motivation and performance. *Journal of Personality and Social Psychology, 75,* 33–52.

Mundt, M. H. (2001). An external mentor program: Stimulus for faculty research development. *Journal of Professional Nursing, 17,* 40–45.

Pellico, L. H., Brewer, C. S., & Kovner, C. T. (2009). What newly licensed registered nurses have to say about their first experience. *Nursing Outlook, 57,* 194–203.

Ragins, B. R., & Kram, K. E. (Eds.). (2007). *The handbook of mentoring at work: Theory, research, and practice.* Thousand Oaks, CA: Sage Publications.

Robert Wood Johnson Foundation. (2009). *Nurse Faculty Scholars.* Retrieved September 4, 2009, from http://www.nursefacultyscholars.org

Studer, Q. (2003). *Hardwiring excellence.* Gulf Breeze, FL: Fire Starter Publishing.

Thiefoldt, D., & Scheef, D. (2004, August). Generation X and the Millennials: Mentoring the new generations. *Law Practice Today.* Retrieved April 6, 2010, from http://www.abanet.org/lpm/lpt/articles/mgt08044.html

Toth, E. (1997). *Ms. mentor's impeccable advice for women in academia.* Philadelphia: University of Pennsylvania Press.

UCSF Academic Affairs. (2009). *Faculty mentoring program.* Retrieved September 3, 2009, from http://acpers.ucsf.edu/mentoring

University of Pennsylvania School of Nursing. (2007). *Faculty manual: Mentoring program.* Retrieved September 4, 2009, from http://www.upenn.edu/provost/images/uploads/Nursing.Mentoring_.pdf

University of Pittsburgh Institute for Clinical Research Education. (2009). *Welcome to the mentoring resources web site.* Retrieved September 4, 2009, from http://www.icre.pitt.edu/mentoring/index.aspx

UVAHS Professional Nursing Staff Organization. (2008). *Ongoing staff and manager development.* Retrieved September 3, 2009, from http://www.healthsystem.virginia.edu/internet/pnso/new/ProfDev/StaffDevelopment.cfm

Vance, C., & Olson, R. K. (Eds.). (1998). *The mentor connection in nursing.* New York: Springer Publishing.

Part III

Leadership as Transformational

Chapter 10

Looking Back to Move Forward

This chapter, which opens the final section of the book, focuses on leadership as transformational. Leadership isn't just a matter of inspiring others or catalyzing a group to achieve existing goals but of moving a profession, an institution, or some aspect of health care down a new path with different expectations, structures, and ways of conceptualizing how to achieve the mission in light of changing conditions. Of course, there have been many nurses who have exerted transformational leadership, beginning in modern times with Florence Nightingale: Clara Barton founded the Red Cross, Mary Breckinridge developed a model rural health care system now known as the Frontier Nursing Service, Margaret Sanger founded the American birth control movement, and Florence Wald brought the hospice movement to the United States.

There are nurses who have changed the shape and direction of our profession: defining our practice (Virginia Henderson), developing advanced-practice roles (Lee Ford, Hildegard Peplau, and Ernestine Wiedenbach), designing new delivery models (Lillian Wald and Ruth Lubic), expanding the research infrastructure (Harriet Werley and Ada Sue Hinshaw), reminding us of our history (Elizabeth Carnegie), and increasing the number of minorities in the field (Hattie Bessent). There are nurses who have redirected institutional policy: emphasizing the needs of the unserved and underserved (Rhetaugh Dumas at the National Institute of Mental Health) and bringing together nursing service and nursing education (Luther Chrisman at Rush University Medical Center).

My goal in this chapter isn't to list all nurses who have exerted transformational influence—that would be a very long list—but to evoke past achievements to energize others to do the same. When you look back at all that our predecessors have accomplished—those who dared to think that they could address an issue in a fundamentally better way—trying to do something different yourself doesn't seem quite as daunting. If six undergraduates could decide in 1922 to found an honorary society for nursing comparable to Phi Beta Kappa in the humanities (and the director of their program could take them seriously enough to help them actualize their dream), thus birthing what is now Sigma Theta Tau International, there's no saying what their 21st-century counterparts might accomplish.

On a day-to-day or week-to-week basis, I can easily get overwhelmed by frustrations and problems. Yet, when I look back on all our profession has accomplished during the course of my career, I am dazzled by the enormity of the change. Quite simply, it is easy to lose sight of what has been achieved when you are living through that history. You tend to take improvements for granted—"obviously we had to do that"—and keep thinking about all that still hasn't been accomplished because you can imagine things even better than they currently are. But going through an exercise whereby you are forced to look at what has been realized in the last few decades can be both enlightening and energizing. Now is a much, much better time to be a nurse than when I started out a half century ago.

"Top 10" Changes—Last Half Century

In 1998, the American Academy of Nursing celebrated its 25th anniversary with the commissioning of four papers meant to describe how much the profession had changed since the organization's founding. I was asked to prepare the one on changes in nursing education over time, and this task convinced me of the value of looking back to move forward. I would, therefore, like to do something similar in this chapter, building on that work (McBride, 1999), but looking back at my beginnings as a nursing student and forward to where I think nursing is now. In that paper prepared for a meeting of the Academy, I used the framework of a "top 10" list to shape my remarks because it forced me to think in terms of a set number of key changes, so I will do the same in this chapter. David Letterman always unveils his "top 10" lists starting at No. 10, and I will do the same. I do not want to say that the transformative importance of the item grows as I move up the list because that isn't necessarily the case, but the changes in the top five spots are still gathering force and haven't yet effected as much large-scale change as they eventually will (see Exhibit 10.1).

Our profession has undergone enormous infrastructure development in the last half century. When I started out, there weren't many journals; now there are so many that most of us don't know the names of

1. Nursing isn't one kind of job; it is a gateway to a series of career opportunities, including the opportunity to exert leadership that isn't discipline specific.
2. There is growing national acceptance of the fact that nurse leadership is essential to the development of safe practice environments and quality care.
3. The informatics revolution means that all aspects of nursing—practice, research, and education—are no longer time and place bound.
4. The emphasis in health care and nursing is less on process and more on outcomes, valuing data as the basis for decision making.
5. Centers of nursing excellence are taking shape, and with their growth, more consortium arrangements will be forged across institutional boundaries.
6. The research base of nursing is visible with the establishment of doctoral education, postdoctoral research training, the National Institute of Nursing Research, the Council for the Advancement of Nursing Science, and regional research societies.
7. Advanced-practice nursing has become established at the graduate level (MSN, DNP), with concomitant acceptance by the public and the growth of specialty organizations and validating certification processes.
8. Nursing students have become increasingly diverse in terms of age, race, gender, learning style, and so forth, so the profession is beginning to reflect the population it serves.
9. Articulation across levels of nursing is increasingly possible and user-friendly (LPN-ASN, LPN-BSN, RN-BSN, RN-MSN, BSN-PhD, etc.).
10. Nursing's literature and infrastructure have greatly expanded with new journals, standards, agreed-upon competencies, and policy statements.

EXHIBIT 10.1 "Top 10" changes—last half century.

most of them. *Nursing Research*, founded in 1952, is no longer the only journal devoted to nursing research, as it was when I entered the field. We now have *Research in Nursing and Health*, *Western Journal of Nursing Research*, *Clinical Nursing Research*, *Applied Nursing Research*, *Journal of Nursing Measurement*, *Research and Theory for Nursing Practice*, *Journal of Nursing Scholarship*, and *Research in Gerontological Nursing*, to mention a few. Springer has been publishing the *Annual Review of Nursing Research* for almost three decades. There have already been two editions of the *Encyclopedia of Nursing Research*, and a second edition of the *Encyclopedia of Nursing Leadership* is in process. Infrastructure development has taken many forms, from the development of scores of new specialty organizations to essential documents describing the core components of various degree programs and from the establishment of a range of recognition programs to statements about the scope and standards of practice for an assortment of specialties from forensic nursing to home health.

What has all this infrastructure development meant for the development of the profession? When I was starting out, you tended to make a case for the richness of the field by discussing possibilities rather than sharing successes. It was the difference between saying "Nursing can make a difference" and "Here's how nursing has made a difference," backing up claims with data. Before, you might have had to argue with skeptics that there is a role for genetics/genomics in nursing; now you can make that case by just sharing a booklet on the scope and standards of that specialty or referring to the essentials of baccalaureate education. A rich infrastructure means that individuals new to the profession have so much to build on; they don't have to start out dealing with both their own knowledge gaps and those of their discipline. They can lean on what's already in place, even as they seek to make contributions of their own. When lots of basics are in place, you can have the fun of not having to start from scratch, so you can get further faster, and this in itself sets the stage for new opportunities.

When I was starting out, diploma education was the norm; nursing was still struggling to be accepted as an academic discipline deserving of the same legitimacy as law or medicine. If you were an RN already and wanted a bachelor's degree, you practically had to start all over again even if you already had a great deal of clinical experience and years of classes, albeit not in a university setting. This attitude has substantially changed as articulation programs provide ways to give credit for previous experience and education (LPN-ASN, LPN-BSN, RN-BSN, and RN-MSN). Although nursing still has not reached consensus on entry into practice, the field has reached some rough accommodation with the fact that there are many ways to enter the profession, including fast-track programs for college graduates.

You don't want any RN to feel unwelcome by virtue of not having done the "right" thing at the start, but you do want all RNs to keep learning, with many getting additional degrees so that they can reach the level of practice that best suits their interests and abilities. We have even gotten better at encouraging particularly gifted individuals to go right from a bachelor's degree to a PhD, realizing that we have to encourage a certain percentage to move in that direction so that we can build our science. I cannot say that we've given up believing that there is one right way to move ahead academically, for we still envy physicians for their one-degree entry into medicine, but we are realizing the advantages of being in a profession that encourages self-improvement and lifelong learning. This approach has advantages if you are in a field still largely peopled by women, thus making us particularly mindful that careers don't unfold in a lockstep fashion.

What is the advantage of this shift? Articulation across levels of nursing means that the individual has more career possibilities than ever before; you are not limited by choices made right after high school. Coming to terms with the fact that there isn't going to be one right way to move ahead academically also means some recognition that nurses aren't the interchangeable workers they have sometimes been treated as—the old notion that a nurse is a nurse is a nurse. Once you realize that you have to ask about individual background, strengths, and limitations, then you are treating the person less like another cog in the organizational machinery and more professionally. The more the person has to explain her or his abilities to a prospective employer, instead of letting mere licensure tell the story, the more that person is likely to be cognizant of personal responsibility. Nurses who move from a bachelor's degree straight through to a PhD will not have the same clinical experience as those who worked in a hospital unit for years before going on to graduate school, but such individuals will, one hopes, be mindful of their limitations and partner with other nurses who are clinically savvy as they take the lead in developing programs of research.

Students have become increasingly diverse in terms of gender, race, age, learning style, and so forth. When I entered nursing school, everyone in my class was young, white, female, and more or less middle class. This has changed considerably, with more of an age range and many more men entering the field. Alas, our profession still remains quite homogeneous, peopled largely by white women (Queneau, 2006), though that is less so with every passing year. Increasing diversity means the profession is beginning to look more like the American public we serve. The more the field doesn't look like the stereotype, the more it is likely that we will be treated in a less stereotyped fashion. This change is starting within the field itself. Compared with perceptions in 1992, newly recruited student nurses one decade later held less stereotyped images of nursing; they no longer saw women as more caring than men, men as more intelligent than women, or women as making better nurses than men (Jinks & Bradley, 2004).

In keeping with the move to a "knowledge economy" (National Research Council, 2002), the RN population has become better educated over time. When I started out, the overwhelming majority of nurses were diploma prepared. By 2004, 33.7% ($n = 981,238$) of RNs held at least an associate degree, 34.2% (n = 994,276) had obtained at least a bachelor's degree, with another 13% (n = 376,901) holding a master's or doctoral degree (Bureau of Health Professions [BHPR], 2007). The number of nurses who are graduate prepared has grown steadily with the development of advanced-practice nursing, up 68% between 2000 and 2008 (BHPR, 2010).

As nursing practice became more complex, specialty preparation developed. As an RN generalist, you can with experience become knowledgeable about a patient population, setting, or common problems, but without specialty preparation you are not likely to understand underlying complexities that shape matters and guide research. Originally, master's degrees prepared the nurse for new functional roles, serving as an administrator or teacher, but eventually graduate education began to focus on higher-level caregiving which could be confirmed through appropriate certification processes.

Whereas RN is a statement of general knowledge and minimum competencies, certification represents specific expertise, enabling individuals to practice more independently on their confirmed authority, for example, in exercising prescription privileges. As specialty practice evolved, a movement to substitute the Doctor of Nursing Practice (DNP) degree for the master's degree has emerged on the grounds that every advanced practitioner needs additional preparation in subject matter that cannot be squeezed into the already-full MSN curriculum, for example, higher-level aspects of quality-improvement methods and informatics.

Advanced-practice nursing changed the focus from the nurse as largely supporting the primary-care provider to the nurse gaining credence as a primary-care provider. Nurse practitioners, nurse midwives, and nurse anesthetists are qualified to practice in their own right; clinical nurse specialists are additionally prepared to help less-educated nurses address complex problems and improve caregiving systems, in many instances providing continuity across settings. Because many advanced-practice nurses have prescriptive privileges and work closely with physician practices, what they are capable of doing is also more obvious to medical colleagues.

Despite anecdotes about tensions between physicians and advanced-practice nurses, there is evidence that the states with more physicians per capita also have more of these professionals per capita, suggesting that advanced-practice nurses complement physicians rather than substitute for or supplant them (BHPR, 2004). Instead of being seen largely as helpers, advanced-practice nurses are increasingly valued for their independent and interdependent contributions, and this makes a big difference in nurses being treated as clinical leaders and viewing themselves that way too. Specialty practice means those nurses don't have to function as a Jack or Jacqueline of all trades, but can strive to be master of some, and that can be a relief. Instead of feeling sometimes inadequate about all you don't know, the focus switches to emphasizing what you do know, and this can make all concerned more aware of their leadership abilities. Generalists profit from specialists too, because they can seek consultation within the field, thus reaffirming that they are part of a vibrant whole.

Concurrent with the development of advanced-practice nursing, the research base began to build. In the 1960s, Virginia Henderson indexed nursing research to date and found much more research on what makes nurses tick than studies of how to improve the focus of nursing, that is, patient care (Halloran, 1996; Simmons & Henderson, 1964). The decades that followed sought to correct the situation and began to focus on clinical nursing research—health promotion and disease prevention, management of acute and chronic illness, and development of effective nursing systems—culminating in 1986 with the establishment of what is now the National Institute of Nursing Research (Merritt, 1986). The 1980s and 1990s were decades that saw the development of regional research societies and research committees in almost every specialty organization, which further supported the advancement of clinical nursing research.

Nursing's scientific progress was fostered by the establishment of doctoral education and postdoctoral research training. At the start of my career, there were very, very few doctorally prepared nurses; I knew two during my undergraduate years and one as a master's student. Nurses prepared at that level usually obtained a doctorate in education (EdD) because that background assisted them in the development of graduate programs, a major task of that period. The next round of doctoral education involved nurses going into other fields to get research training via the PhD, and then using that preparation in a related area to build programs of clinical nursing research. I belonged in that camp; in the 1970s, I chose to get a doctorate in developmental psychology because it complemented my specialty preparation in psychiatric–mental health nursing.

Many of the first doctoral programs in nursing were Doctor of Nursing Science (DNS or DNSc) degrees because nursing faculty often did not believe their university's graduate school would be supportive of a PhD in nursing, because the doctorally prepared nurse was then considered by many to be an oxymoron concept (schools of nursing can award professional degrees described as nursing, but the PhD is a research degree awarded only by a university's graduate school). So solid is nursing's reputation now that the overwhelming majority of research doctorates in nursing are PhD degrees; there was only one at the start of the 1960s, and there were 64 by the end of the century (American Association of Colleges of Nursing [AACN], 2001).

Once significant numbers of nurses were research prepared and ready to orchestrate their own programs of scholarship over a career, the science began to build around focus areas. Institutional research training and center/program grants enabled excellence to take shape as like-minded researchers worked together on clinical problems of shared interest. For example, the University of Washington's School of Nursing got some of the first funding to establish a Center for Women's Health Research, an area in which they continue to excel. Collaborative arrangements across institutional boundaries began to be forged so strength could build on strength in tackling major issues. For example, the University of Iowa College of Nursing and Mennonite College of Nursing at Illinois State University offer a collaborative PhD program in aging.

Collectively, the development of a vibrant research presence and centers of excellence means that the profession is finally able to document both what works under controlled conditions and what works in real life and to disseminate the "best practices" so that they shape standards of care, what is taught to health care providers, and what is mandated and reimbursed by institutional/governmental policies. We are moving from being a field with good ideas but relatively few tested successes to having our initiatives disseminated broadly and to influencing the very design of health care (Naylor et al., 1999). Because we have a "home" within the National Institutes of Health, the nation's funding agency for health-related research, the profession has a scientific respectability that seemed beyond our grasp a half century ago.

Health care professionals—dentists, nurses, nutritionists, physical therapists, physicians, psychologists, social workers, and so forth—are most highly differentiated on entry into their fields; each profession socializes its members to look at patients and their families through a discipline-specific lens. These professionals, who then go on to become researchers, have much more in common with each other because science is science no matter what the field. Whether you use qualitative or quantitative methods, you are still governed by considerations of validity and reliability. Once you have a shared commitment to rigor, then you are likely to pay even more attention to each other's findings because knowledge doesn't know disciplinary boundaries, setting the stage for fresh recognition of the contributions of nurses.

The emphasis in nursing and health care is now less on process and more on outcomes. It isn't that processes are ignored or unappreciated; getting effective ones in place remains challenging in the best of circumstances. However, in these times of scarce resources, the focus has shifted to proving that what's in place is achieving desired results. It's the difference between being appreciated for working hard and being appreciated because you make a demonstrated difference. This shift to an outcomes orientation has been prompted by a growing public skepticism that resources are being used wisely and by a "show me" attitude that values data over rhetoric. This turn of events can be difficult for nurses who weren't taught to calculate their effectiveness using accepted measures, but this change offers the profession a golden opportunity to demonstrate the value-added difference it makes. Aiken is one of several nurses who have studied the impact of nursing on patient outcomes—patient satisfaction, mortality, and morbidity—providing the field with solid evidence of its effectiveness (Aiken, Clarke, Sloane, Sochalski, & Silber, 2002; Clarke & Aiken, 2006; Kutney-Lee et al., 2009).

Thankfully, the shift to an outcomes orientation is occurring at a time when advances in information and communications technology (ICT) make it possible to aggregate data relatively easily so that patterns can emerge. Nursing has long held goals—document observations and interventions subsequently undertaken, foster continuous quality improvement, use research findings to improve care, evaluate achievement of desired outcomes, monitor needs of vulnerable populations, and integrate clinical and financial data in strategic planning—that were never fully achievable before the dawn of 21st-century ICT (McBride, 2010). Before the advent of standardized ways to measure phenomena of concern to nursing and the move to an electronic health record, data collection was erratic; it wasn't regular and uniform enough to permit comparisons across practices. Now that this is changing, you don't have to invent a way of measuring differences when you wish to prove that nursing makes a difference. ICT makes possible online dissemination of constantly changing standards and policies, and then permits benchmarking local outcomes against national averages for similar institutions (Bakken, Cimino, & Hripcsak, 2004). Being able to document differences made on nurse-sensitive indicators—reduction in infections, ulcers, and falls—and to compare progress with that of competitors gives nursing a value in CEO offices that it has not historically enjoyed.

The informatics revolution under way also means that nursing is no longer completely time and place bound (McBride, 2005). For example, the Veterans Health Administration's new Care Coordination and My HealtheVet programs make possible continuous communication between patients and nurses, thus eliminating routine clinic visits and focusing instead on seeing patients when necessary (Perlin & Roswell, 2004). Nurses can monitor patients' well-being and provide care over distances too vast to traverse in one day (Whitten, Doolittle, Mackert, & Rush, 2003). Educational resources can be pooled across institutions to address problems creatively.

Concerned about how little geriatric nursing was taught in baccalaureate programs, the John A. Hartford Foundation partnered with New York University's College of Nursing to create materials that are available to all faculty wishing to strengthen their offerings on care of the elderly. Such easily available resources have demonstrably enriched undergraduate education over time (Berman et al., 2005). In another example, five universities who are members of the Committee on Inter-Institutional Cooperation—Indiana University, The University of Iowa, The University of Michigan, The University of Minnesota, and The University of Wisconsin–Madison—have formed a consortium to pool graduate offerings in nursing informatics. No school has many faculty members knowledgeable in this area, but together the consortium has substantial expertise. The benefits have been significant—more robust curricular offerings, student access to a broader set of expertise, and additional peer support available to students and faculty alike (Delaney et al., 2006).

Freed of in-person constraints and with most people having access to computers, nurses can be creative in imagining the future. The early leadership research was dominated by a preoccupation with relations-oriented behaviors—Does the leader demonstrate care and integrity?—and task-oriented behaviors—Does the leader clarify tasks to be performed and monitor progress? Now there is increasing emphasis on a third dimension, that is, the way leaders initiate change and encourage organizational innovation (Yukl, Gordon, & Taber, 2002), and ICT holds the promise of simultaneous transformation of all aspects of nursing (Lang, 2008). Not all nurses are prepared to realize this promise, but the profession is increasingly viewed as having leadership potential, and this is a big change.

In 2004, the Institute of Medicine (IOM) devoted an entire volume, *Keeping Patients Safe: Transforming the Work Environment of Nurses*, to the proposition that nurses must function as knowledge workers and their work environments must strive to display the hallmarks of a learning organization. This IOM report supported the importance of strong nurse leadership if quality and patient safety are to be realized and recommended additional education so that nurses can meet new expectations, particularly around ICT-enhanced knowledge management and the design of work to reduce error. Publication of this report, because it honors the work of nursing as essential to quality care and urges that the work environment of nurses be improved to support the nursing staff, was a watershed event in that it elevated nursing leadership to a national priority. It wasn't just nurses laying claim to being knowledge workers; an IOM report was maintaining the position and urging preparation for that eventuality.

It remains to be seen how much nurses will seize this opportunity. After decades of feeling not fully appreciated for our contributions, we are finally being recognized as indispensable in areas that will only grow in importance as health care institutions seek, in part for financial reasons, to develop an organizational culture that strengthens patient safety. Can we mobilize our considerable strengths—the ability to work collaboratively, intra- and interdisciplinarily; an understanding of systems; creativity demonstrated in a long record of savvy work-arounds; and a commitment to facilitating quality of life and functional ability—to take the lead offered to us at this period of time? It's too early to tell, but the fact remains that we have never before had the opportunities we have now.

It is these opportunities that constitute the biggest change in the last half century. Nursing is no longer one kind of job; it is a gateway to a series of career opportunities. Nurses are needed in a broad array of settings from acute care to long-term care and everything in between, from military preparedness to community-based schools and programs, and from workplace to think tank. Nurses function as clinicians, educators, managers, chief executives, researchers, consultants, entrepreneurs, and policy makers. They can provide care themselves, design new caregiving products, and oversee the systems in which care is given.

Paradigm Shifts: From the 20th Century to the 21st Century

The changes that have taken place since I started out reflect a shift in paradigms as 20th-century conceptualizations gave way to 21st-century expectations. As you can see in Table 10.1, health care delivery is changing, prompted in large measure by the IOM's (2000, 2001, 2003, 2004) quality reports. For example, these reports emphasize that safety is a system concern; work-arounds (you improvise when the right equipment and dosage are not available) only add dangerous variation into the mix; best practices need to be uniformly incorporated into routine expectations; and interdisciplinary communication is essential if accidents are to be avoided. Where before you were taught to emphasize the importance of the provider–patient relationship, now the emphasis is shifting to whether the setting has structures and policies that encourage individuals to do their best and catch their mistakes before they become catastrophic.

I have already talked about process orientation giving way to one focused on outcomes; the nurse being seen as a primary-care provider, not just as someone helping the physician; and care not being time and place bound. I was educated to assess and then meet all of a patient's

TABLE 10.1 Shifting Paradigms

20th-Century View	21st-Century View
Health Care Delivery	
Process oriented (what a professional does)	Outcomes oriented (value of what is done)
Meet all of a patient's needs oblivious to costs	Triage needs mindful of costs
Nurse supports primary-care provider	Nurse provides primary care
Nursing = direct care	Nursing = direct care, promoting self-care, directing care given by others, managing patient services, and designing models of care and caregiving products
Doing no harm is an individual responsibility	Safety is a system concern
Focus of care = patient compliance	Focus of care = best practices
Care time and place bound	Telecare
Work-arounds commonplace	Variation monitored
Organized into professional silos	Interdisciplinary collaboration
Academia	
Emphasis on teaching	Emphasis on learning
Teacher = "sage on stage"	Teacher = "guide by side"
Memorization of facts	Use of information for decision making
Time and place bound	"Virtual university"
Research = study of nurses	Research = study of phenomena of concern to nursing
Centralized administration	Responsibility-centered management
Salaried	Increasingly entrepreneurial
Organized into professional silos	Interdisciplinary collaboration

needs unconcerned about costs; now the focus is on triaging needs (what's important and critical, and what needs to be addressed at this point in recovery) while being mindful of resources. You still put first things first, but you do the best you can in understanding that patients aren't in hospitals very long and even good insurance has reimbursement limits, so you have to be creative in follow-through, for example, telephoning the patient after discharge to check on how she or he is doing at home.

In my day, being a nurse was equated with providing direct personal care. There is still the tendency to think of that first because such caregiving is at the heart of patient-focused care, but nursing is increasingly meaning other things too—promoting self-care, directing care given by others, managing patient services, and designing models of care and caregiving products. When a new view is ascendant, it doesn't mean that the old one has no use. Processes—meeting as many needs as possible, assuming personal responsibility for patient care rendered, and being concerned about patients following the prescribed treatment regimen—all remain important. The new view is a corrective, reminding one and all that the original framing of the issues led to unintended consequences when played out to their ultimate conclusion.

The primacy of the provider–patient relationship is being questioned on the grounds that often it encouraged an improvisation that led to unsafe variation rather than quality care; this relationship remains vitally important, but now the outcomes are being monitored in order to determine if the provider needs to make course corrections. No matter how perceptive or thoughtful you might be with individual patients, you still need unit-level information about how your infection rate fares in comparison to analogous units elsewhere in order to know whether you are doing the best you can at this point in time.

The health care delivery system isn't the only major social structure undergoing shifting expectations. Academia is changing in many of the same directions, for example, it is no longer bound by time and place. The switch from an emphasis on teaching to an emphasis on learning reflects the overall societal shift away from a process orientation (teaching) to an outcomes orientation (learning). Complementing this move is a corresponding emphasis on the teacher as less "sage on stage" performing and more "guide by side" coaching. The old emphasis on memorization needs to be rethought given the knowledge explosion, because it is impossible to remember every fact so that you can retrieve it as needed. Instead, the stress increasingly is on knowing where to find correct information for just-in-time decision making, and this is where ICT expedites matters.

Both health care and academia have been historically organized so that the various disciplines didn't interact much with each other; hospitals had separate dining rooms just for physicians, and universities had separate courses for each of the health professions even when they needed to know the same subject matter. Now, interdisciplinary collaboration is being encouraged in teaching, research, and practice, and that is why Chapter 13 is devoted to this important subject.

There are two paradigm shifts that I alluded to in Chapter 8 under the heading of resource development that bear reprising. One is the move away from centralized administration in favor of responsibility-centered management. Nursing service and nursing education have historically been run centrally in a hierarchical fashion with the top administrator having the final say on just about all decisions. One reason this happened is that that person often was the best educated nurse in the building. Now that many nurses are well-educated and they have different specialties and expertise, the administrative style that is likely to make best use of their capabilities is one where day-to-day decisions that don't change policies are made by those most familiar with and responsible for the circumstances.

Even though policy changes still need a sign off from the top administrator, they now are more often arrived at through some collective discussion of pros and cons that makes use of the range of talents in the overall group. The advantage of this shift is that the decisions are likely to be better. If you are the top administrator responding to dozens of persons who each think the final decision is yours, then everyone else is not particularly engaged in finding creative solutions to problems and all you can ever do is be responsive. You are a prisoner of what they tell you because you don't have the wherewithal to check out basic assumptions and don't have a system whereby the ideas get "cooked" by debate before they reach you. With responsibility-centered management, there is more likelihood that good ideas will surface throughout the organization, and as individuals get more empowered they also have a tendency to become more entrepreneurial in thinking about how to realize their ideas so that they see the light of day. Thus, the resourcing of new initiatives ceases to be the responsibility of only one person, the top administrator, and becomes instead a shared responsibility, making it more likely that someone will figure out a way to make things happen.

What I have hoped to do in this chapter is to use our history as a stimulant to envision our future. If so much could change for the better in the last half century, then imagine the change for the better that's possible in the next half century. The nursing workforce is now three times larger than it was back then, so the changes have been both qualitative and quantitative. Major changes in recent decades have transformed the profession into a force capable of additional societal change, most likely to be realized if we fully comprehend and act on the paradigm shifts taking place in the societal systems in which we operate.

I remember the chancellor, to whom I reported, reminding the deans repeatedly that we didn't want to wind up like train tycoons or Hollywood moguls in this country; they didn't fare well with the advent of automobiles/planes and television. They hadn't seen themselves in either the transportation or entertainment business, and so did not think beyond current ways of doing things (Levitt, 1974). He also reminded us that every generation has opportunities if we can but see them, and sometimes an institution without much history or distinction can achieve in a new area because the personnel are not hampered by "we've always done it this way" thinking.

Applying this kind of thinking to nursing, I would say that we need to keep abreast of major shifts so that we don't shrivel up trying to keep on doing what we were educated to do years ago even though the world is changing. Nursing's commitment to the optimization of health and ability; the alleviation of suffering; and advocacy in the care of individuals, families, communities, and populations doesn't change (American Nurses Association [ANA], 2003, p. 6). Values endure, but how they get expressed will vary as new sensibilities and knowledge become available.

To be a transformational leader means that you cannot get so distracted by particulars—whether nurses dress a certain way, whether they use pen and paper or a computer to document, whether all nurses need a year of medical–surgical nursing before specializing, whether you have to be center stage to be an effective teacher or leader—that you cannot be playful in imagining other ways of achieving the same goals (Scoble & Russell, 2003). For each one of the major changes that has taken place, there were hundreds of nurses unafraid to imagine and then try something else, and their collective courage has led us to a point in time where even the IOM, part of the National Academies of Science and established by the U.S. Congress, expects us to exert transformative leadership in creating safe health care environments. If important others do not see us as constrained, then we shouldn't act as if we are.

Key Take-Away Points

- Transformational leadership means moving a profession, an institution, or some aspect of health care down a new path with different expectations, structures, and ways of conceptualizing how the mission can be achieved in light of changing conditions.

- Looking back on all that nursing has achieved in the last half century can be energizing; it makes trying to do something different yourself not seem quite as daunting.
- Nursing is much stronger now as a profession than it has been in the past—larger, better educated, somewhat more diverse with a solid infrastructure, demonstrated outcomes, specialty expertise, a growing research base, more opportunities, and no longer time and place bound.
- Conceptual shifts have driven many of these changes, the most important one being an emphasis on outcomes (the value of what a professional does) over processes (what the professional does), which itself reflects a research shift away from studying nurses in favor of studying how to improve what they do.
- Nursing's commitment to the optimization of health and ability, alleviation of suffering, and advocacy hasn't changed over time; values endure, but how they get expressed will vary as new sensibilities and knowledge become available.
- Even the IOM expects nurses to exert transformational leadership.

REFERENCES

Aiken, L. H., Clarke, S. P., Sloane, D. M., Sochalski, J., & Silber, J. H. (2002). Hospital nurse staffing and patient mortality, nurse burnout, and job dissatisfaction. *Journal of the American Medical Association, 288,* 1987–1993.

American Association of Colleges of Nursing. (2001). *Indicators of quality in research-focused doctoral programs in nursing.* Retrieved October 14, 2009, from http://www.aacn.nche.edu/Publications/positions/qualityindicators.htm

American Nurses Association. (2003). *Nursing's social policy statement* (2nd ed.). Washington, DC: Nursesbooks.org.

Bakken, S., Cimino, J. J., & Hripcsak G. (2004). Promoting patient safety and enabling evidence-based practice through informatics. *Medical Care, 42,* II49–II56.

Berman, A., Mezey, M., Kobayashi, M., Fulmer, T., Stanley, J., Thornlow, D., et al. (2005). Gerontological nursing content in baccalaureate nursing programs: Comparison of findings from 1997 and 2003. *Journal of Professional Nursing, 21,* 268–275.

Bureau of Health Professions. (2004). *A comparison of changes in the professional practice of nurse practitioners, physician assistants, and certified nurse midwives: 1992 and 2000.* Retrieved October 13, 2009, from http://bhpr.hrsa.gov/healthworkforce/reports/scope/scope1-2.htm

Bureau of Health Professions. (2007). *The registered nurse population: Findings from the 2004 National Sample Survey of Registered Nurses.* Retrieved October 16, 2009, from http://bhpr.hrsa.gov/healthworkforce/rnsurvey04/2.htm

Bureau of Health Professions. (2010, March). *The registered nurse population: Initial findings from the 2008 National Sample Survey of Registered Nurses.* Retrieved March 20, 2010 from http://bhpr.hrsa.gov/healthworkforce/rnsurvey/initialfindings2008.pdf

Clarke, S. P., & Aiken, L. H. (2006). More nursing, fewer deaths. *Quality and Safety in Health Care, 15*(1), 2–3.

Delaney, C. W., Brennan, P. F., McDaniel, A. M., Jones, J. F., Keenan, G. M., & Abdoo, Y. M. (2006). Leveraging through cooperation: CIC—Committee on Inter-Institutional Cooperation. In C. A. Weaver, C. W. Delaney, P. Weber, & R. L. Carr (Eds.), *Nursing and informatics for the 21st century: An international look at practice, trends, and the future* (pp. 210–214). Chicago: Healthcare Information and Management Systems Society.

Halloran, E. J. (1996). Virginia Henderson and her timeless writings. *Journal of Advanced Nursing, 23,* 17–24.

Institute of Medicine. (2000). In L. T., Kohn, J. M. Corrigan, & M. S. Donaldson (Eds.), *To err is human: building a safer health system.* Washington, DC: National Academies Press.

Institute of Medicine. (2001). *Crossing the quality chasm: A new health system for the 21st century.* Washington, DC: National Academies Press.

Institute of Medicine. (2003). In A. C. Greiner & E. Knebel (Eds.), *Health professions education. A bridge to quality.* Washington, DC: National Academies Press.

Institute of Medicine. (2004). In A. Page (Ed.), *Keeping patients safe. Transforming the work environment of nurses.* Washington, DC: National Academies Press.

Jinks, A. M., & Bradley, E. (2004). Angels, handmaiden, battleaxe or whore? A study which examines changes in newly recruited student nurses' attitudes to gender and nursing stereotypes. *Nurse Education Today, 24,* 121–127.

Kutney-Lee, A., McHugh, M. D., Sloane, D. M., Cimiotti, J. P., Flynn, L., Neff, D. F., et al. (2009). Nursing: A key to patient satisfaction. *Health Affairs, 28,* w667–w669.

Lang, N. M. (2008). The promise of simultaneous transformation of practice and research with the use of clinical information systems. *Nursing Outlook, 56,* 232–236.

Levitt, T. (2004, July–August). Marketing myopia. *Harvard Business Review, 82,* 138–149.

McBride, A. B. (1999). Breakthroughs in nursing education: Looking back, looking forward. *Nursing Outlook, 47,* 114–119.

McBride, A. B. (2005). Nursing and the informatics revolution. *Nursing Outlook, 53,* 183–191.

McBride, A. B. (2010). Informatics and the future of nursing practice. In C. A. Weaver, C. W. Delaney, P. Weber, & R. L. Carr (Eds.), *Nursing and informatics for the 21st century: An international look at practice, trends, and the future* (2nd ed., pp. 5–15). Chicago: Healthcare Information and Management Systems Society.

Merritt, D. H. (1986). The National Center for Nursing Research. *Journal of Nursing Scholarship, 18*(3), 84–85.

National Research Council. (2002). In P. A. Graham & N. G. Stacey (Eds.), *The knowledge economy and postsecondary education: Report of a workshop.* Washington, DC: National Academies Press.

Naylor, M. D., Brooten, D., Campbell, R., Jacobsen, B. S., Mezey, M. D., Pauly, M. V., et al. (1999). Comprehensive discharge planning and home follow-up of hospitalized elders. A randomized clinical trial. *Journal of the American Medical Association, 281,* 613–620.

Perlin, J. B., & Roswell, R. H. (2004). Why do we need technology for caregiving of older adults in the U.S.? *Public Policy and Aging Report, 14*(1), 22–24.

Queneau, H. (2006). Changes in occupational segregation by gender and race-ethnicity in healthcare: Implications for policy and union practice. *Labor Studies Journal, 31,* 71–90.

Scoble, K. B., & Russell, G. (2003). Vision 2020, part 1: Profile of the future nurse leader. *Journal of Nursing Administration, 33,* 324–330.

Simmons, L., & Henderson, V. (1964). *Nursing research survey and assessment.* New York: Appleton-Century-Crofts.

Whitten, P., Doolittle, G., Mackert, M., & Rush, T. (2003). Telehospice carries end-of-life care over the lines. *Nursing Management, 34*(11), 36–39.

Yukl, G., Gordon, A., & Taber, T. (2002). A hierarchical taxonomy of leadership behavior: Integrating a half century of behavior research. *Journal of Leadership and Organizational Studies, 9,* 15–32.

Chapter 11

The Vision Thing

These days, whenever a new leader is appointed, there usually is some snickering because the first thing the person inevitably does is initiate a process of strategic planning. The individual is intent on putting his or her mark on the organization, but any benefit produced by this collective rethinking about where the organization should be heading isn't always obvious. Onlookers see this as a period of dislocation to be endured and might have a few choice words to say about "the vision thing." The vision thing gets dismissed as more hallucination than inspiration because the intention behind the exercise isn't always clear. But make no mistake, the point behind the exercise is important.

The reality is that leadership has to include more than doing what's been done all along, only better. These days, leadership must involve facing the challenges occasioned by living in this piece of time, recognizing where the world is going, avoiding problems that can be anticipated, and seizing the opportunities that might now exist that weren't heretofore realizable. Easier said than done because most of us don't welcome change no matter how innovative we may see ourselves as being. Even if we don't like some aspects of what we're doing, we like the predictability that goes with the status quo. There's always the niggling worry that we might guess wrong about where to head.

The truth of the matter is that organizations, professions, and people that keep on doing what they've always been doing, even if they have been doing it well, aren't likely to keep up, much less progress, because there will always be new realities. That nothing stays the same is a truism that most of us prefer not to think about too much because we're reluctant to venture beyond our comfort zone of familiar faces and set routines, but tastes change. Expectations rise. New technologies emerge. External forces—war, shortages, recession, climate change, immigration patterns, new microbes, and regulations—impinge. Funding streams evaporate. Sensibilities shift—seat belts and helmets become accepted, drunken driving is no longer tolerated, and smoking is banished from restaurants and bars. The very meaning of health and aging keeps evolving. Organizations, professions, and people will thrive only if they recognize how easy it is to grow stale and be left behind if you keep clinging to old realities when it's a different world.

Strategic Planning

I don't think that basic values change; that's why you keep holding on to them in contemplating any change. But how these values will be manifested or achieved must adapt to changing circumstances. The vision thing at its best involves periodically embarking on a process of strategic planning whereby you examine how your professional or organizational mission is being affected by changing circumstances, and then set short-term and long-term goals with concrete actions and a timeline that move you in desired new directions. No planning would be complete without also figuring out what resources—funding, training, consultation, social support, space, equipment, technical assistance, and the like—are needed to realize the various goals, and how you will know you've been successful, that is, what are the expected outcomes? The steps I have outlined are essentially the same whether you are putting together an individual-development plan or a plan for an organization. Both would also begin with some analysis of strengths because you always get further by building on strengths (Rath & Conchie, 2008) rather than wasting time mastering what you had no inclination to do in the first place, one of the major points in Chapter 2.

What I am advocating begins with some version of a SWOT analysis whereby you assess internal (to the person or organization) *strengths* and *weaknesses* and external (to the person or organization) *opportunities* and *threats*, in order not to be undone by weaknesses and to leverage strengths to seize opportunities and avoid threats. SWOT analysis, which began as a business strategy (Andrews, 1971; Learned, Christensen, Andrews, & Guth, 1969), has a value no matter whether you are planning your next career move or trying to figure out how to move your organization to its next level of development. In either instance, the strategy works best if you solicit the opinions of key stakeholders—subordinates, peers, and superiors; different generations and backgrounds; deliverers and consumers of services; those in your field; and those who work with your field—so you are not misled by your own perspective. If you do not involve key stakeholders, you are likely to be blinded by your beliefs and experience, thinking that your point of view is the one that prevailing opinion holds most dear, when that may not be the case.

As I've implied, earlier I didn't grow up thinking in terms of strategic planning. Once I made the decision to become a nurse, I thought my career planning was essentially over because I had already made the really big decision. Even subsequent decisions to get graduate education were more a matter of responding to opportunity rather than creating a thought-through future. I was similarly socialized to think in terms of responding to organizational changes rather than setting them in motion. What redirected me to think more strategically was noticing the changes taking place in Sigma Theta Tau in the 1970s and 1980s. Soon after Nell Watts became its first executive director, Sr. Rosemary Donley became president, and both began to ask themselves and others the question, "After membership, what?" They realized that the honor society for nursing could be so much more than it was if it only harnessed the talents of its members to elevate the profession and improve health care.

Carol Lindeman, who succeeded Donley as president, spearheaded development of the Ten-Year Plan, the first strategic plan of any nursing organization, which focused the society away from only being concerned about honoring members and onto making the most of them to develop, disseminate, and use nursing knowledge. With a compelling sense of direction, the reenergized society focused efforts on developing the needed infrastructure to realize the vision—expanding the membership, establishing chapters outside the United States, developing structures that facilitated goal attainment (e.g., launching a series of writing workshops to help members publish, strengthening the *Journal of Nursing Scholarship*, establishing a series of awards to recognize different kinds of excellence, founding what is now *Reflections on Nursing Leadership* as a way to communicate with members, and inaugurating a series of international research congresses), and determining to build a headquarters featuring an electronic library (Watts, 1997).

What I learned from both observing and contributing to this endeavor is that you can really make profound changes if you dare to dream, think through ways to realize next steps, and then communicate your vision in a way that causes others to get excited about possibilities ahead and work with you to develop the needed resources. If you analyze in hindsight what made Sigma Theta Tau so successful during this period, you can see that the leaders built the strategic plan on an appreciation of trends that were only going to gain importance in the years ahead: the need for knowledge workers in an information age, more emphasis on career development now that most women were working outside the home, the globalization of health care, and the growth in information and communications technology. They understood that you needed to put in place an infrastructure to facilitate the work of the organization and that both nurses and non-nurses will respond generously if they buy into the vision. They used regional assemblies to tell the membership about the plan and to prepare chapter officers for the work ahead. Watching this transformation unfold convinced me that people really want to be part of an organization on the move. We all hope that we can look back and say, with pride, "That was an exciting time to be there and part of important developments."

Before I leave the subject of Sigma Theta Tau International, a word is in order about Nell Watts, the first executive director, because she was a transformational leader without being the kind of charismatic figure you so often identify with leadership. She didn't dress in an attention-grabbing way or speak in a riveting voice, nor was she the type to be the life of the party, but she turned a sleepy organization, with 16,110 members and 56 chapters in 1973, into the largest nursing organization in the United States (187,120 members and 323 chapters) by 1993. How did she do that?

First of all, she was deeply committed to the organization and its values, believing that she was doing something very important, so she was always mission driven. She didn't hesitate to make use of consultants to help her think through ideas that went beyond her expertise, so she was never limited in what she could do by her own abilities. She listened hard for good ideas, always noticing when one surfaced that seemed to address what she had already identified as an issue; then she didn't hesitate to try something new, knowing full well that not all good ideas work out equally well. This made her more venturesome than most because she didn't expect every innovation to be successful, and occasional failures didn't stop her from experimenting because she expected a certain percentage of efforts to be unsuccessful. Once she knew where she was going generally, she then always tried to figure out all the steps the organization needed to take to get there, so she unfailingly joined vision with practicality, an unbeatable combination. She really believed that problems were "opportunities in disguise," so she remained optimistic even when severely stressed. She didn't care if she got the credit, so long as her organization thrived. If certain personalities annoyed her, she didn't let her feelings get in the way of using those individuals to the organization's advantage. I learned a tremendous amount from her approach.

The next time I was deeply engaged in strategic planning was in the 1990s when I became dean of Indiana University's School of Nursing. The institution had a proud history dating back to 1914 and a national reputation for strong academic programs and innovation (e.g., the founding of Sigma Theta Tau in 1922 and leadership in mobility education). The school, however, needed at this point to become research intensive—because what is now called the National Institute of Nursing Research had already been established—and to become better aligned with both the university and the health science center.

The strategic-planning effort set in motion reviewed trends, and eventually all concerned decided to use Boyer's (1990) notion of valuing different kinds of scholarship as the organizing framework for describing key goals. We resolved to build on existing strengths and develop a scholarly reputation in defined areas. The overall mission of the school remained to develop the workforce and knowledge base to meet the various health care needs of the state and beyond, but the conventional tripartite university mission of teaching, research, and service was restated more specifically as a commitment to the *scholarship of teaching* stressing creative pedagogy and use of information technology, the *scholarship of discovery* emphasizing the facilitation of quality of life in those struggling with chronic illness (with particular concern for patients/families struggling with cancer), and the *scholarship of application* focusing on development of healthy communities and healthy families. The overarching emphasis on scholarship signaled that all faculty would be held to similar standards (Glassick, Huber, & Maeroff, 1997), but it also broadened the notion of what counted as scholarship (American Association of Colleges of Nursing [AACN], 1999).

The three focus areas built on existing assets, connected to the latest thinking about faculty work, and dovetailed with emphases in the larger university and health sciences campus, which stressed interactive learning, informatics solutions, excellence in cancer care and control, and community involvement. The administrative makeup of the school was restructured to advance growth in these focus areas. Every annual report and state-of-the-school address was similarly organized to communicate progress in these areas—for example, the number of distance-learning offerings, presentations, publications, funding, the number of students helped so as to present/publish and obtain funding, mothers receiving care through our MOMmobile, the number of professionals prepared by our faculty for the state's healthy-families program, national rankings, and awards recognizing excellence in these areas.

Faculty and staff who were leaders in these areas of scholarship became members of university committees and advisory groups concerned with these matters, so the school was more knowledgeable about what was going on interprofessionally and became more influential through these forums. Merit-pay increases were meted out in terms of the three different kinds of scholarship, but fund-raising was also structured to encourage donations that strengthened these areas, too. All prospective faculty members received information about the school's commitment in these defined areas, in order to allow them to decide for themselves whether there was a fit between their interests and the direction in which the school was heading; so new hires generally entered the organization already committed to moving in these directions, which helped us move faster in building overlapping interests that deepened preexisting strengths.

During my tenure as dean (1991–2003), Indiana University's School of Nursing operated as a multicampus school with offerings on eight Indiana University campuses, two of which were research intensive but six of which were comprehensive campuses (McBride, Yeager, & Farley, 2005). Accordingly, the scholarship of discovery was emphasized more on the former, with the scholarship of teaching and the scholarship of application emphasized more on the latter. Because all the campuses shared a strong commitment to quality undergraduate education, our system-wide faculty retreat and communication network stressed creativity in this direction. It was challenging for all concerned to craft a vision, a strategic plan, and faculty evaluation criteria for tenure and promotion that allowed for mission differences by campus, yet encouraged a shared school-wide commitment to excellence across campuses, but this kind of challenge is one that leaders regularly face when they are asked to provide direction across units or hospitals with different purposes. It takes a certain amount of cognitive gymnastics to sort out how to articulate a shared vision that inspires excellence across the performance spectrum, but the ability to articulate where an organization is one system and where the units (hospitals or campuses) can function sensitive to community differences is increasingly an expectation of leadership as we operate in progressively more intricate organizations.

The world of nursing—hospitals and other clinical and community agencies, universities, government, and business—is complex, interconnected, interdependent, and diverse (Lindberg & Lindberg, 2008). Thus, nurses are increasingly being called upon to create a vision and set goals that emphasize clarity of purpose, connection to core values, collaboration across sundry stakeholders, and respect for differences. It is this level of strategic planning that I can see in my current assignment as a member of the board for a statewide hospital network with small community hospitals, suburban facilities, regional centers, and large metropolitan hospitals that deliver the most complicated possible medical treatment. As a board, we strive constantly to predict the future, so that we can be prepared for new pressures, changes in regulations and reimbursement, the aging of the population, and the latest developments in technology and best practices. Obviously, we do not have a crystal ball, so the future remains ill-defined, yet this constant concern with forecasting serves the very real purpose of helping us evaluate whether we would be prepared for the various new twists and turns that might be anticipated.

As chair of the board's Committee on Quality and Patient Safety, I am particularly engaged in helping to push the envelope in this important area. We have used a SWOT analysis to get clearer about our strengths (a CEO and top leadership committed to quality and safety; an annual plan and our infrastructure in support of quality and safety), our weaknesses (desired hard-to-achieve changes difficult to sustain; need for more systematic processes), opportunities (a reputation for quality and safety is likely to increase market share), and our threats (a discomfort with initiating crucial interprofessional conversations about safety). We used the SWOT findings to set board priorities, particularly in how we would get "on board" with the Institute for Healthcare Improvement's campaign in this direction (IHI, 2009).

Because there was a perceived need for more systematic processes, we went through another round of soliciting opinions, this time to reach agreement about the variations that we needed to eliminate from our system-wide hospital network. The leadership was surveyed about where we wanted to be as one health system with regard to quality and safety. The findings showed that there was strong agreement (≥80%) about how we should proceed in developing a culture with shared quality expectations, a common computerized order entry system, a shared formulary for drugs and devices, and a collective minimum data set regarding standards. This exercise not only provided some direction about how to proceed but also energized the network to move in this direction because there was more agreement about next steps than had been predicted beforehand.

Board membership, because boards set organizational policy, requires many of the leadership skills that are associated with transformational leadership—forecasting, setting direction, strategic planning, developing the message, and then staying on it so others can hear the message. Alas, women dominate the labor force in health care and social assistance (79.1%) but are still underrepresented on boards (12.5%); nurses (2.3%) are even more dismally represented on hospital boards (Catalyst, 2009; Hunt, 2009; Meyers, 2008). Because most boards look for directors who have had executive experience of some kind, this situation may change as women in general and nurses in particular assume these roles. However, interdisciplinary boards are not likely to choose nurses if they haven't participated in interdisciplinary forums—that's how people in other fields get to know nurses—and nurses have historically been more comfortable staying in their own circles.

This certainly was the case earlier in my own career. I pretty much equated being a nurse leader with exerting leadership in nursing and didn't fully understand the importance of interdisciplinary involvement. Some of this was me and some was our profession. Being interdisciplinary in my day often involved being the only woman or the only nurse in a group, so it was simply more comfortable to be in the company of those like me, where I didn't have to work hard to explain myself or my profession. Nursing also has some history of cold-shouldering those who assume positions outside the profession: lots of murmurings about the person "leaving the field" and being no longer identified with nursing. I can understand the emphasis on being proud to be a nurse. What I cannot understand is why the field hasn't always taken proportional pride in nurses exerting interdisciplinary leadership while still claiming such individuals as our own, but this is shifting as nurses increasingly see themselves as agents of change in major circles (Flowers, 2008).

I'm also not sure that we have prepared nurses who assume managerial, executive, and board positions within their profession—becoming a unit manager, department chair, the chief nurse officer, dean of nursing, or president of a nursing organization—for the interdisciplinary leadership that they will have to assume from those positions. The unit manager has to interface with everyone who interacts with patients in making any changes. A chief nurse officer needs to hold his or her own negotiating with the chief informatics officer or chief fiscal officer. The dean of nursing has to make presentations to the board of trustees and is involved in planning for the campus/university. The president of the American Nurses Association or of the American Academy of Nursing is regularly called upon to interact with her/his opposite number in non-nursing organizations. I think we have done a better job of telling nurse leaders what they have to do to move the profession forward, than we have of describing the role you have to be able to play from these leadership positions in moving forward larger world views that honor nursing values. In all these situations, you need broad knowledge about trends, the ability to make sense and give sense to strategic change, and a familiarity with how to enable others to work together to achieve higher levels of purpose (Smith, 2008).

Developing a Sense of Strategy

I mentioned earlier in the book that I have become something of a student of leadership, watching how others handle challenges and responsibilities, for the purpose of learning what works and what doesn't. I have admired those who inspire and those who move their organizations to become more effective, but along the way I've come to appreciate particularly those who have strategic sensibilities, individuals who seemingly know how to do an environmental scan and select those issues that are bound to grow in importance over time. It's as if they have a special ability to cut through the noise and clutter and identify the most important trends. They are the ones who read the early quality reports put out by the Institute of Medicine and realized the implications before the rest of us, for example, understanding that the importance of safety and quality would rise one day to be on par with fiscal solvency as reimbursement for services began to be tied to achievement of the highest levels of quality. They are the ones who were ahead of the curve in appreciating that computers, the Internet, and electronic records weren't just destined to be the toys of the technologic few, but would be important pieces of a new, highly interactive way of providing care and facilitating learning.

Is a strategic sensibility something that you can develop? Although people vary in whether they are initially wired to think out of the box, I think it's something that can be developed by reading broadly, going to a variety of meetings in and out of the profession, and deliberately looking out for trends. Sometimes the burden of keeping up with what has to be read to maintain one's practice becomes an excuse for not reading other things, but curiosity about the larger world has to be cultivated if you aspire to exert leadership (Brown, 2010). Staying abreast of the news provides some sense of social and political trends. Joining various professional and governmental list-serves is a way to learn about a variety of developments. Reading strategic plans and position papers—of the university, professional organizations, the National Institutes of Health, and various Washington think tanks—can be enormously helpful in figuring out how what you do fits into the larger scheme of things and in understanding different perspectives.

For decades, I have been a subscriber to *Science* magazine, less for the articles which tend to be more technical than I care to read and more for the news about broad scientific developments and editorial opinions. My first inklings about the globalization of science came from realizing that *Science* had more and more stories about research institutes and scientific developments outside the United States. As a faculty member, I got used to scanning regularly *The Chronicle of Higher Education* to learn about matters affecting other universities that might shed light on what was happening in my school. Once I got over the schoolgirl habit of feeling guilty when I didn't read every newspaper, journal, or book from cover to cover, I was freer to develop my scanning abilities—reading carefully the introduction and last chapter of books because that's where arguments are usually summed up, learning to scan reference lists to see who and what are most cited in an area of interest so I could at least become familiar with classics, using the table of contents as a quick-and-dirty snapshot of what's being discussed in a field, and figuring out what journals (e.g., *Health Affairs*) most shape health policy, and glancing through them regularly.

Being generally knowledgeable serves several interrelated purposes. First, you can contribute to the discussion when you are part of broad strategic planning because you have some sense of the issues facing society in general. If you have a sense of what's only going to become more important in the future, then you are able to take advantage of the opportunities that exist when something new is introduced. For example, believing that communication and information technology were only going to grow in importance, I offered our school up as a test site when the campus was encouraging units to become wired and paperless. As a test site, we got resources that I didn't think would be available later on when moving in that direction became an expectation for every unit, and in the process we developed a reputation within the university for being innovative. Being generally knowledgeable also prepares you for fund-raising; knowing a little bit about a lot of things makes you less self-conscious when you have to interact with a range of potential donors/sponsors.

Convincing Others to Move in a New Direction

Once leaders have a good sense of future trends, the task becomes that of helping others understand why a new direction is important. Unless you are in an emergency situation and time is of the essence, you cannot just tell colleagues you're moving in a new direction and expect them to cooperate when they are not convinced of the need for the change. Indeed, the more educated and experienced colleagues are, the more they will resist anything that feels like being ordered to do something that seems against their better judgment. I have found it useful to remind myself regularly that there is a big difference between (a) getting myself clear about what to do, and (b) getting things done because the latter requires some strategy for moving even the best of ideas forward.

I tend to "float balloons" when I'm trying to effect change. When I thought my colleagues didn't fully appreciate how much a new trend was taking shape, I might send out an e-mail message after attending a key meeting and say, "I was just at the meeting of _____ and was surprised about how many schools are moving to _____, so I thought I would share this information with you." I might follow that up by bringing materials to share at a committee meeting that described the trend and how that development was affecting programs. Familiarizing others with new ideas, before asking them to be supportive of specific changes, is a way of getting others used to new thoughts so that they don't seem too far-out or too preposterous. The point that I'm making is that actually moving in a new direction has to begin with some attention paid to convincing others about the wisdom of doing so. Float some trial balloons and you can get a sense of whether what you are talking about already has supporters or not; this helps you figure out who might be engaged to be an early innovator in launching a new effort. Knowing who is deeply opposed is also very useful information because it helps to know what the opposition is concerned about in formulating a change strategy.

I am convinced that reasonable people can come together to think through the actions needed for moving in a new direction, a timeline for proceeding, and necessary resources. What you particularly need a leader for is to make and give sense to the new direction (Anderson & McDaniel, 2008; Gioia & Chittipeddi, 1991). It is the leader who has to make sense of the needed move by explaining why redirection is necessary and how the proposed move dovetails with both the profession's aspirations and a particular organization's mission and values. It helps if you use history to neutralize concerns being voiced about how the move supposedly runs counter to long-standing traditions by linking, for example, the current importance of nursing research to Nightingale's development of public health statistics during the Crimean War. You can counter arguments about nursing research being elitist and unconnected to practice by contending that nursing research has long been fundamental to the profession and to the evaluation of its effectiveness. Such tests of effectiveness (aka research) are an important part of making sure that you are investing limited resources in what actually works.

The leader not only makes sense of the need to reposition in a new direction but also is responsible for explaining why a proposed move is important to the well-being of the larger university or hospital: What pressures is the institution facing? What problems need to be addressed? What outcomes are being sought by the board of trustees or state legislators? It is so easy for people suspicious of authority—a characteristic, I would argue, of American society—to dismiss an idea on the grounds that the boss is just jerking us around or hasn't thought through this latest directive. That is why it is important for nurse leaders to explain what went into setting a new institution-wide agenda and how this move can be advantageous to the nursing faculty or nursing service. For example, a hospital's push to eliminate costly hospital-acquired infections can be framed as an opportunity for the profession to showcase the value of nursing (Buerhaus, Donelan, DesRoches, & Hess, 2009).

Leaders who aspire to exert a transformational influence must understand the role that they play in preparing others to be open to change. They consequently have to monitor whether they are giving mixed messages, urging change in words but questioning it in their nonverbal behavior. They are likely to enhance acceptance of the new direction by admitting at the start that all concerned will need additional preparation to meet the challenges ahead, including the leadership.

One of the major reasons individuals are reluctant to accept change is the fact that they know how unprepared they may be to move in a particular direction and they are reluctant to have their ignorance or ineptness exposed. Spelling out the resources that will be needed to accomplish something new goes a long way in convincing colleagues that change won't automatically be accomplished on their backs and is a necessary step in actually getting those resources. It also helps to remember that change usually doesn't have to be all or nothing, and well-placed pilot testing can be useful in working out kinks, learning from mistakes, building support, and strengthening the case for change with real data.

Learning to Cut to the Chase

In both developing a strategy for the future and getting others to move in that direction, you have to learn to trust your own creativity and that of others. You need to develop the ability to bracket traditional assumptions and ideas so that they are in suspended animation, as you take a fresh look at the issues. To do this, you need to have the ability to cut through barnacled practices accumulated over time and ask yourself, "What is the core issue and are we addressing it in the best possible way?" It takes daring to ask the question, and many of us don't start out confident enough to trust our better judgment because we are unsure of ourselves or of how what we might say will be received by others, but going through the exercise of letting yourself and others think "new" thoughts as part of planning processes can be very useful in unleashing the creativity buried in each one of us (Wakefield, 1996).

There was a period in my life when I was writing my first book. It wound up becoming one of the first books to look at motherhood in light of the women's movement, but when I was writing it, I was obsessed with the notion that if it were really a good idea, then someone else would have come up with it before, and because no one had written that book yet, then that must be proof positive that the ideas didn't make sense. Thankfully, even I could see that that was crazy thinking, only likely to kill any new ideas, and since that time I've tried hard to give myself time to think "What if . . .?" The best ideas usually keep coming back in greater detail, and eventually you decide to insinuate them into a conversation or a memo.

Strategic planning requires the ability to be playful with ideas. Can you imagine different assumptions operating other than the ones you learned in school? Can you take conceptual pieces and rearrange them so that they form a different pattern? How can you reach agreement about what to pursue when you are working across different fields? When I was on the National Advisory Mental Health Council, I was the only nurse, so I was unlikely to generate interest in nursing research as such, but when I framed the priority as behavioral research, I was able to interest the consumer representative, the psychologist, the social worker, the sociologist, and several psychiatrists in lobbying for more resources in that direction. So often you can get fixated on one way of stating things about which there is a difference of opinion, but if you go up the conceptual hierarchy, sometimes you can get joint creativity, which was absent before. For example, social work, medicine, and nursing have different perspectives on "discharge planning" because the phrase means something different to each one of them (from getting social services and taking prescriptions correctly to lifestyle change), but if you reframe the issue as managing the first month of transition between hospital and home, this view may open everyone up to new and more comprehensive views of how to proceed by working together.

I have long thought that one of the great ironies of life is that you go to school to learn the jargon of your profession and how to write scientifically, but leadership requires you to speak and write jargon-free and simply. To be taken seriously at the start, you need to be able to demonstrate to yourself and others that you have learned the conventions of professional behavior, but leadership entails something else—an ability to inspire across groups—which requires the ability to get to the heart of the matter and touch everyone. It's not unlike the definition of nursing which is helping others do what they would do for themselves unaided if they knew what to do and could do it. On the face, it sounds like common sense, but we forget that sense is not common. It takes years of education and experience to look as if you just naturally know what to do. Similarly, a big piece of leadership is framing the task and the reason for moving in this direction simply and clearly (cutting to the chase), so it makes common sense, but doing so takes a great deal of practice.

In my experience, the way you frame things is also shaped by your view of change. Do you believe in revolutionary or incremental change? I am not as keen on revolutionary change as some of the leadership books suggest you should be. You can change things quickly if you have enough resources to put in place something new, but I've never had the capital to do so. I've seen new leaders come in, telling everyone that they aren't good enough and have to move in a new direction, but their behavior didn't generate the positive change they envisioned; it produced rounds of anger and recrimination that got in the way of actually moving forward.

Incremental change has been misunderstood, in my opinion, because it too often gets equated with moving slowly, only one inch at a time. As a leader, I think you go for inches until symbolically you have 12 of them; then you start talking metaphorically about going for feet until you have three of them, after which you switch the focus onto yards, and then on to symbolic miles. I think that the leader has to begin by conceptualizing the immediate goal as something reachable but also headed in a new direction, constantly reconceptualizing the immediate goal in more challenging language as colleagues become more comfortable with moving in a new direction and can begin to see progress. How many rounds of change any leader is willing to oversee will vary with the person, but there is some evidence that the experienced tend to become less experimental over time—a cautionary note for how long any person should stay in one position (Finkelstein, Hambrick, & Cannella, 2009).

Revising the Link Between Nursing Education and Practice

In Chapter 10, I sketched out some trends gathering force at this point in time that will be shaping nursing practice and nursing education in the 21st century, but I think the area where we most need to have vision is in bringing practice and education back together in new ways (Benner, Sutphen, Leonard, & Day, 2009). Originally, the two were intertwined when hospital-based programs were the major route to becoming a nurse. Although the move away from apprenticeship training and to university-based education is understandable as an important component of professionalization, a gulf that is counterproductive in a practice profession developed. The 1970s saw the development of some unification models that sought to bridge the divide by merging leadership for the two-in-one person (Nayer, 1980), but they did not catch on for a variety of reasons, not the least of which was the difficulty of expecting one person to juggle both sets of responsibilities when one set included 24-hour coverage. (Because medicine is segmented by appointments and procedures, it is somewhat easier in that field to set boundaries when combining practice and education.)

The time is ripe, however, to launch new efforts to bridge practice and education for a variety of reasons—this is an era of system change, and educators will not be able to teach about safety procedures, quality initiatives, and use of information technology if they are not familiar with what is going on in a particular system; the electronic health record is making vast amounts of data available, and hospitals need graduate students who can ask important clinical questions of these large data sets as part of their studies; as reimbursement moves toward capitated payment, hospitals all the more need nurse-researched models to manage chronic care and avoid expensive rehospitalization (Cave, 2005).

In recent years, there have been a number of attempts to bridge practice and education in preceptoring students (Myrick & Yonge, 2005), developing academic-community partnerships (Lough, 1999), preparing students to use a hospital's electronic health record (Connors, Weaver, Warren, & Miller, 2002), providing transitional care (Naylor et al., 2004), and stimulating innovation (Dreher, Everett, & Hartwig, 2001). Some of the most promising collaborations have used research—broadly conceived as knowledge development, dissemination, and utilization—as the intersection point where practice and education can work together to determine best practices and move them to bedside and community.

One recent and intriguing effort to bridge practice and education is the move at three universities (Duke University, The University of California at Davis, and Columbia University) to give the new dean of nursing the title of Vice Chancellor for Nursing Affairs, Associate Vice Chancellor for Nursing, or Senior Vice President within the health sciences center. How this authority will shape a new integrated view of nursing leadership remains to be seen, but it is a development that promises new influence.

The reason that I'm convinced we need to bring practice and education together in new ways is because separately these two aspects of our profession have often lacked the clout to shape the larger institutional agenda but jointly they can be a force for transformational change. Historically, the dean of nursing was able to speak independently but may not have known enough about what was going on in the hospital to voice an opinion when the time was right. The chief nurse officer, on the other hand, knew everything that was going on clinically but was constrained in speaking up because she worked for the organization, and the obligation to serve the institution robbed her of an independent voice. If, however, practice and education espouse a common agenda with a shared commitment to distinction in particular areas, then together they may be able to compound their influence and build excellence.

Key Take-Away Points

- Strategic planning involves examining how the professional or organizational mission is being affected by changing circumstances, setting goals with concrete actions and a timeline, and then figuring out needed resources and expected outcomes.
- Strategic planning often begins with some version of a SWOT analysis—assessing internal (to the person or organization) *strengths* and *weaknesses* and external *opportunities* and *threats*.
- Transformational leaders are deeply committed to the organization and its mission/values, make use of consultants so that they are not limited by the boundaries of their expertise, are willing to try something new knowing that not all good ideas work out, combine vision with practicality in figuring out how to operationalize the change process, and know how to use a range of individuals to the organization's advantage.
- Board membership requires many of the skills expected of transformational leaders—broad knowledge about trends, the ability to make sense of and give sense to strategic change, and the skill to help others work to achieve higher levels of purpose.
- A strategic sensibility can be developed by reading broadly, going to a variety of meetings in and out of the profession, and deliberately looking out for trends.
- Once leaders have a sense of the course correction that is needed, the task becomes that of helping others understand why a new direction is important.

- Incremental change doesn't mean that you have to move slowly; it means that you move forward deliberately, ready to embellish the plan as others are ready to attend to particulars.
- The area where nursing most needs vision is in bringing nursing practice and nursing education back together in new ways to craft a common agenda that builds excellence.

REFERENCES

American Association of Colleges of Nursing. (1999). *Defining scholarship for the discipline of nursing*. Retrieved December 20, 2009, from http://www.aacn.nche.edu/Publications/positions/scholar.htm

Anderson, R. A., & McDaniel, R. R., Jr. (2008). Taking complexity science seriously: New research, new methods. In C. Lindberg, S. Nash, & C. Lindberg (Eds.), *On the edge: Nursing in the age of complexity* (pp. 73–95). Bordentown, NJ: Plexus Press.

Andrews, K. (1971). *The concept of corporate strategy*. Homewood, IL: Irwin.

Benner, P., Sutphen, M., Leonard, V., & Day, L. (2009). *Educating nurses: A call for radical transformation*. San Francisco: Jossey-Bass.

Boyer, E. L. (1990). *Scholarship reconsidered: Priorities of the professoriate*. San Francisco: Jossey-Bass.

Brown, G. (2010, Spring). A curious mind. *Johns Hopkins Nursing, 8*(1), 24–27.

Buerhaus, P. I., Donelan, K., DesRoches, C., & Hess, P. (2009). Registered nurses' perceptions of nurse staffing ratios and new hospital payment regulations. *Nursing Economics, 27*, 372–376.

Catalyst. (2009, December). *Women in U.S. health care and social assistance*. Retrieved December 19, 2009, from http://www.catalyst.org/publication/156/women-in-us-health-care-and-social-assistance

Cave, I. (2005). Nurse teachers in higher education—Without clinical competence, do they have a future? *Nurse Education Today, 25*, 646–651.

Connors, H. R., Weaver, C., Warren, J., & Miller, K. L. (2002). An academic-business partnership for advancing clinical informatics. *Nursing Education Perspectives, 23*, 228–233.

Dreher, M., Everett, L., & Hartwig, S. M. (2001). The University of Iowa nursing collaborator: A partnership for creative education and practice. *Journal of Professional Nursing, 17*(3), 114–120.

Finkelstein, S., Hambrick, D. C., & Cannella, A. A. Jr., (2009). *Strategic leadership: Theory and research on executives, top management teams, and boards*. Oxford, UK: Oxford University Press.

Flowers, L. (2008, February). Leadership: A conversation with Joanne Disch, AARP board chair. *American Nurse Today, 3*(2), 28–29.

Gioia, D. A., & Chittipeddi, K. (1991). Sensemaking and sensegiving in strategic change initiation. *Strategic Management Journal, 12*, 433–448.

Glassick, C. E., Huber, M. T., & Maeroff, G. I. (1997). *Scholarship assessed: Evaluation of the professoriate.* San Francisco: Jossey-Bass.

Hunt, V. W. (2009, September 21). Overlooked ingredient. *Modern Healthcare.* Retrieved December 20, 2009, from http://www.modernhealthcare.com/article/20090921/SUB/309219990

Institute for Healthcare Improvement. (2009). *Get boards on board.* Retrieved December 19, 2009, from http://www.ihi.org/IHI/Programs/Campaign/BoardsonBoard.htm

Learned, E. P., Christensen, C. P., Andrews, K. P., & Guth, W. (1969). *Business policy: Text and cases.* Homewood, IL: Irwin.

Lindberg, C., & Lindberg, C. (2008). Nurses take note: A primer on complexity science. In C. Lindberg, S. Nash, & C. Lindberg (Eds.), *On the edge: Nursing in the age of complexity* (pp. 23–47). Bordentown, NJ: Plexus Press.

Lough, M. A. (1999). An academic-community partnership: A model of service and education. *Journal of Community Health Nursing, 16*(3), 137–149.

McBride, A. B., Yeager, L., & Farley, S. (2005). Evolving as a university-wide school of nursing. *Journal of Professional Nursing, 21,* 16–22.

Meyers, S. (2008). A different voice: Nurses on the board. *Trustee, 61*(6), 10–14.

Myrick, F., & Yonge, O. (2005). *Nursing preceptorship: Connecting practice and education.* Philadelphia: Lippincott Williams & Wilkins.

Nayer, D. D. (1980). Unification: Bringing nursing service and nursing education together. *American Journal of Nursing, 80,* 1110–1114.

Naylor, M. D., Brooten, D. A., Campbell, R. L., Maislin, G., McCauley, K. M., & Schwartz, J. S. (2004). Transitional care of older adults hospitalized with heart failure: A randomized, controlled trial. *Journal of the American Geriatrics Society, 52,* 675–684.

Rath, T., & Conchie, B. (2008). *Strengths-based leadership.* New York: Gallup Press.

Smith, W. E. (2008). *The creative power. Transforming ourselves, our organizations, and our world.* New York: Routledge.

Wakefield, D. (1996). *Creating from the spirit. Living each day as a creative act.* New York: Ballantine Books.

Watts, N. J. (1997). *The adventurous years: Leaders in action 1973–1993.* Indianapolis, IN: Center Nursing Press.

Chapter 12

Choosing Excellence

If you are going to have a vision, it might as well be for excellence. Sounds deceptively straightforward, but I don't think many health professionals have been prepared to think in those terms. We may have sought good grades or merit-pay increase or to avoid mistakes or even to capture some prize, but excellence seems so unreachable, the kind of goal that ordinary mortals feel is beyond their grasp. When the health care system has countless challenges and universities seem to be in a downward spiral because of money problems, you tend to think that survival—getting by and staying afloat—makes more sense as an achievable goal. From the Hippocratic Oath on, the focus has been on "doing good" but not necessarily on excellence.

Doing good is at the center of all professional education and socialization. You are trained to respond to your patients and students as best you can. This approach usually emphasizes the importance of doing no harm, acting with integrity, and staying up to date, with the emphasis being on personal responsibility. The assumption is that if everyone does her or his best, then some semblance of excellence will prevail. But it doesn't work that way because all the good people might be working at cross-purposes, each seeing a different part of the proverbial elephantine institution. These days, good isn't good enough (Kerfoot, 2009a). When all the health professionals interacting with patients look at them through their own lenses, they might individually be doing their best, but what they are doing doesn't necessarily add up to quality care; it is more likely to result in well-meaning fragmentation of effort. Being even thoughtfully responsive will never add up to being transformative.

As a mental health nurse steeped in nursing-process thinking, I may have had particular difficulty early in my career in understanding the limits of responsive behavior because I was specifically trained to focus more on individual therapeutic relationships (Orlando, 1961) rather than on transforming the lot of whole groups of people or organizations. As I started to assume various leadership roles, however, I started thinking that my nursing preparation—I can spot a putdown or a problem at 1,000 paces—sometimes even got in the way of my doing something substantial to direct or redirect efforts in addressing the challenge. It was as if the troubling vibrations given off by the situation were sufficiently disturbing that they affected my equilibrium in moving forward.

Too often I went from seeing the problem to holding myself responsible for the problem, and this sense of personal accountability actually got in the way of being analytic enough to take the information I was receiving and turn it into some resolution that went beyond the here and now. To really change matters, you have to be strategic, and if you are paralyzed by the reactions of others, then you are not prepared to motivate them to go down another path. All my professional focus on process—group process, family process, and teaching process—although valuable for assessment and evaluation purposes, needed to be deliberately harnessed toward some conceptualization of excellence, and I didn't always understand that.

I am not repudiating the value of being able to "see" problems, but in hindsight I think my intense socialization to be healing and alert for difficulties sometimes left me with a tendency to be mired in the present without enough energy left over to address the future. This phenomenon holds to some extent for all nurses, because we have been uniformly prepared to function as first responders and all staff nurses are held responsible for failure to rescue. Because we are metaphorically schooled to notice the grain of the trees, we may not see the forest, and transformative leadership requires that you see larger realities and keep your eye on the whole (Gardner, 1990). Ironically, nursing emphasizes being holistic, but in the execution this too often gets translated as paying attention to all the parts, and you can get overwhelmed by the many pieces. Collins-Nakai (2009) has also talked about a similar problem in medicine, whereby a long-standing orientation toward the patient-provider relationship limits the exercise of the transformative leadership needed, which of its very nature requires system thinking, what Heifetz (1994) called "the balcony perspective."

Clustering Excellence as a Leadership Strategy

Exerting transformational leadership requires some understanding that you have to harness the pieces in a defined direction. Transformational leadership isn't merely reactive or responsive; it is proactive in encouraging high performance (Wolf, Boland, & Aukerman, 1994). Individual transactions are not the end point; these transactions have to be in service to matters of consequence (Bass, 1985; Burns, 1978). The biggest issue of consequence is excellence. Are we all working intentionally to be the best in class, whatever that means for our setting or service at this point in time?

This kind of thinking, however, doesn't come easily to a profession that has spent decades building infrastructure because the focus of those years was sometimes more on development than on how you act differently once fully developed. (Perhaps the best example of this quandary is the nurse who completes the doctorate at great personal cost and is delighted to have achieved that goal but doesn't then use the doctorate to practice differently.) Even though the central focus of the last half century has been on development, the good news now is that this orientation has really accomplished what it was supposed to do—transform the profession—making nursing now prepared better than ever before to exert transformative leadership.

I do not want to discount the achievements of the hundreds of thousands of nurses "doing good" throughout those decades, nor the brilliance of those individuals who transformed the field along the way, for it is because of them that we now fully understand the career journey from novice to expert, making us ready as never before to exert the transformative force of excellence. And I am well aware that many of us still find ourselves in situations in dire need of further development, but this is still different from our past when we didn't have enough of an infrastructure to provide a road map for how to proceed. These days, nurses in clinical settings have Magnet Hospital criteria to guide them in changing their circumstances and nursing faculty have models in place for what a core curriculum should include and how to support research development, so collectively we have a much better sense of how to redirect our part of nursing in the direction of excellence.

How much did I aim for excellence in my own leadership endeavors? Certainly, I tried to do my best in various situations. In positions held, I tried to move a department or an organization in a direction I thought would only grow in importance over time. I knew enough about "the vision thing" to try to mobilize existing strengths to the next level of development. But I didn't fully appreciate the strategic importance of clustering excellence as a leadership strategy before I read Porter (1998). He sees the economic world as being dominated by clusters, critical masses of unusual competitive success. Cluster formation allows each person in the network to benefit from the information, resources, and talents of the others. Together they are greater than the sum of their parts. He argues that by building excellence in defined areas, you get more productivity as people play off of each other's ideas, and together you are collectively in a better position to seize opportunities as they arise.

What Porter argues from a business viewpoint made sense to me from both a clinical and academic perspective because I had ample experience with trying to make changes stick, only to see them disappear when the key person was no longer there. A unit runs well, then the manager takes another position, and everything slides back to the way it used to be before she or he worked there. A faculty member who is a prolific writer and grant getter retires, and the school's research productivity—not all that high in the first place—is cut by a third. The only way to set in motion lasting change is to move from an emphasis on individual achievement to one emphasizing some aspect of organizational excellence. That doesn't mean that individual achievement isn't important and worthy of celebration. Indeed, it is through harnessing these achieving individuals that organizational excellence is forged.

Haven't nurses always known that individual achievement must be in service to cultural excellence? Yes and no. Nurses who are salaried workers have long viewed their professional abilities as in service to the organization's mission. But the more independent certain nursing roles became, the more that individuals in them were rewarded for their personal successes and advised not to get enmired in organizational matters or their productivity would decline. For example, junior faculty in research-intensive environments have sometimes been counseled not to get involved in committee work lest their research will suffer, with the unspoken message being that personal productivity is more important than good citizenship.

Administrative opportunities have come to hold less appeal now that assuming organizational responsibilities is no longer the only route to a pay increase. Why become a director or chair a committee when it takes time away from meeting personal goals? As the profession became transformed, we were understandably proud that we now had advanced-practice nurses lauded on CNN for meeting primary-care needs, nurse scientists with decades of continuous NIH funding for their research, and nurses who won interdisciplinary policy fellowships, then parlayed their expertise into major policy positions. We were delighted that some of us could compare favorably with the best in other fields, so there were times when promotion of individual achievement seemed to become an end in itself.

As personal achievement for nurses seemed more possible, institutional excellence also began to seem more impossible. With limited resources, clinical agencies and schools of nursing have been pushed to provide coverage and address basic workforce needs. These challenges, so fundamental in nature, tend to forestall anyone thinking loftier or more futuristic thoughts about excellence. You feel too much in a crisis mode to change the situation. If anything, there is some tendency to use crises as an excuse to repeal advances—"We don't have the luxury in these hard times to try to make needed improvements." But crises will always be with us, so the answer cannot be to wait until there is a perfect time to mount new efforts. Instead, I think that the answer lies in separating out what the activities of daily life are that simply need to be managed as well as possible—patients nursed, students taught, and accreditation visits that end successfully—and what the areas are in which the organization is going to aspire to excellence.

Aspiring to Be the Best in Some Areas

It is impossible to be excellent in all areas, but becoming excellent in some has a way of changing the culture, making it greedy to become excellent in more areas. Focus relentlessly on long-term excellence, all the while tackling the short-term objectives needed to achieve the sought-after milestones, and the results can be transformative (Jones, 2008). It is when you don't do anything well that you are most likely to believe that aiming for excellence is foolhardy, so you don't move in that direction and it becomes a self-fulfilling prophecy because the lack of momentum causes things to slide.

If infection is the biggest problem on a particular service, then what are nurses on the unit going to do collectively, both in adopting best practices and in trying new strategies, to get the infection rate down and then sustain the change? Sustain the change and other people and places will be interested in how you did it, and this positive attention will only make you more interested in sustaining the change. If you teach in a nursing program situated in a rural community, what research or academic initiative are you going to launch so that you become excellent in something important to your institution? Become excellent in some aspect of rural health and a large portion of the world will beat a path to your door to find out more about what you did.

Too often we think of excellence in terms of becoming like another better-known institution, and then breathe a sigh of regret knowing our workplace cannot compare. And that's true. You have to grow where you are planted. You can only become excellent in some area if you focus on what makes sense for your setting and circumstances. Nurses have to aspire, I think, to become excellent in areas of importance to the institutions in which they work, so any decision to move in a certain direction should begin with some analysis of the mission and goals of the larger institution. The advantage of beginning with some thought to what is important to your organization is that achievement of excellence in that area is likely to be noticed, praised, and rewarded.

What would happen if every nursing service or school of nursing decided to become excellent in some area? It would have a transformative effect on health care. The research conducted by investigators working together in an area of shared interest is likely to be more substantive than that of any one supertalented scientist. Together, they are more likely to conduct research that actually moves new discoveries into treatment advances in record time—moving from studying key factors to designing and testing interventions, and then finding out if the new approach works in real-life situations with diverse patient populations (Collins, 2010). Known for excellence in this area, a school is likely to offer doctoral and postdoctoral training with that focus, attracting individuals to the institution who are interested in that subject and can then be recruited to form the next generation of faculty leaders in this area. When the most productive investigator retires, the program is not likely to disappear, because successor talent is in place.

Clustering excellence can have a cascading effect. A hospital committed to excellence in critical care may also have a foundation receptive to the development and funding of nurse fellowships in critical care. These fellowships are likely to require learning experiences that encourage innovation, so participating in these projects may positively influence patient satisfaction ratings. If an innovation introduced on one unit proves workable, the new practice may be adopted throughout the hospital, and soon become the subject of a paper presented at the annual meeting of the American Critical-Care Nurses Association. Interest in the paper at the meeting may cause some nurses in attendance to relocate so that they can work at a center of excellence, thus building the cadre of talent available. Other nurses may come for a site visit so they can reproduce the results at their institutions. Critical care nursing that helps the hospital expand its reputation regionally or nationally doesn't go unnoticed by influentials, strengthening the high regard in which nurses are held within the institution and their ability to be sought after as change agents in the future.

My own thinking about excellence has been shaped by many factors, but none more so than watching how our hospital network has tackled the safety-quality challenges of this last decade. A new CEO took office with the vision that quality was destined to become as important to the well-being of the institution as financial solvency— since then, it has even been documented that a CEO and board who think that way are more likely to be found in high-performing hospitals (Jha & Epstein, 2010). He looked at organizational efforts and started to question the traditional approach, "Our previously stated goal was 50th percentile to claim excellence. So, we said having half better than us was ok. Would you recommend an 'average' hospital or health care provider to your own family?" He challenged the hospital network to aim for excellence, defined as in the top 90th percentile for every important parameter. Saying we need to move in a certain direction isn't the same thing as getting everyone to head that way, but it is the first step in everyone's starting to believe that preeminence is possible.

Challenged to be excellent, more and more of the professional staff came to believe that they were capable of moving in that direction, and that sense of being "on the move" further energized all concerned. This entire effort was, in turn, shaped by concrete steps to facilitate this progress—*development of an infrastructure:* leadership charged with responsibility for moving quality forward and bonuses tied to improved outcomes, annual quality-safety goals, and service-based and hospital-based quality-safety structures; *benchmarking linked to measures identified by national organizations:* The Joint Commission, Centers for Medicare and Medicaid Services, The Institute for Healthcare Improvement, Leapfrog, Anthem, Healthgrades, The National Database of Nursing Quality Indicators, and others; and *hardwiring culture-building processes:* using keywords at key times, following up consistently, rounding regularly, sharing stories that connect to purpose, and writing thank-you notes (Studer, 2003).

Much of what was done dovetailed with the Institute for Healthcare Improvement's recommendations for exerting leadership in this area—build capability, engage everyone from housekeepers to board members, and make the right thing easy to try and do (Reinertsen, Bisognano, & Pugh, 2008). Linking the hospital network's goals with national initiatives reinforced the notion that the organization was operating at a high level, playing a national game. But as I watched and participated in the changes taking place, I was impressed with how important it was for the CEO to say every day in every way, on and off the premises, that the organization intended to become preeminent; his language varied by group but the message stayed the same. You never doubted his commitment, so your own commitment strengthened, and without even realizing it, you began to repeat his points and elaborate on his themes.

There were many times when the rhetoric and reality weren't in sync. So the question always became, "How can we do better?" Individuals who early on thought, "This too shall pass" began to get engaged in the conversation: "I'm not good in this area but I've just hired someone who is." There were successes and they were celebrated—one of the hospitals was rated the top hospital in the country for quality by the University HealthSystem Consortium two out of three years running—and those successes drove other units/hospitals to show their competitive pluck. There were failures and they reminded us that being well-intentioned wasn't enough, so new strategies were tried as all concerned rededicated themselves to becoming preeminent. There were movements to add detail in the hope of becoming more comprehensive; then there were adjustments meant to simplify so everyone would grasp the fundamentals, and as an organization we learned how difficult it is to sustain change as we settled in to shape the long run.

Over time, the CEO's generally hopeful style took hold, generating additional hopefulness in return. Muttering and dissatisfaction didn't disappear, but there was considerably less general acceptance of mere discontent that didn't lead to some new recommendation for improvement. The transformation has been in keeping with Gladwell's (2000) notion of how many little things all heading in the same direction can make a difference, leading to a cultural tipping point. Getting to the tipping point had elements of Sisyphus' struggle, moving the rock uphill, only to have it fall back at the end of the day, because new directions don't have tread at the start. But once you reach a tipping point, then everyone in the organization starts reinforcing the values, and moving in the desired direction becomes more likely than it originally was, so additional gains are propelled by the momentum that has gathered force. At this point, the leader isn't so much driving the change as reinforcing it because elevated expectations have become part of the fabric of everyday behavior.

Partnering for Additional Gains

Once you have some areas of excellence, I think you become more inclined to form alliances and partnerships, and this tendency is itself generative, likely to beget additional gains. When you are solid but not particularly excellent, you are more self-conscious about potential collaborations because you may be embarrassed to find out your exchange value. If you are strong in an area, you are more inclined to collaborate with others who are similarly strong because you don't have to be convinced that success can breed success. But interestingly, I also think that you are more inclined to collaborate with others who excel in areas that you do not because you know that no institution can be good at everything. Make strategic alliances, and the excellence of others can move your efforts forward with greater speed.

We are beginning to see more collaboration within hospital networks as nurses on different services and in different kinds of hospitals become first-rate in a particular area, share their successes with colleagues at across-unit or across-hospital meetings, and wind up serving as consultants when the innovation is disseminated more broadly. One variation of this multiplicative effect is for a mistake at one hospital to trigger a root-cause analysis of what went wrong, with the understanding being that any subsequent improvements will be broadly disseminated to units that have not yet experienced the problem. Once you are committed to excellence, I think you are less likely to dismiss the problems of others as not your problem, and more likely to welcome learning from others with shared commitments.

If you think about stages of organizational development, certainly for schools of nursing, which I know best, the most developed ones have moved over time from a stage dominated by *infrastructure development*—hiring doctorally prepared faculty, launching a doctoral program, and creating mechanisms to support grant writing and data analysis; to a stage of *faculty development*—more faculty supports are in place and some individuals build research programs that are excellent by any standards and then start mentoring others; to a stage of *program development*—mentoring is institutionalized and postdoctoral research training, institutes, and centers are established around areas of emerging institutional excellence; to a stage of *collaboration* across schools, institutions, and continents with investigators juggling multiple grants, some as principal investigator and others as co-investigator. Over time, individual achievement is forged into enduring programmatic excellence. Some version of this progression is reported by the University of Washington's School of Nursing (2010).

The subject of alliances is important because current economic woes make it impossible to sustain the pretense that any one organization can be all things to all people. I have seen nursing programs in my part of the country band together to create and test simulation scenarios, using an agreed-upon template for design and evaluation, so that all the schools involved can use all the cases in their teaching without having to do all the work. Where once it was expected that the gifted educator would teach a course using only materials that he or she had developed, much as the virtuous homemaker was expected to bake a cake from scratch, there is now a growing realization that excellence may even be more possible if you take full advantage of what others have accomplished (Watson, 2009).

One transformative initiative in nursing that was built on this principle and an overall commitment to excellence as a change strategy is the Hartford Geriatric Nursing Initiative (HGNI, 2010). The John A. Hartford Foundation is a foundation dedicated to improving health care for older Americans, and their first venture within this overall nursing initiative was establishing the Hartford Institute for Geriatric Nursing at the New York University (NYU) College of Nursing. The vision of the NYU founders (Mathy Mezey and Terry Fulmer) and the Hartford Foundation creator (Donna Regenstrief) was for that institute to become a portal to high-quality teaching materials that could be used by baccalaureate nursing faculty nationally. In a similar spirit, practitioner-friendly materials ("the Try This" and "How to Try This" series) were developed next and made available so that common clinical problems could be tackled with state-of-the-science assessment tools and intervention strategies. The overall approach of this institute has been to develop and disseminate materials that allow educators and clinicians around the country (really around the English-reading world) to have access to and use the best products in their work even if they are not themselves experts in geriatric nursing, thus taking steps to ensure that excellence within the profession as a whole isn't limited by individual abilities. If you think about it, this is a truly revolutionary strategy because the mandate to do "our best" and the warning during our school years not to plagiarize both seemed to stress personal responsibility and made us predisposed to reinvent rather than use the best of others, an integral part of any clustering technique.

The next HGNI initiative—conceived by Claire Fagin, Cory Rieder, and Donna Regenstrief—was the Building Academic Geriatric Nursing

Capacity (BAGNC) Program, a partnership with the American Academy of Nursing. It supported predoctoral and postdoctoral research training and established what are now 10 Centers of Geriatric Nursing Excellence at universities located across the country—Oregon Health and Sciences University, University of Arkansas Medical Sciences, University of California at San Francisco, University of Iowa, University of Pennsylvania, Arizona State University, Pennsylvania State University, University of Minnesota, University of Utah, and University of Oklahoma (the last funded by the Reynolds Foundation). The intention behind this program was to build the geriatric nursing workforce by preparing the geriatric nursing faculty of tomorrow, nurse scientists capable of expanding the knowledge base to address the pressing clinical problems of the 21st century.

Because the center directors meet regularly and know what each other is doing, they have been able to take advantage of what the others do best, for example, sharing recruitment materials and inviting scholars elsewhere to take advantage of a training opportunity not available at their universities. The center directors have repeatedly joined forces to accomplish what they cannot do alone. A Nursing Home Collaborative, funded by the Atlantic Philanthropies, was developed to improve practices in nursing homes, with the Mayday Fund supporting a special initiative within this effort to manage pain more effectively in nursing homes. Three of the centers—in Arkansas, Iowa, and Pennsylvania—launched a Geropsych Initiative aimed at establishing a core set of geropsychiatric nursing competencies for all levels of nursing education (see www.geriatricnursing.org/collaborative/hcgne-collaboration.asp).

Without necessarily planning to do so, the directors have begun to address the difficult problem of successor preparation. Because they work closely with each other, they know the talent out there and have used their network to recruit and to mentor each other's new directors. Not only has the profession's image of geriatric nurses changed for the better—it looks like one of the more vibrant specialties to enter—but the interdisciplinary image has changed too. Because the annual leadership conference for the BAGNC Program is deliberately scheduled just before the annual meeting of the Gerontological Society of America in order to promote attendance there, the visibility of nursing in the program and within that organization has dramatically increased (McBride, Fagin, Franklin, Huba, & Quach, 2006).

In addition to the programs that I've already mentioned, a number of other programs have been launched as part of the HGNI, all in partnership with various nursing organizations—the American Association of Colleges of Nursing, the National League for Nursing, and Sigma Theta Tau International—and collectively they demonstrate the power of clustering excellence. As all these projects were funded, there was a conscious attempt made to have the whole add up to more than the sum of the pieces. A Web site (www.hgni.org) and an e-newsletter (www .hgni.org/newsletter.html) for use across programs were developed to share news and resources, craft a common calendar, exchange opinions, debate issues, and seek consultation. Attention was paid to branding the "look" of the disparate pieces so that they all existed separately but shared a swelling identity each time a presentation was made or a paper published. In recent years, all the program directors have come together annually to discuss how they can collectively address common problems and mount needed new efforts. As a result, they have used each other as resources in learning how they might additionally harness the philanthropic appeal of geriatric nursing to attract new resources.

The HGNI has been generously funded (>$75 million), so there might be some tendency to say, "Put that much money into anything and you will get results." But that certainly isn't the case. We all know of instances where money was poured into a project or series of projects that didn't add up to anything substantial, certainly not enduring. With regard to just the BAGNC Program, there are now data on the achievements of the first nine cohorts through January 2009: about 200 scholars/fellows have gone on to teach 23,000 students, produce 976 peer-reviewed articles, and obtain $36.9 million in grant funding afterward (Watman, 2010). These outcomes are substantial by any standard, providing a model for how to cluster excellence and thereby leverage additional outcomes.

We are living in a time when we are all being asked to do more with less, and increased productivity is too often solely defined as a numbers game (Triangle Associates, 2010): Can you take care of more patients? Can you teach more students? This approach stretches people to their limits with more likelihood of breaking down than building up the organization because expansion is usually pushed without reexamining underlying assumptions. The advantage of choosing to focus on excellence is that it turns the conversation away from focusing on "more of the same" to the energizing notion of "value added"—higher patient/student satisfaction, fewer readmissions, better resolutions, and the achievement of Magnet Hospital status (Porter-O'Grady, 2009). Excellence is increasingly a necessity rather than a luxury (Royer, 2007) because there aren't enough resources available to chance having them swallowed up by status quo mediocrity, which itself doesn't come cheap.

If you don't head toward excellence, what you permit becomes de facto what you promote (Kerfoot, 2009b).

Hard to Argue With Excellence

What I also like about excellence as a change strategy is that it is diffi-cult to argue with; the focus isn't so much on the person making a case for the proposed innovation but is on the fact that it is necessary for the sake of others: Don't our patients or our students deserve the best we can provide? Aren't the people of the state or our alumni expecting us to act in their best interests? In asking such questions, you dem-onstrate your "servant leadership," a phrase first coined by Robert Greenleaf (Greenleaf, 1977; Greenleaf Center for Servant Leadership, 2008). He believed that you act differently if you are first a servant (of the people or organization) then channel your leadership on behalf of others, rather than a leader first who is perhaps more focused on personal performance/benefit than on public service. If you are acting to help others, a stance with which nurses are comfortable, then your drive isn't an expression of personal will as much as it is a statement of responsibility in action. If you further couch your recommendations in terms of similar ones made by an organization known to stand for excellence and be above politics (e.g., the Institute of Medicine or an accrediting agency), then you reaffirm that the move is for the com-mon good, which makes what you have to say more important and acceptable.

The challenge is not to get railroaded right away by all the objec-tions that inevitably arise about whether we can collectively really achieve excellence. Remind colleagues that some kind of excellence is in everyone's reach (Gardner, 1961). Talk about it as a "stretch" goal, so that the emphasis is on having aspirations in a needed direction, rather than on the likelihood of immediate success. The reality is that if every-one stretches a little, then the shape of the organization can become transformed. I think we all need aspirational goals just to stay energized. Whether we realize everything we intend to accomplish is not as impor-tant as to get moving in a needed direction. If you aim metaphorically for an A+ and only wind up with a B–, chances are that you wouldn't have gotten even that far without leaving your comfort zone. Even if you achieve only one-third of what you wanted, you are still ahead of where you were when you started, and this difference can be just the upstream redirection needed to achieve something even more substantive downstream.

I think it is very important for leaders to remind everyone regularly about both progress made—complete with over-time graphs and data—and what the next challenge has to be on the way to getting where they want to go. Most people forget, rather quickly, the starting point because what is now in place has begun to be familiar. They think, "It was never that bad, was it?" and start minimizing the distance covered, so they need to be reminded of progress to date because every promise fulfilled becomes a promissory note for what else is possible. If we could get this far, imagine what else we can accomplish! I think regular reminders of how matters have improved is needed so that all concerned don't lose heart and revert to "ain't it awful" thinking.

A regular recitation of victories to date is also important in keeping the leadership invigorated. I was one of the few people at my university who liked having to put together an annual report because the finished product always made me feel that progress was being made. When you are in the thick of things, you sometimes just feel tired and forget that your fatigue may be the result of having accomplished a great deal. Recall the achievements, and you are likely to regain your enthusiasm for the journey.

Not only does the leadership have to remind all concerned about progress, but it is also important to link your statement of steps forward with the next steps in the journey to excellence. You cannot assume that others will see the next steps that you now do without some direction because they are focused on what they do, not on where the organization is headed. If you don't bring the next steps to everyone's attention, then you run the risk of resting on achieved laurels and coming to a halt. You have to be on guard against letdowns that derail further progress, and the more you are able to identify some major next steps, the more others have confidence that you know where you are headed.

Every time you move forward, what you can now see on the horizon changes. If you didn't just accomplish _____ (fill in the blank), you wouldn't "see" that _____ (fill in the blank) now needs to be addressed. There is some sense in which progress is a process of revelation. When I came to regret, as I often did, "not having known better" at the start of a project, I always felt more upbeat if I reminded myself that I couldn't have known what I do now without going through the steps that I did.

No matter how brilliant you are, it is, of course, highly unlikely that you do know all the next steps, so this should also be the time you humbly and wisely declare, "Since we are a 'learning community' committed to constant improvement, what next steps do you see that I have failed to mention?" Being part of a learning community means that everyone concerned needs to be part of trying to figure out how to make what happens at this point in time something of value. The beauty of choosing excellence as the destination is that no one would be expected to have a cookbook notion of how to proceed. Choosing excellence can never be simply some regurgitation of what's been done before, even though you learn from those experiences, because excellence in one setting and piece of time can never mean simply cutting and pasting what's been done elsewhere in other periods.

If you have any aspirations to leadership or even if you are a reluctant leader thrust into some position out of necessity, it is important to keep in mind that choosing excellence is a tried and true way to proceed. Moving in that direction makes clear that you are values driven, have a preference for action over the status quo, support innovation, and are committed to quality improvement—themes that have gained in currency over the last quarter century (Peters & Austin, 1986; Peters & Waterman, 1982). Nurses are now collectively prepared in the 21st century to move toward excellence because they are better prepared than ever before and know what quality encompasses. Positioned to exert leadership within what has historically been their domain, they are also more likely to be asked to wield leadership beyond their traditional spheres of influence.

Key Take-Away Points

- If you are going to have a vision, it might as well be for excellence.
- "Doing good" is the prime directive of health profession education, but everyone doing her or his personal best is no guarantee that excellence will prevail.
- Building clusters of excellence, you get more productivity as resources are shared and people play off of each other's ideas, positioning all concerned more effectively to seize new opportunities.
- The only way to set in motion lasting change is to move from emphasizing individual achievement to stressing some aspect of cultural excellence. It is, however, in harnessing these achieving individuals that cultural excellence is forged.
- Once you have some areas of excellence, you are more inclined to form alliances both with those who are similarly strong and with those who excel in areas that you do not.
- Some kind of excellence is within everyone's reach.

- Excellence is a "stretch" goal, but if everyone stretched a little, the shape and quality of the organization would be transformed.
- Even if you achieve only a small portion of what you wanted to accomplish in the name of excellence, this improvement can be just the upstream redirection needed to achieve something even more substantive downstream.
- Excellence is a journey full of next steps that can only be seen as you move forward and are able to catch a glimpse of what is now on the horizon.

REFERENCES

Bass, B. M. (1985). *Leadership and performance beyond expectations.* New York: Free Press.

Burns, J. M. (1978). *Leadership.* New York: Harper & Row.

Collins, F. S. (2010, January 1). Opportunities for research and NIH. *Science, 327,* 36–37.

Collins-Nakai, R. (2009). Leadership in medicine. *McGill Journal of Medicine, 9*(1), 68–73.

Gardner, J. W. (1961). *Excellence: Can we be equal and excellent too?* New York: Harper & Row.

Gardner, J. W. (1990). *On leadership.* New York: Free Press.

Gladwell, M. (2000). *The tipping point: How little things can make a big difference.* Philadelphia: Little, Brown.

Greenleaf Center for Servant Leadership. (2008). *What is servant leadership?* Retrieved January 18, 2010, from http://www.greenleaf.org/whatissl

Greenleaf, R. K. (1977). *Servant leadership: A journey into the nature of legitimate power and greatness.* New York: Paulist Press.

Hartford Geriatric Nursing Initiative. (2010). *HGNI Program Descriptions.* Retrieved January 9, 2010, from http://www.hgni.org/091008%20HGNI%20 Project%20Descriptions.pdf

Heifetz, R. A. (1994). *Leadership without easy answers.* Cambridge, MA: Harvard University Press.

Jha, A., & Epstein, A. (2010). Hospital governance and the quality of care. *Health Affairs, 29,* 182–187.

Jones, G. (2008). How the best of the best get better and better. *Harvard Business Review, 86*(6), 123–127, 142.

Kerfoot, K. M. (2009a). Good is not good enough: The culture of low expectations and the leader's challenge. *Nursing Economics, 27,* 54–55.

Kerfoot, K. M. (2009b). What you permit, you promote. *Nursing Economics, 27,* 245–246, 250.

McBride, A. B., Fagin, C. M., Franklin, P. D., Huba, G. J., & Quach, L. (2006). Developing geriatric nursing leaders via an annual leadership conference. *Nursing Outlook, 54*, 226–230.

Orlando, I. J. (1961). *The dynamic nurse-patient relationship, function, process and principles.* New York: G. P. Putnam.

Peters, T. J., & Austin, N. K. (1986). *A passion for excellence. The leadership difference.* New York: Warner Books.

Peters, T. J., & Waterman, R. H., Jr. (1982). *In search of excellence: Lessons from America's best-run companies.* New York: Harper & Row.

Porter, M. E. (1998, November–December). Clusters and the new economics of competition. *Harvard Business Review, 76,* 77–90.

Porter-O'Grady, T. (2009). Creating a context for excellence and innovation: Comparing the chief nurse executive leadership practices in magnet and non-magnet hospitals. *Nursing Administration Quarterly, 33,* 198–204.

Reinertsen, J. L., Bisognano, M., & Pugh, M. D. (2008). *Seven leadership leverage points for organization-level improvement in health care* (2nd ed.). IHI Innovation Series white paper. Cambridge, MA: Institute for Healthcare Improvement. Available from www.IHI.org

Royer, T. C. (2007). Excellence is a necessity, not a luxury. *Frontiers of Health Services Management, 23*(4), 29–32.

Studer, Q. (2003). *Hardwiring excellence.* Gulf Breeze, FL: Fire Starter Publishing.

Triangle Associates. (2010, January). *Leading trends. Emerging issues in organizational leadership. Getting to the heart of the productivity issue.* Retrieved January 20, 2010, from http://www.ta-stl.com/LeadingTrends012010.pdf

University of Washington School of Nursing. (2010). *The office of research. About the office.* Retrieved January 9, 2010, from http://www.son.washington.edu/research/internal/AboutTheOffice/AboutTheOffice.asp

Watman, R. (2010, January 25). Personal communication.

Watson, H. (2009, August 26). *100 useful online libraries for nurses and nursing students.* Retrieved January 9, 2010, from http://www.nursingschools.net/blog/2009/100-useful-online-libraries-for-nurses-and-nursing-students/

Wolf, G. A., Boland, S., & Aukerman, M. (1994). A transformational model for the practice of professional nursing. Part 2, implementation of the model. *Journal of Nursing Administration, 24*(5), 38–46.

Chapter 13

Beyond the Discipline Specific

Doris Merritt, whom I've mentioned earlier in the book, frequently talks about her MD degree as really standing for "magic degree" because you can do so much with it—anything from running a hospital and overseeing research at a drug company to serving as president of a foundation/university or governor of a state. Lawyers have similarly known that the JD not only prepared them for various positions in the legal profession but also for many of the positions that do not belong to any one field. Something comparable is increasingly happening in our profession, particularly to those who have obtained graduate degrees. Nurses are first successful in positions within their field, and then some are recruited to positions that go well beyond the discipline specific because the larger world needs their skill sets.

This development is enormously important because the exercise of transformational leadership requires that you be able to shape opinions and policies that are broader than the purview of any one field— topics like access to health care, what long-term care will be covered by insurance, support of higher education, research priorities at NIH, and the design of community-based services and web portals. You get to participate in these larger debates by understanding and valuing what your profession contributes to the world of ideas, developing a personal reputation for being accomplished, and then operating increasingly in interdisciplinary forums, knowing that you may eventually assume positions that are boundary spanning of their very nature. Hospital CEOs, university presidents, and U.S. senators come from a range of disciplines; these are positions that do not belong to any one field.

Interdisciplinary Collaboration

It has been said that working in interdisciplinary teams is a core competency all health professionals will need in the 21st century; they need to be able to collaborate, coordinate, and, most of all, communicate with one another in order to optimize care and maximize operational excellence (Institute of Medicine [IOM], 2003). We already know that when colleagues fail to communicate openly and effectively with each other, mistakes are likely to be made that can even kill; it has been estimated that about 60% of medication errors are the result of poor communication (Maxfield, Grenny, McMillan, Patterson, & Switzler, 2005). Moreover, we are living in a time when what is known by one provider, no matter how gifted, isn't enough to address the complexity of today's problems, so we need to pool our knowledge and skill sets for the best outcomes (Porter-O'Grady, 1997).

Americans have a checkered history of interdisciplinary collaboration. There have been repeated attempts to encourage interprofessional education and practice—the community health center movement of the 1960s, primary care and geriatric team building in the 1980s, and rural initiatives in the 1990s—but interdisciplinary collaboration too often disappears when special funding for that purpose evaporates (Baldwin, 2007; Hassmiller, 1995). It's as if working across professions is an intellectual good, but one that doesn't stick, because it takes people out of their comfort zones, so they revert back to silo-like behaviors when incentives disappear. At the present time, the concept is resurfacing once more with renewed force, not just as important to community, geriatric, or rural health, but as essential to preventing large numbers of adverse events in expensive acute care—so the need for interdisciplinary collaboration may now be more likely to take hold because it is being espoused as vital to the most hierarchical and costly part of health care (Fewster-Thuente & Velsor-Friedrich, 2008).

There are renewed efforts to encourage interdisciplinary education on the grounds that it is impossible to function well as a member of a team after graduation if you haven't had some experience in that direction beforehand (Barnsteiner, Disch, Hall, Mayer, & Moore, 2007; Francis & Humphreys, 1999). Students in the health professions who had been exposed to an interdisciplinary patient safety curriculum were found to start off with substantially different perspectives but generally came to hold similar values after completing shared instruction (Cox et al., 2009). Joint simulation exercises are increasingly being used to foster interdisciplinary collaboration; working together on a simulated case, student nurses and medical students come to appreciate the strengths the other discipline brings to the situation (Dillon, Noble, & Kaplan, 2009; Reese, Jeffries, & Engum, 2010).

In practice, examples of interdisciplinary collaboration have included everything from the blurring of occupational boundaries that occur in community mental health (Brown, Crawford, & Darongkamas, 2000) to the establishment of daily nurse–physician planning meetings (Ashton, Shi, Bullot, Galway, & Crisp, 2005). Even though Fagin said in 1992 that collaboration between physicians and nurses was no longer a choice but a necessity, interdisciplinary teamwork is still in its infancy, and all concerned need to work on how their prejudices and identities impede or facilitate care to patients and their families (Goldsmith, Wittenberg-Lyles, Rodriguez, & Sanchez-Reilly, 2010). At the hospital of the University of Pennsylvania, nursing's professional practice model stresses collaboration, with a particular emphasis on how partnership between the chief nurse officer (CNO) and the chief medical officer (CMO) can facilitate a level of clinical excellence otherwise not possible (Dietrich et al., 2010). When the CNO and CMO work collaboratively, it sets a tone for interdisciplinary collaboration at other levels of the organization.

Universities are encouraging ever more partnership across discipline-specific boundaries in education, service, and research (Mitchell et al., 2006). There is particular emphasis on interdisciplinary research because of the importance placed on this subject by the National Science Foundation's Integrated Graduate Education and Training Program and the National Institutes of Health's (NIH) Roadmap (2004). NIH's Office of Research on Women's Health has partnered with various NIH institutes to invest heavily in interdisciplinary research training programs and interdisciplinary research centers (ORWH, 2010). For example, the Specialized Center of Research on Sex and Gender Factors developed at the University of Michigan (2007) seeks to improve care for women who experience pelvic floor dysfunction after birth trauma and involves four schools, one of which is nursing. While some investigators at the center are doing very basic research to understand birth biomechanics, some of the nurse scientists have investigated behavioral interventions that prevent urinary incontinence (Sampselle et al., 2005). Together, all the collaborators have a more complicated view of the subject as a result of their interactions with each other.

Understanding increasingly complex phenomena—minimizing morbidity when living with a chronic health problem and addressing childhood obesity—requires an interdisciplinary line of attack; hence NIH designed the Institutional Clinical and Translational Awards to encourage research approaches that go from bench to bed to community (Knafl & Grey, 2008; Loeb et al., 2008). If you look around the country, nurse scientists are building on our profession's long-standing translational skills—explaining to patients what's involved in following the medical regimen prescribed by their physicians—to take the lead in translating research to the community (Duke Translational Medicine Institute, 2010; Yale Center for Clinical Investigation, 2009).

Even when interdisciplinary collaboration is encouraged, it is not easy (Clark, Dunbar, Aycock, Blanton, & Wolf, 2009). The basic education of all health professionals continues to prepare them for a particular practice that is then validated by state licensure; thus, the initial socialization is toward differentiation rather than collaboration. The disciplines may still eat in different parts of the hospital cafeteria and often have different school calendars. Appointments typically require a discipline-specific home base; in universities tenure and promotion guidelines support ownership of research by a particular department or school. Both isolation within discipline-specific buildings and governance structures, and the status differences between and among the various professions, further limit collaboration. Even perceptions of collaboration are not the same for nurses and physicians, with the latter regarding themselves as much more collaborative than the former believe to be true (Broome, 2007).

Although all health professionals have some training in communication effectiveness, none of the professions are schooled sufficiently in the complex skills necessary for team building—understanding the lens through which the other person views matters; being able to talk about the same thing from a discipline-specific point of view and also from an interdisciplinary perspective; establishing shared goals based on common values; setting direction in a way that enables all concerned to achieve their professional priorities (e.g., each member of the team is able to contribute at a level senior enough to build a reputation in his or her specialty); handling tensions; fostering consensus; enabling the voicing of criticism without defensiveness; and celebrating shared achievements. Despite these formidable obstacles, there is growing evidence that interdisciplinary respect is emerging as being of critical importance to professional development and satisfaction (Taylor, Karnieli-Miller, Inui, Ivy, & Frankel, in press). Good nurse-physician relationships certainly result in improved nurse retention (Rosenstein, 2002).

Although I have used the word "interdisciplinary" (or interprofessional) to describe generally any collaboration across the health professions, teaching, research, and practice operate on a continuum from *multidisciplinary* with several disciplines working on common problems, each seeing matters through their own lens, to *interdisciplinary* with disciplines working together from a shared overall framework to, *transdisciplinary* addressing recalcitrant problems, the disciplines collaboratively creating new models and methods that are more all-encompassing and effective than traditional approaches (Grey & Mitchell, 2008; Mitchell, 2005). This range of possibilities suggests that the most transformative leadership would be exerted when operating at the transdisciplinary level because the emphasis in this approach is on results adding up to something fresh and innovative, not just on mere coordination, which is itself a good starting point if no synchronization is currently in place.

Interdisciplinary Collaboration Needs to Start Early

How much of an interdisciplinary person have I been over my career? The first portion of my career focused largely on nursing; however, over time I became much more interdisciplinary. I came of age professionally in an educational system where student nurses were instructed not to talk with medical students or physicians directly; they were supposed to speak with their nursing instructors who, in turn, conveyed any messages to the head nurse, who then communicated with medical students/physicians as necessary. This process said to me, "Don't bother busy men/physicians . . . they are not interested in what you have to say . . . and will only get riled up if you bother them." It was not unlike the message that my mother communicated to me about my policeman father, so I absorbed it with the same combination of feelings—respect was tinged with resentment at having to kowtow and with scorn because men/doctors needed to be protected from ordinary give and take. What I am describing is reminiscent of what Stein (1967) later called the doctor–nurse game, whereby nurses are supposed to be indirect in describing what they think and grateful to physicians who take note of their recommendations.

Once I was an RN, although I spoke regularly with physicians, I was also a trifle wary of how they would treat my observations and comments. I had my share of being yelled at for not helping a physician fast enough for his liking (even when I wasn't responsible for his patients), and those encounters just made me want to avoid them. At various times, there was some talk of the "team," but there were constant reminders that physicians were always heads of teams and non-physicians were "just staff" meant to support them—not an approach likely to encourage resourcefulness in the team but one likely to leave you feeling on the defensive. The more educated that I became, the more I had the luxury of acting relatively independently (in fact, that's one of the reasons I sought graduate education), and what I had to say was taken more seriously. The more I worked on projects with colleagues in other fields, the more I realized that I had something to contribute, and the more I opened up and contributed. The more I contributed, the more I was positively reinforced for participating. Over time, I became more oriented to interdisciplinary approaches because my interests led me to committees and efforts that were, of their very nature, boundary spanning.

I look back on those early years and wish in hindsight that I had had some counseling or coaching to exorcise the residual wariness that limited my interdisciplinary participation in the impression-formation portion of my professional life. The world changed with the feminist revolution that questioned male-female and doctor-nurse stereotypes, but that doesn't make one's learned guardedness disappear overnight. Even if you give the impression of being personally forceful and confident, which I generally did, there may still be a gap between external bravado and core confidence.

I have often described my feminist journey as moving from being pleased when told, "You're so smart, you could be a doctor," to a stage where I argued vociferously at such remarks: "What do you mean . . . nurses are smart too . . . and they can even become doctorally prepared!" Even when I quarreled with the stereotype, I think I continued to preen inside at the compliment, taking pride in being seen as out of the ordinary ("You're not a fluff head like the others"). It is only when I moved to the third stage, stopped being combative, and kept repeating, "I don't understand what you mean; there's nothing that I can do that other nurses aren't also good at," that I really came up with an effective response because it put the other person on the defensive and it was grounded in my deep-seated belief that there isn't anything worthy in my person that isn't replicable in many other nurses. I'm not being humble when I say that, but it's true that many nurses ordinarily do the extraordinary. By the time I genuinely thought that way, I had developed a different kind of confidence, one that was no longer just on the surface; it was now the kind of assurance that comes from truly believing that you are part of an important and knowledgeable profession. Your abilities are magnified by those your colleagues have, so you are not dependent just on what you personally know in order to be successful; you can call on them to help you. And it is that kind of assurance that, I think, you need to be effective in interdisciplinary forums.

Embarrassed about how self-conscious I had been early in my career, I did try some self-analysis and came up with some insights that helped me move ahead and shaped my later behavior. Recognizing that nurses were encouraged to be passive, I came to realize that many of us were consequently inclined to be passive-aggressive because we were discouraged from being forthright, so I tried hard not to succumb to those tactics, concluding that being straightforward was more effective in the long run. A particularly destructive part of being passive-aggressive is the tendency on the part of some nurses to be the first to berate other colleagues, as if being critical of them absolves you of being part of the nurse stereotype, when not standing up for your own just confirms it.

I came to realize that, except for those situations when statutory authority is at issue, what discipline you belong to isn't necessarily the best predictor of who will contribute the most to resolving a problem or facilitating a project, and this insight boosted my confidence and caused me to reevaluate my strengths and those of my profession more honestly. I also realized that the more you self-consciously get obsessed by the doctor-nurse game, the more you may lose opportunities to partner creatively with others—social workers, psychologists, physical therapists, ethicists, engineers, economists, pharmacists, and the like—because you start to treat them with the same "We're not noticing" attitude nurses have often received at the hands of physicians. Partnering with other non-physicians can, in fact, be a surefire way to get your ideas heard even if they are pooh-poohed by physicians.

What changed me the most from prickly to positive was the experience of being helped by individuals in other fields; their investment in me had the effect of confirming my worthiness. When I served on the National Advisory Mental Health Council and tried to lobby for more research resources to support psychiatric nurses, it was one of the physicians on the council who helped me think through a strategy likely to succeed, and when the approach we talked about worked, he was the first to offer both me and my profession congratulations. I never forgot his help and, many years later, nominated him for something prestigious, hoping to help him realize dividends on his investment in nursing.

The number of colleagues in other fields who have been generous in their support of my career and my interests is now quite large. Having learned how important it is for colleagues in other fields to offer support, I try to pass on to others the gifts I've received. You expect those who are in your specialty to more or less support you but you are never quite sure if what you have to say makes sense to those not in your field. That's why it is so important early on to interact with other professions to build skill in sharing your perspective on common concerns. When you start out professionally, you may care more about nursing's being heard, but with experience, you realize that what you say should be framed in terms of overriding values and interests because interdisciplinary communication is best delivered in a nonpartisan way.

If my early socialization to hierarchy rather than collaboration was one major hurdle in comfortably exerting leadership in interdisciplinary forums, a less obvious one was nursing's traditional emphasis on becoming a Jack or a Jacqueline of all trades rather than master or mistress of one. Although I specialized relatively early in my career, I didn't think in terms of building an area of expertise so much as I thought of preparing myself to help a particular patient population. I didn't set out to become an expert in something and I wasn't particularly encouraged to think of myself that way, but I now know that you need to work at seeing yourself as authoritative in some defined area because appointment to the most interesting interdisciplinary committees and projects isn't just a matter of representing your field. (When health-oriented committees are constructed to represent various disciplines, the powers that be are only likely to pick one person, not several, from the same field, although they still see each medical specialty as needing representation in a way that they do not see other nonphysicians as needing to be represented.)

I have probably overstated things to make a point, which is that I come out of a tradition where all that you do professionally is described as nursing, so you are predisposed to think in terms of representing your field and not likely to see that you will be more interesting in interdisciplinary circles if you have developed some identifiable expertise. When the Institute of Medicine (IOM) puts together a committee to create a report on a particular subject, staff members are always careful to say that no appointment is by virtue of field; all the appointments have been vetted to assemble the expertise needed to address various aspects of the problem. There is some assumption, I think, that mere representation only gets you multidisciplinary collaboration; an assemblage of expertise is more likely to yield transdisciplinary collaboration and a new view on the subject.

It's not that nurses don't have expertise, but they are not schooled to think that they are authorities on medication reconciliation, screening techniques, fall prevention, or preventing cognitive loss, even when they have had an enormous amount of experience in these areas. It's the difference between physicians being traditionally socialized to exude authority and nurses being prepared to help. In some sense, I am repeating the theme of Chapter 5, where I urged that each one of us understand what we contribute to where we work because if you think that way you are likely to be able to articulate how you might contribute to interdisciplinary efforts in a way that assists others in understanding your know-how (Clifford, 1991). Because nurses have been frequently deployed to provide coverage on the unit and in the classroom, they may take pleasure in being effective in many different situations, but when you are always a pinch hitter, then you will not be likely to be invited to participate in an effort to effect permanent change.

Early in my career, I didn't see an involvement in interdisciplinary forums as something I should prepare for or as something to seek deliberately, perhaps because my generation was so focused on the development of the nursing profession. I responded to opportunities, but I wasn't proactive the way I now think nurses need to be. Nurses need an interdisciplinary plan from the start of their careers. For example, I now advise nurses interested in an academic career to think about making interdisciplinary connections at every career stage; Table 13.1 builds on the career stages discussed earlier in Chapter 4, highlighting the importance of interdisciplinary collaboration throughout a career (McBride, 2010).

Joining Interdisciplinary Organizations

Nurses should join nursing organizations but they also need to be active in interdisciplinary organizations right from the start because their work will have a broader impact if it is presented at those annual meetings and published in those journals. Seek an adjunct appointment in another school and you are forced to develop the skill of being able to talk about your work in different ways—explaining why it is of central concern to nursing while also pointing out ways in which it is of broader interest, too. Centers are an excellent way of getting involved in interdisciplinary research (Heitkemper et al., 2008).

As nurse scientists become active in interdisciplinary organizations and become known for their expertise, some will eventually

TABLE 13.1 Career Stages and Interdisciplinary Development

Stage	Central Developmental Task	Means	Interdisciplinary Development
I. Preparation	Learning—assimilating values, knowledge base, and inquiry skills of chosen field	• Analysis of personal strengths and limitations • Formal education • Socialization experiences • Mentoring	• Clarify nature of own contributions • Interdisciplinary course work/research training • RA experience on interdisciplinary team • Interdisciplinary advisors • Join interdisciplinary research organizations
II. Independent Contributions	Moving from novice to competence—demonstrating ability to establish own program of research and become effective teacher/mentor	• Obtain external funding, refereed publications, and presentations • Hone team-building skills • Develop collegial network intra- and interdisciplinary efforts • Mentor less experienced and less educated	• Adjunct faculty appointments • Membership at interdisciplinary center • Meet interdisciplinary benchmarks of success • Participate in interdisciplinary efforts
III. Development of Home Setting	Moving from competence to expertise—assuming responsibility for development of others and of setting	• Expand purview of own research • Lead curriculum/program initiatives • Build home setting's resources, infrastructure, and image • Mentor in more complex aspects of role	• Shape interdisciplinary training • Guide interdisciplinary research • Address institutional barriers; incentivize interdisciplinary research

IV. Development of Science	Shaping health care and field—exercising power of authority and creating a vision for the future	• Consult in area of expertise • Serve as advisor/officer to local, regional, national and/or international efforts and organizations • Set research agenda • Shape policy/practices	• Leadership in interdisciplinary efforts and organizations • Articulate transdisciplinary models, methods, and foci • Interdisciplinary honors • Consensus efforts
V. The Gadfly Period	Continuing to shape health care and field when no longer constrained by institutional obligations	• Coach current generation of leaders • Take on special projects that require high-level integrative abilities • Articulate strong positions that might not have been possible when constrained by institutional affiliations	• Interdisciplinary leadership development • Expand appreciation for complexity of human condition

Source: This table first appeared in McBride, A. B. (2010). Toward a roadmap for interdisciplinary academic career success. *Research and Theory for Nursing Practice: An International Journal,* 24(1), 73–84.

become presidents of interdisciplinary organizations, just as Martha Hill (American Heart Association) and Terry Fulmer (Gerontological Society of America) already have. Along the way, some of us serve on interdisciplinary advisory boards—Joanne Disch chaired AARP's board; Patricia Brennan is on the editorial board of the *Journal of the American Medical Informatics Association*; Victoria Champion is a member of the National Cancer Institute's advisory board; and Pam Cipriano serves on the board of the National E-Health Collaborative—and we win major interdisciplinary honors: Kathryn Barnard and Ruth Lubic have both received IOM's prestigious Lienhard Award for making outstanding contributions to patient care. They even take the lead in developing transdisciplinary research training (McDaniel, Champion, & Kroenke, 2008), so it should come as no surprise that the director of Health Policy Education and Fellowships at the IOM is a nurse, Marie Michnich.

I can remember a time in the 1970s when nursing faculty, unless they were actually teaching, largely defined their jobs as working "in their offices," so they would be there for students who wanted to see them. I heard colleagues in other fields actually say about them, "They are nice ladies, but I don't know what they do." These nursing faculty members didn't feel valued by the larger academic community, but they weren't visible around campus either. We have changed a great deal since then, becoming active in and leading many university initiatives, and nurses are increasingly exerting interdisciplinary leadership—as heads of university-wide faculty governance, as Vice President for Engagement (Divina Grossman, Florida International University), as Senior Vice Chancellor for Academic and Student Affairs (Karen L. Miller, University of Kansas Medical Center), as Vice Provost for Academic Policy and Faculty Resources (Carole Anderson, The Ohio State University), as Provost and Vice President for Academic Affairs (Mary Ann Swain, Binghamton University), and even as President (Carol Z. Garrison, University of Alabama at Birmingham).

Interdisciplinary collaboration is equally important in clinical agencies, something public health and school nurses have known for a long time. Most clinical agencies have discipline-specific governance structures to set policies relevant to physicians or nurses, but they also have many interdisciplinary committees where they consider subjects that cut across disciplines—utilization review, information technology, space allocation, and human-resources policies. Nurses haven't always been interested in serving on such committees, thinking that those assignments took them away from their real work and forgetting that nurses need to have a voice in those matters if their so-called real work is going to be properly resourced.

Work on such committees and you get to know colleagues in other fields, individuals on whom you can call when you need help at other times. You also get to know more about boundary-spanning subjects—strategic planning, budget, technology, and community involvement—and this background makes you an attractive candidate for other high-level appointments. The Advisory Board Daily Briefing (2007), a membership-based news service, has reported that 132 nurses served as hospital CEOs nationwide and this number is only going to grow now that care quality and service excellence top hospital agendas; for example, San Francisco General Hospital has had two "nurse as" CEOs in recent years—Gene O'Connell and Sue Currin (UCSF School of Nursing, 2009).

It isn't just in academia and in clinical agencies that nurses are assuming interdisciplinary leadership. I mentioned earlier that President Obama appointed Mary Wakefield as the head of the Health Resources Service Administration, which is the principal federal agency for improving services to people who are uninsured, medically vulnerable, and isolated; among other things they do, this agency oversees 1,100 health centers that operate 7,500 clinics and oversees Maternal and Child Health Service Block Grants to all states. Marilyn Tavenner was recently named the principal deputy administrator of the Centers for Medicare and Medicaid Services, making her the second-ranking official at this important agency that shapes guidelines for most of health care reimbursement.

Many other nurses have worked for or are currently working for federal agencies in positions that are not focused on nursing per se— for example, Carole Hudgings at the National Institute of Allergy and Infectious Disease and Taylor Harden at the National Institute on Aging. At the Agency for Healthcare Research and Quality, Kathie Kendrich directs strategic planning, program development, and evaluation activities; Sally Phillips runs the Public Health Emergency Preparedness Program; and Beth Collins Sharp is in charge of the evidence-based Practice Centers Program.

At the start of the 111th Congress, three representatives were nurses—Carolyn McCarthy, Lois Capps, and Eddie Bernice Johnson (Wikipedia, 2009). A number of nurses have been elected to state legislatures (Dailey, 2008; Hall-Long, 2009), and nurses increasingly are being appointed to top health-policy positions in state government. For example, Virginia Trotter Betts was appointed the commissioner of the Tennessee Department of Mental Health and Developmental Disabilities,

Susan R. Cooper is that state's Commissioner of Health, and Linda Spoonster Schwartz is the Connecticut State Veterans Commissioner. My intention is not to name-drop or to come up with some exhaustive listing but to draw attention to some of the interdisciplinary leadership that nurses are already exerting around our country, which still goes largely unnoticed in public discussions and nursing circles.

Nurses are involved in providing interdisciplinary leadership, but not all of them continue to identify themselves as nurses, once they are in these positions, nor are they always permitted to mention that aspect of their background because there is some fear that being so identified will cause the upwardly mobile person to lose status. For quite a while, being recognized as "Jane Doe, PhD," was thought to confer authority, while being described as "Jane Doe, PhD, RN," was thought to weaken the power conferred by the doctorate. I understand the argument that the RN isn't an academic degree the way MD, PharmD, and MSW are, but this point wasn't always the real issue. Being a nurse came to be so narrowly defined that you couldn't retain that identity if you assumed responsibilities that weren't in keeping with how nursing was pigeonholed; if you advanced to another level of responsibilities, you were often described as a former nurse even by other nurses, when you didn't see yourself that way.

I believe that such parochial thinking is changing, but slowly. As nursing has become a better-paying career and more professional, being an RN no longer means constrained circumstances, and the more others see the career potential, the more the nursing identity will stay with the person even when she or he assumes interdisciplinary responsibilities. How fast this happens will be determined by whether all of us become more comfortable with proudly alluding to our nursing heritage in circumstances when we are asking colleagues in other disciplines to use their backgrounds in tackling wide-ranging challenges.

It would be remiss on my part if I didn't also mention the special advantages that nurses have in interdisciplinary collaboration. They are used to function as facilitators bridging disciplines and settings; their training prepares them to understand system issues. We hear so much these days in political circles about the need for leaders to "connect the dots," and nurses have extensive experience in making connections. At all levels of education, nursing emphasizes extensive preparation in other disciplines. Before the development of scores of doctoral programs in nursing, nurses went to other fields to obtain research training, so the field has considerable experience in the boundary-spanning abilities of nurse physiologists, nurse epidemiologists, nurse psychologists, nurse historians, nurse sociologists, nurse ethicists, and the like, not to mention the sizable number of nurses with MBA degrees. A former dean of law once told me that he would recommend an undergraduate degree in nursing to anyone interested in going on to do health law because this preparation provides both a sound basic education—a combination of humanities, social sciences, and basic sciences—and a thorough understanding of how the health professions interact with patients in various settings.

Just about everything that I have said about interdisciplinary collaboration and opportunities has implied working with other health professionals or other academics. There is, however, another aspect of interdisciplinary collaboration where nurses have an advantage, and that is with their community connections. So much of what we do puts us in touch with community organizers, consumer advocates, government officials, legislative aides, vendors, philanthropists, and media types, and working with them via community foundations, fraternal organizations, neighborhood initiatives, and social and women's groups is yet another way to make the connections that can lead eventually to important board appointments or task forces. Local and regional United Way boards want competent volunteers, but those volunteers get a great deal in return as they interact with one another and build a leadership network of their own.

Interdisciplinarity—Part and Parcel of Orchestrating a Full Career

The advantages nurses have can only be fully realized when all of us start thinking that we have careers, not just jobs, and act accordingly, knowing that holding positions with the word "nurse" in them are not our only options. If you are career-minded, you don't dawdle with education, stretching it out over many years; you get what will be your final degree as soon as you can manage, so you are prepared for opportunities ahead. Get graduate preparation in your 50s and you are less likely to advance to interdisciplinary positions; complete your education by the age of 30 and you can spend the next 20 years building your discipline-specific expertise, so you are ready for interdisciplinary challenges of the highest order by the age of 50.

I am certainly not saying that the majority of nurses should plan at some point in time on moving from nursing positions to interdisciplinary ones. I myself chose not to move in that direction even though I was asked on several occasions to apply for such positions. They weren't right for me when those inquiries came my way, but I can imagine matters being different if I had moved further faster in my career. Not everyone wants to pursue each and every possibility for a variety of reasons, from family and health reasons to a lack of interest in upward mobility for its own sake, to simply liking what you are doing in your current position. My main point is that nurses can now consider, and benefit from, such options; you never know what you will want later on, so it's good to have choices and alternatives. Even if you are not inclined toward interdisciplinary positions, you will want to participate in interdisciplinary boards because the most important matters are decided in those venues, since larger "solutions" by their very nature must span a range of interests.

Interdisciplinary opportunities provide more occasions to change matters fundamentally than discipline-specific opportunities do. CEOs and provosts/presidents can shape the very direction of their institutions. When Shirley Chater became president of Texas Women's University, she was able to promote new programs for students with children, receiving national recognition for her efforts. When Joan Austin was elected the first nurse to serve as president of the American Epilepsy Society, she was able to encourage a new appreciation for the behavioral perspective in the assessment and treatment of childhood epilepsy, a slant visible in subsequent convention programs and in the Hoyer Lecture she delivered to 4,000 professionals at the completion of her presidency (Austin, 2009). When Margaret Grey served on the board of the American Diabetes Association, she was instrumental in developing standards of behavioral care for youth with diabetes. In all these instances, nurses didn't leave nursing so much as they finally were in positions to move values forward that are dear to our profession.

When I write about interdisciplinary collaboration and the possibilities of interdisciplinary positions, I can almost hear some old tapes playing in my head: Why encourage nurses to spend time in interdisciplinary forums if they don't have enough time even now to participate in nursing meetings? Why should you promote interdisciplinary positions if we don't have enough nurses now to fill positions in nursing?

First of all, why is it that we don't think that way about a shortage of physicians? No one urged either Indiana Governor Otis Bowen or Senate Majority Leader Bill Frist to go back to the practice of medicine when they were in those positions. The assumption was that they could do more for the public good in those government positions, and this is how we need to view nursing. As the first nurse serving as president of AARP, Jennie Chin Hansen can do more to improve services to the aging than she even did when she transformed a small Chinatown-based agency in San Francisco, On Lok, into an innovative model of full-spectrum services for seniors, assisting 20,000 people by the time she left the agency.

Going beyond the discipline-specific isn't a repudiation of our profession. It offers those considering a career in nursing an energizing sense of the many possibilities now available over a professional lifetime. It provides new challenges to seasoned nurses who are feeling stale in their current positions. It enables one to take nursing's perspective and insinuate it into larger debates where what we have to say can be heard by many others and attract additional public support. As nursing emerges from an intense period of professionalization with vision and a commitment to excellence, our discipline is in a better position than ever before to exert transformative leadership—creating interdisciplinary research teams, offering new models of chronic-care management, using communication and information technology in ways that customize care while simultaneously managing whole patient populations, designing new structures and services for seniors, and delivering education in ways that are no longer bounded by time and place. Everything I have predicted for the future already exists to some extent in our present, so we shouldn't shy away from dreaming about what else is possible.

Key Take-Away Points

- The execution of transformative leadership requires that you be able to shape opinions and policies that are more extensive than the purview of nursing.
- You attain this point by understanding what nursing contributes to the world of ideas, developing a personal reputation for being accomplished, and then operating increasingly in interdisciplinary forums, knowing that you may one day assume a position that isn't owned by any one field.
- It is not easy to function well as a member of a team after graduation if you haven't had some experience in that direction beforehand.
- Although all health professionals have had some training in communication effectiveness, too many of them are not proficient in the skills necessary for team building, something we must all seek to remedy.
- To be transformative, interdisciplinary collaboration cannot stop at mere coordination or synchronization of efforts but must strive to create new models and methods that are improvements over traditional approaches.

- Nurses need to be active in interdisciplinary organizations from the start of their careers.
- Nurses have many advantages in interdisciplinary collaboration— sound basic education in humanities, social sciences, and basic sciences; many community connections; and experience in facilitating care across different providers.
- Interdisciplinary opportunities provide more prospects for effecting large-scale change than discipline-specific opportunities do.
- Moving beyond the discipline specific doesn't mean that nurses leave nursing; it mean they assume positions in which they can now advance the perspective of nursing in ways that others can appreciate, while attracting additional public support.

REFERENCES

Advisory Board Daily Briefing. (2007, June 15). From CNO to CEO: Former nurse executives discuss skills to make the leap. *Nurse Executive Watch.*

Ashton, J., Shi, E., Bullot, H., Galway, R., & Crisp, J. (2005). Qualitative evaluation of regular morning meetings aimed at improving interdisciplinary communication and patient outcomes. *International Journal of Nursing Practice, 11,* 206–213.

Austin, J. K. (2009). The 2007 Judith Hoyer lecture. Epilepsy comorbidities: Lennox and lessons learned. *Epilepsy and Behavior, 14,* 3–7.

Baldwin, D. C., Jr. (2007). Some historical notes on interdisciplinary and interprofessional education and practice in health care in the USA. *Journal of Interprofessional Care, 21,* 23–37.

Barnsteiner, J. H., Disch, J. M., Hall, L., Mayer, D., & Moore, S. M. (2007). Promoting interprofessional education. *Nursing Outlook, 55,* 144–150.

Broome, M. E. (2007). Collaboration: The devil's in the detail. *Nursing Outlook, 55,* 1–2.

Brown, B., Crawford, P., & Darongkamas, J. (2000). Blurred roles and permeable boundaries: The experience of multidisciplinary working in community mental health. *Health and Social Care in the Community, 8,* 425–435.

Clark, P. C., Dunbar, S. B., Aycock, D. M., Blanton, S., & Wolf, S. L. (2009). Pros and woes of interdisciplinary collaboration with a national clinical trial. *Journal of Professional Nursing, 25,* 93–100.

Clifford, J. (1991). The practicing nurse as a leader. *American Journal of Maternal Child Nursing, 16*(1), 18–20.

Cox, K. R., Scott, S. D., Hall, L. W., Aud, M. A., Headrick, L. A., & Madsen, R. (2009). Uncovering differences among health profession trainees exposed to an interprofessional patient safety curriculum. *Quality Management in Health Care, 18,* 182–193.

Dailey, M. A. (2008, September). Those who served: Nurse members in the PA House of Representatives. *Pennsylvania Nurse, 63*(3), 9–11.

Dietrich, S. L., Kornet, T. M., Lawson, D. R., Major, K., May, L., Rich, V. L., et al. (2010). Collaboration to partnership. *Nursing Administration Quarterly, 34*(1), 49–55.

Dillon, P. M., Noble, K. A., & Kaplan, L. (2009). Simulation as a means to foster collaborative interdisciplinary education. *Nursing Education Perspectives, 30,* 87–90.

Duke Translational Medicine Institute. (2010). *Duke Translational Nursing Institute.* Retrieved August 31, 2010, from http://dtmi.duke.edu/about-us/organization/duke-transitional-nursing-institute

Fagin, C. M. (1992). Collaboration between nurses and physicians: No longer a choice. *Academic Medicine, 67,* 295–303.

Fewster-Thuente, L., & Velso-Friedrich, B. (2008). Interdisciplinary collaboration for healthcare professionals. *Nursing Administration, 32,* 40–48.

Francis, B., & Humphreys, J. (1999). Combined education for nurses and doctors. *Nursing Standard, 13*(39), 42–44.

Goldsmith, J., Wittenberg-Lyles, E., Rodriguez, D., & Sanchez-Reilly, S. (2010). Interdisciplinary care team narratives: Collaboration practices and barriers. *Qualitative Health Research, 20,* 93–104.

Grey, M., & Mitchell, P. H. (2008). Guest editorial: Nursing and interdisciplinary research. *Nursing Outlook, 56,* 95–96.

Hall-Long, B. (2009). Nursing and public policy: A tool for excellence in education, practice, and research. *Nursing Outlook, 57*(2), 78–83.

Hassmiller, S. (1995). The primary care policy fellowship: An innovative model for interdisciplinary collaboration. *Journal of Health Administration Education, 13,* 277–286.

Heitkemper, M., McGrath, B., Killien, M., Jarrett, M., Landis, C., Lentz, M., et al. (2008). The role of centers in fostering interdisciplinary research. *Nursing Outlook, 56,* 115–122.

Institute of Medicine. (2003). The core competencies needed for health care professionals. In A. C. Greiner & E. Knebel (Eds.), *Health professions education: A bridge to quality* (pp. 45–74). Washington, DC: National Academies Press.

Knafl, L., & Grey, M. (2008). Clinical translational science awards: Opportunities and challenges for nurse scientists. *Nursing Outlook, 56,* 132–137.

Loeb, S. J., Penrod, J., Kolanowski, A., Hupcey, J. E., Haidet, K. P., Fick, D. M., McGonigle, D., & Yu, F. (2008). Creating cross-disciplinary research alliances to advance nursing science. *Journal of Nursing Scholarship, 40,* 195–201.

Maxfield, D., Grenny, J., McMillan, R., Patterson, K., & Switzler, A. (2005). *Silence kills: The seven crucial conversations for healthcare.* Provo, UT: VitalSmarts. Executive summary retrieved January 28, 2010, from http://www.silencekills.com/UPDL/SilenceKillsExecSummary.pdf

McBride, A. B. (2010). Toward a roadmap for interdisciplinary academic career success. *Research and Theory for Nursing Practice: An International Journal, 24*(1), 73–84.

McDaniel, A. M., Champion, V. L., & Kroenke, K. (2008). A transdisciplinary training program for behavioral oncology and cancer control scientists. *Nursing Outlook, 56,* 123–131.

Mitchell, P. (2005). What's in a name? Multidisciplinary, interdisciplinary, and transdisciplinary. *Journal of Professional Nursing, 21,* 332–334.

Mitchell, P. H., Belza, B., Schaad, D. C., Robins, L. S., Gianola, F. J., Odegard, P. S., et al. (2006). Working across the boundaries of health professions disciplines in education, research, and service: The University of Washington experience. *Academic Medicine, 81,* 891–896.

National Institutes of Health. (2004). *NIH roadmap for medical research. Research teams of the future.* Retrieved January 26, 2010, from http://nihroadmap. nih.gov/researchteams

Office of Research on Women's Health. (2010). *Interdisciplinary research.* Retrieved January 26, 2010, from http://orwh.od.nih.gov/interdisciplinary.html

Porter-O'Grady, T. (1997). Quantum mechanics and the future of healthcare leadership. *Journal of Nursing Administration, 27,* 15–20.

Reese, C. E., Jeffries, P. R., & Engum, S. A. (2010). Learning together: Using simulations to develop nursing and medical student collaboration. *Nursing Education Perspectives, 31*(1), 33–37.

Rosenstein, A. H. (2002). Nurse-physician relationships: Impact on nurse satisfaction and retention. *American Journal of Nursing, 102*(6), 26–34.

Sampselle, C. M., Messer, K. L., Seng, J. S., Raghunathan, T. E., Hines, S. H., & Diokno, A. C. (2005). Learning outcomes of a group behavioral modification program to prevent urinary incontinence. *International Urogynecology Journal and Pelvic Floor Dysfunction, 16,* 441–446.

Stein, L. I. (1967). The doctor-nurse game. *Archives of General Psychiatry, 16,* 699–703.

Taylor, A. C., Karnieli-Miller, O., Inui, T. S., Ivy, S. S., & Frankel, R. M. (in press). Appreciating the power of narratives in healthcare: A tool for understanding organizational complexity and values. In C. N. Candlin & S. Sarangi (Eds.), *Handbook of communication in professions and organisations.* Berlin: Mouton de Gruyter.

UCSF School of Nursing. (2009, Fall). Alumni focus. *Science of Caring, 21*(2), 8–9.

University of Michigan. (2007). *Theme: Birth, muscle injury and pelvic floor dysfunction.* Retrieved January 31, 2010, from http://www.niams.nih.gov/ Funding/Funded_Research/abs_michigan.pdf

Wikipedia. (2009, March). *Members of the 111th United States Congress.* Retrieved January 31, 2010, from http://en.wikipedia.org/wiki/Demographics_of_ the_United_States_Congress

Yale Center for Clinical Investigation. (2009, June 11). *YCCI collaborates with YSN to bring research results to the community.* Retrieved January 30, 2010, from http://ycci.yale.edu

Toward the Future

This book has been largely retrospective, reflecting on leadership lessons learned in the last half century. However, it cannot end there because these lessons have been learned in order to change the future. I do many presentations on what it means to have a full career, during which I always say this: "It has taken me my entire career to be able to discuss key stages in a career, but now that I can describe what it means to have a full career, it means that future generations can use this framework as a road map. If you see the possibilities ahead, you can get much farther faster."

An epilogue is of course a short section at the end of a book or a film that typically describes the fate of the major characters. What happened to them years later, long after the author penned the last chapter or the director shot the last scene? In a similar fashion, I would like to comment on what I hope happens to nursing in the decades ahead. Do nurses plod along making incremental improvements in status or do they move boldly to transform health care and perceptions of their power and influence?

Read the March 29, 2010, issue of *Newsweek* and you wonder if the future holds much change—". . . the four most common female professions today are secretary, registered nurse, teacher, and cashier— low-paying 'pink collar' jobs that employ 43 percent of all women. Swap 'domestic help' for nurse and you'd be looking at the top female jobs from 1960 . . ." (Bennett, Ellison, & Ball, 2010). Equating the RN with the cashier as a pink-collar job is disheartening to say the least. Now, read the findings of the 2008 National Sample Survey of Registered Nurses (Bureau of Health Professions [BHPR], 2010), which came out the same month, and you are impressed with how our profession is steadily growing in numbers (over 3.1 million); diversity (16.8% are non-white; since 1990, one-tenth of the new nurses have been men); pay (average = $66,973, up 15.9% from 2004); and education (between 2000 and 2008, advanced degrees increased by 68%). The RN workforce in this composite image is substantial and increasingly learned. The big difference between the two portrayals is that the *Newsweek* view is a lingering perception, whereas the survey results are fundamental facts.

And to my way of thinking, what we must continue to do is keep changing what is true of us, so that residual stereotypes fade for good. Instead of getting sidestepped by misperceptions, and by the resulting anger, each one of us must take responsibility for laughing at how dated views of nursing remain in some circles (the *Newsweek* piece was written by women journalists who decried how patriarchal corporate culture remains, although much has been accomplished, by spouting some stereotype themselves). I would argue that we are now such forces for change that we can afford to chuckle at how old-fashioned some views still are. Indeed, there is no power play better than expressing amusement at something preposterous (like equating RNs with cashiers), always followed by, "I don't understand why you would say something like that, which hasn't been true for eons."

But do we all know what truths need to be emphasized? Do we continue to argue about entry into practice—what constitutes the correct first degree—or do we focus instead on how career opportunities expand with education, enticing one and all to further their education no matter where they start? Do we continue to recruit and support individuals who are mainly detail-oriented and perform best when assignments/situations are well defined, or do we actively recruit and develop men and women who thrive on innovation and are receptive to thinking critically about the entire system of care? (Benner, Sutphen, Leonard, & Day, 2010; Kalisch & Begeny, 2010; Oliver, 2010). Do we concentrate on what we cannot do because of constraints or on the examples of innovative practice compiled by the American Academy of Nursing (2010), which are ready for wide-scale replication? Do we continue to debate on who is the "real" nurse or do we talk increasingly about what the intraprofessional nursing team—aides, LPNs, RNs, APNs, nurse researchers, and nurse administrators—can collectively accomplish as we collaborate with an array of colleagues in other fields?

The 21st-century reality is that we no longer have to settle for discussing our good intentions; we can direct attention to our impact. Recently, the Robert Wood Johnson Foundation commissioned Gallup to survey opinion leaders ($n = 1,504$) throughout the United States about the role nurses are currently playing in planning, policy making, and management of health systems and services (RWJF, 2010). About half said nurses already have a great deal of influence in preventing medical errors and providing quality care, but ≥80% said that they would like nurses to have even more influence than they now do in preventing medical errors, providing quality care, promoting wellness, increasing efficiency, coordinating patients, and addressing the needs of an aging population. That is a mandate of sorts, I believe, for us to act on our current authority and extend our influence further. It is interesting to note what these opinion leaders thought was the greatest barrier to seizing this power and that was the fact that at present nurses are not important decision makers. This problem is eminently fixable as nurses increasingly move into decision-making positions that are interdisciplinary in purview. Nine nurses made *Modern Healthcare's* 2010 list of 100 most powerful people in health care when only four of them had made it the year before—Linda Aiken, Polly Bednash, Barbara Crane, Sr. Carol Keehan, Beverly Malone, Rebecca Patton, Sr. Mary Jean Ryan, Pam Thompson, and Mary Wakefield (ANA, 2010)—so there is reason for optimism.

The health care system of the 21st century will value prevention, patient safety, quality outcomes, coordinated care, teamwork, appropriate use of information technology, encouragement of patient self-management, maximization of quality of life and functionality, and population-based approaches to major problems. I would argue that we collectively are in an excellent position to move in these directions. That's not a "We're better than others" statement of bravado, as much as it is an affirmation that what our profession has accomplished in the last half century has prepared us well for assuming that kind of leadership in the next half century.

As someone who has played a role in the development of theoretical underpinnings for women's health (McBride & McBride, 1981), I have seen that enormous area of scholarship move from *critique*—of women not included as subjects in health care research and their concerns being unstudied—to *assertion*; meaning a focus on new problems using new methods (McBride & McBride, 1993). In a comparable fashion, I think nursing has moved from the critique phase, where we focused more on remedying what wasn't yet in place, to an assertion phase, where we are focused on what we are going to change or make happen. This switch means that we will be looking less inward and more to the changing horizon, a shift in focus that will require each one of us to act boldly on the authority we have and to exert leadership that is transformational in impact. I so wish I could be around to see all of the next half century.

REFERENCES

American Academy of Nursing. (2010). *Edge runners*. Retrieved March 29, 2010, from http://www.aannet.org/i4a/pages/index.cfm?pageid=3303

American Nurses Association. (2010, August 24). *ANA's Patton, other nurse leaders recognized in* Modern Healthcare's *100 most powerful people in health care*. Retrieved September 1, 2010, from http://www.medicalnewstoday.com/articles/198727.php

Benner, P., Sutphen, M., Leonard, V., & Day, L. (2010). *Educating nurses: A call for radical transformation*. San Francisco: Jossey-Bass.

Bennett, J., Ellison, J., & Ball, S. (2010, March 29). Are we there yet? *Newsweek*, 42–46.

Bureau of Health Professions. (2010, March). *The registered nurse population. Initial findings from the 2008 National Sample Survey of Registered Nurses*. Retrieved March 20, 2010, from http://bhpr.hrsa.gov/healthworkforce/rnsurvey/initialfindings2008.pdf

Kalisch, B. J., & Begeny, S. (2010). Preparation of nursing students for change and innovation. *Western Journal of Nursing Research, 32,* 157–167.

McBride, A. B., & McBride, W. L. (1981). Theoretical underpinnings for women's health. *Women and Health, 6*(1/2), 37–55.

McBride, A. B., & McBride, W. L. (1993). Women's health scholarship: From critique to assertion. *Journal of Women's Health, 2,* 43–47.

Oliver, G. M. (2010). Wanted: Creative thinkers. *Western Journal of Nursing Research, 32,* 155–156.

Robert Wood Johnson Foundation. (2010, January 20). *Nursing leadership from bedside to boardroom: Opinion leaders' perceptions*. Retrieved April 8, 2010, from http://www.rwjf.org/humancapital/product.jsp?id=54491

The Leader

Dreamer . . .
mover . . . shaker . . .
Eyeing new horizons
through the lens of values. Birthing
fresh hope.

Common
touch mixed with truth
telling. Creating a
climate uncommonly healing
for all.

Index